Motivating and Rewarding University Teachers to Improve Student Learning

Motivating and Rewarding University Teachers to Improve Student Learning

A Guide for Faculty and Administrators

Donald R. WOODS

City University of Hong Kong Press

ISBN: 978-962-937-189-0

Published by
   City University of Hong Kong Press
   Tat Chee Avenue
   Kowloon, Hong Kong
   Website: www.cityu.edu.hk/upress
   E-mail: upress@cityu.edu.hk

Printed in Hong Kong

Table of Contents

Detailed Chapters Contents

3.   The skills — The five basic skills that usually are not rewarded explicitly

4.   The skills — Excellence in teaching: Measuring and gathering evidence

5. The skills — Excellence in research in teaching and subject knowledge: Measuring and gathering evidence

6. The skills — Excellence in administration and service: Measuring and gathering evidence

7. Make it happen — Intrinsic incentives to improve teaching

8. Actions for individuals — Using intrinsic motivation to improve teaching

9. Actions for administrators — Creating an atmosphere for intrinsic motivation

13.   Actions for individuals — Extrinsic motivation

14.   Ideas for administrators for coping with underperformance

Preface

Broad coverage, based on research and experience, nitty-gritty details, checklists of actions to take, many examples, practical forms, building trust — this book offers so much to help you in your career.

Many excellent books have been written for administrators about motivating faculty. Some books have been written about being an academic. Books have been written about the reward system. Others have been written on improving student learning. Boyer has written about the scholarship of teaching. Some books have been written on measuring effective teaching. Some books are written only for administrators; others, only for individual faculty. None have been written so as to integrate all of these and address them as a whole. This book does. Both faculty and administrators will benefit from this book.

One overall theme of this book is that we can and should improve student learning. Many articles and books have been written that are chock full of interesting, effective ways to improve students learning. But numerous surveys show that the way to get teachers to change what they do in the classroom is not more ideas — it is the reward system, the culture and inadequate assessment that usually offers no support and little incentive for dedicated teachers to work hard to improve student learning. The rewards tend to be for research in the subject domain. Concerning the assessment process, many of the published policies I have seen lack measurable criteria and a description of the expected forms of evidence. In other words, the five principles of assessment rarely seem to be applied to Mission and Vision statements, P&T policies and annual performance reviews. Guidelines and examples are given on how to do this well.

A second theme is that all faculty should do research. Some prefer to do research-in-teaching but, to date, this effort still lacks credibility. In the past, for example, the credibility for research-in-teaching has been damaged because some diddle around, try one thing or another, publish this and claim it to be scholarship. In this book we explore the issue of what is research-in-teaching, why it is important, how excellence in teaching differs from excellence in research-in-teaching and offer suggestions (and remedies) as to why research-in-teaching fails to be recognized and rewarded: Section 5.7 with remedies in Chapters 11 and 12.

The culture or the system in which each of us works is critical to our success. We offer a definition of "culture," suggest how one might probe the institution to uncover the real culture and offer suggestions to administrators about how to create a culture to nurture student learning.

This book is structured around four basics:

- the five principles of assessment
- a seven-step process for intrinsic motivation
- fundamentals of how to improve student learning
- Kreber's research identifying the processes used by academics not the products.

This book is based on the five fundamental principles of assessment. Motivation comes from self-assessment and reflection. Rewards, merit, tenure and promotion come from peer assessment of our performance based on evidence related to criteria. Most of the angst I have observed in the university context occurs because academics and administrators do not understand and apply the fundamental principles of assessment.

Intrinsic motivation is powerful. A seven-step process, based on the classic book *Motivational Interviewing*, is used as a model. Details are given as to how to use this model for individuals to improve student learning (Chapter 8) and for chairs to motivate individuals (Chapter 9) and for administrators to eliminate under-performance (Chapter 14).

Guidelines are given for individuals on how to improve student learning and to have an exciting and rewarding career path within the culture of your institution. This isn't an oxymoron nor are these two mutually exclusive.

Kreber's research on academic responsibilities identifies seven dimensions of successful academics. These include 1) skill in teaching and facilitating student learning, 2) skill in research (or the scholarship of discovery) and 3) skill in planning, administration and decision-making (the traditional teaching, research and service) plus four basic skills (that are not usually acknowledged or rewarded explicitly): 4) enthusiasm, 5) integrity and ethics, 6) skills in problem solving, assessment, team work, critical thinking, creativity, and 7) expertise in subject discipline. To these latter four we add 8) contributing to the vitality of the university/citizenship. For these latter five, criteria and forms of evidence are suggested so that these can rightfully be included in performance assessment. Checklists of target behaviors and suggestions on how to improve these skills are given. Table 1.3 summarizes this perspective and forms the basis for the first half of this book where terms are defined, goals suggested, measurable criteria are created and examples of evidence are given. Graduate and undergraduate teaching are intimately mixed.

What's unique?

1. Frames out the multifacets of an academic career. This is introduced via Table 1.3 that provides an overall structure.

2. Based on research fundamentals of assessment, intrinsic motivation, learning and academic processes.

3. Addresses eight dimensions of successful academics and elaborates on the five characteristics beyond the traditional *teaching, research and service.*

4. Provides details about academic integrity and ethics.

5. Gives practical advice, with examples, of how to intrinsically motivate yourself to improve student learning (Chapters 7 and 8).

6 Suggests how to develop a colleague's confidence that he/she can make a change.

7. Addresses ambivalence as an issue in making a change.

8. Offers guidance to identify your University's culture or "the system."

9. Gives a variety of instruments that can be used to provide evidence about the quality of the student learning and the learning environment: Queen's Exit Survey, MRIQ, Teaching Load, CPQ, ASQ, student course evaluation, Perry, and PEEP.

10. Gives self-help details for skills needed by an academic — but rarely emphasized or evaluated — enthusiasm, integrity, process skills (problem solving, communication, interpersonal, team, leadership), lifelong learning and enthusiastic contributor to the vitality of the institution.

11. Suggests criteria and forms of evidence for measuring performance in citizenship and contributing to the vitality of the University.

12. Gives a rich set of criteria and evidence for assessing teaching effectiveness.

13. Extends "teaching" to include the supervision and teaching of graduate students.

14. Provides criteria and evidence to assess performance in service and administration.

15. Illustrates how to create an effective *Teaching Dossier.*

16. Addresses the issue of scholarship in teaching: what it is and is not, differentiates from "excellence in teaching," lists ratings for scholarly journals in education and differentiates between "research-in-teaching" (where the discovery process is applied to improving learning) and "diddlin' around" (where one tries one thing, then another in the classroom without formally evaluating effectiveness).

17. Demonstrates how to prepare a "Performance Summary" as evidence.

18. Gives practical advice on how to build trust.

19. Gives frequent reflections and easy-to-use "key ideas" introduction at the beginning of each Chapter.

20 Addresses the issue of effectively working with underperforming faculty.

21. Presents an action checklist for faculty and for administrators, given in Preface Too.

Here is the layout of the book.

Preface Too lists the major ideas for each of the 14 Chapters. For individual faculty members, there is a convenient checklist of ideas and actions. For administrators, a convenient list of ideas and actions is given.

Chapter 1 describes the context in which academics function. It gives a "job description" of an academic, an overview of the many activities expected of an academic and reminds us of the tension between the concepts of "teaching" and of "research." Boyer's work, and extension thereof, and Kreber's research form the background for the analysis in Table 1.3 that illustrates how the skills and attitudes of an academic are applied. Each Chapter closes by asking for reflections and a reaction to the ideas presented in the Chapter.

Chapter 2 addresses ten myths and realities related to teaching and education. The first five myths are those described by Terenzini and Passcarella (1994). Myths six to ten focus on assessment, efforts to improve teaching and the reward system.

Chapter 3 lists five attributes characteristic of successful faculty: enthusiasm; integrity; skilled in problem solving, communication, assessment, and interpersonal skills; expert in subject domain and contributes explicitly to the vitality of the institution. Suggestions are given for criteria and evidence pertinent to assessment of performance.

Chapter 4 focuses on skill in teaching. The skill is defined and 12 goals are listed, about 50 criteria are given to measure excellence in teaching and over 15 forms of evidence are described. Details are given on how to prepare a Teaching Dossier as one form of evidence.

Chapter 5 focuses on skill in research (or the scholarship of discovery). The skill is defined and nine goals listed, about 20 criteria are given to measure excellence in research and about a dozen forms of evidence are described. When the research is applied to teaching, as in research-in-teaching, 1) care is needed to differentiate between in-class teaching and research-in-teaching, 2) credibility in research-in-teaching needs to be increased because some claiming to be researchers-in-teaching have diddled around exploring teaching options without applying the research process, 3) many colleagues are unaware of the reviewing standards used by top tier journals publishing papers on research-in-teaching and 4) funding for research-in-teaching is not available in all countries. A listing is given of ratings for refereed journals publishing articles about research-in-teaching.

Chapter 6 defines service and administration. For service, nine criteria are given and about a dozen forms of evidence are described. For administrative service over 15 criteria are listed and a wide range of evidence given.

Chapter 7 discusses intrinsic motivation which is the most powerful force to harness and use. A seven-step process for intrinsic motivation is given. These steps are: understand the context; be realistic in setting goals to improve student learning, acknowledge ambivalence, overcome ambivalence, build confidence that you will succeed in reaching your goals, draw on your support system, develop a plan and implement.

Chapter 8 gives actions for individuals to use the seven-step process for intrinsic motivation. Suggestions are given for each step: understand the context; be realistic in setting goals to improve student learning, acknowledge ambivalence, overcome ambivalence, build confidence that you will succeed in reaching your goals, draw on your support system, develop a plan and implement. Probably the most important issues presented in this Chapter are 1) ideas on how to understand your University's culture or "the system;" 2) set goals to improve learning that are pertinent to your current place in your career, and 3) include elements of research-in-teaching in your plan. The merits of self-assessment and preparing a Private Teaching Dossier are given. The Private Teaching Dossier is compared with the Teaching Dossier that is used as evidence for performance review. Ideas are given to improve student learning via your role as a teacher of undergraduate students and your role as a research supervisor.

Chapter 9 presents an action plan for administrators to create an environment to intrinsically motivate faculty to improve student learning.

Chapter 10 stresses extrinsic motivation should support and nurture intrinsic motivation. The fundamental principles of assessment provide an environment of accountability and equity. Motivational items include prestige and money. Three external motivators include accreditation agencies, external surveys and external awards.

Chapter 11 lists a variety of models that can be used for tenure, promotion and annual performance review. The differences among the models are the way research-in-teaching is considered. Criteria and forms of evidence are presented.

Chapter 12 demonstrates actions for administrators which include the creation of mission and vision statements and policies about promotion and tenure and annual performance review. Resources should be available to empower faculty to be excellent teachers and researchers. Celebrations are important.

Chapter 13 presents actions for individuals. It focuses on getting tenure first and then working to improve credibility for excellence in teaching and in research-in-teaching. An effective document to prepare is a Performance Summary. Suggestions are given on how to present your case effectively in an interview.

Chapter 14 gives administrators ideas on how to cope effectively with underperformance. Symptoms are listed; possible causes are given. For each cause suggestions are given.

The **Appendices** provide free, eight inventories and questionnaires that can be used to improve and monitor teaching.

Thanks to Chris Knapper, Instructional Development Centre, Queen's University, Kingston and Paola Borin, Erika Kustra, and Dale Roy, Centre for Leadership in Learning, Heather Sheardown, Kim Jones, Phil Wood and Shiping Zhu, Chemical Engineering Department, Barb Love and Linda O'Mara, Nursing, Brian Baetz, Civil Engineering, Stacey Farkas, Financial Services, Andrianna Timperio and Robert Tangney, Human Resources, McMaster University, Georgine Loacker and Austin Doherty, Alverno College; Trevor Holmes, University of Waterloo; Dianne Dorland, Rowan University and the many who responded to my e-mail requests for assistance in writing this book. The reviewers provided very helpful suggestions: Dendy Sloan, Colorado School of Mines, Golden; Suzanne Kresta, University of Alberta, Edmonton; Rich Noble, University of Colorado, Boulder.

I thank Carolin Kreber, University of Alberta for sharing her research with me. I am grateful for the input from the many participants of my workshops for motivating and rewarding faculty presented in the United States and Canada.

I thank Linda O'Mara, School of Nursing McMaster University for letting me use her Teaching Dossier as a guide for Table 4.6.

Don Woods
Waterdown, Spring, 2011

Preface Too

I want you to succeed in your career, as a faculty member, as an administrator or as both roles. That's why I share my experience with you. To try to help you the most, I provide — here, right at the beginning — a list of the "points to ponder" and a checklist of practical actions you might take. Details of each are given in the text; together with anecdotes, stories and more suggestions.

Here's the experience I can share: as a faculty member, member of P&T committee and the University Planning Committee, chair, director of a program, frequent external referee for cases of promotion and tenure, expert witness in law case, and presenter of over 400 workshops on motivating and rewarding faculty, on improving student learning, on using PBL and on developing process skills.

I hope these ideas inspire and help you.

Points to Ponder

1. Caroline Kreber's research provides neat insight about what we do as academics.

2. Apply the five principles of assessment (described in Section 2.8). The university "culture" usually holds a number of myths. Sort out your myths about academia.

3. As an individual, acknowledge and enrich your five unrecognized and unrewarded skills needed by an academic: be enthusiastic, show integrity, possess well-developed process skills, be a lifelong learner and add to the vitality of the institution. As an administrator, nudge the system to value these five skills explicitly.

4. Excellence in teaching can be measured. Use the *Course Perceptions Questionnaire*. Critique the student/course evaluation form used by your Faculty.

5. Research is research (regardless of the context). Clearly distinguish between excellence in teaching and excellence in research-in-teaching. Don't *diddle around* and call it research-in-teaching.

6. Effective service is more than a list of committees responsibilities. We can measure excellence in service.

7. Be intrinsically motivated to improve student learning; follow a seven-step model and, in particular, acknowledge and overcome ambivalence.

8. Get a sense of the culture/system in which you work. Say "I want to and I can improve my teaching."

9. Here's what administrators might do to intrinsically motivate faculty to improve student learning. Learn goals of faculty colleagues. Build trust.

10. The culture should promote equity in rewarding performance. Base policies and practices on the principles of assessment.

11. How to get research-in-teaching recognized and rewarded. Distinguish clearly between "teaching" and "research-in-teaching;" use a reward system where *research-in-teaching* is considered research.

12. Create an overall environment that focuses on student learning through well-crafted Mission and Vision statements designed on the five principles of assessment. For Deans, change the P&T and performance review documents to correctly promote effective teaching. For Chairs, have an annual private performance interview with each Departmental Colleague.

13. Learn how to present your performance more effectively. As a young faculty member, be a researcher in your subject discipline and get tenure first.

14. As an administrator, facilitate the process of intrinsic motivation. As an individual, be sensitive to the symptoms and, as appropriate, revisit Chapters 7 and 8.

This book is meant to help you succeed in your career, as a faculty member or as an administrator or as both roles. To help you gain the most from this book, I provide these checklists.

Individual's checklist

Attitude checklist		Chapter
1	Relationship between teaching and research	Section 1.3; rate Section 1.8
2	Compare your attitude with the ten myths	Table 2.3
3	How extensively does your view clash with the University culture?	Table 2.3
Skills checklist		**Chapter**
4	Enthusiasm	Section 3.1
5	Integrity	Section 3.2
6	Trust	Table 3.1
7	Anticipate and handle dishonesty well	Section 3.2
8	Communication	Table 3.3
9	Listening	Table 3.4
10	Problem solving	Table 3.5
11	Creativity	Table 3.6
12	Critical thinking	Table 3.7
13	Interpersonal skills	Table 3-8
14	Group/team skills	Table 3.9
15	Assessment skills — 5 principles	Section 3.3.5
16	Proactive lifelong learning	Table 3.11
17	Contribute to the vitality of the University	Section 3.5
Please send me an e-mail saying that you have completed all the above in Chapters 1, 2 and 3. <woodsdr@mcmaster.ca>		
Your intrinsic motivation		**Chapter**
18	Write long term goals	8.1.1
19	Understand the "culture" or system so that you act knowingly	8.1-2; 13.2
20	Put your goals in the context of your life	8.1.3
21	Write goal to improve teaching	8.2
22	Start simply	8.2.4
23	Get tenure before embracing ambitious goals to improve learning	8.2.4
24	Acknowledge ambivalence	8.3
25	Overcome ambivalence	8.4

... continue

Your intrinsic motivation		Chapter
26	Build confidence: *"I want to and I can"*	8.5
27	Be competent	8.5.1
28	Build support from students	8.5.2
29	Use skill in supervising graduate students	8.5.3
30	Manage time well re getting ready to teach	8.5.4
31	Identify and use support network	8.5.5
32	Manage stress / maintain high self esteem	8.5.6
33	Develop a plan	8.6
34	Use self assessment	8.7.1
35	Use a *Private Teaching Dossier*	8.7.2
36	Get tenure	13.1
37	Understand the culture/system via interview with chair and mentor	13.2; 8.1.2
38	Build credibility for excellent teaching	13.3
39	Build credibility for research-in-teaching by learning details about it	13.4.1
40	Build credibility for research-in-teaching through your own research; don't diddle around	13.4.2; 9.7
41	Be a change agent	13.5
42	Use the resources to improve effectiveness	13.6
43	Keep chair and dean informed	13.7
44	Learn how to gather evidence	13.8
45	Keep good records of what you do	13.8.1
46	Keep records of what you were invited to do but couldn't	13.8.2
47	Gather information needed for performance review	13.8.3
48	Create *Performance Summary* for teaching, research and service	13.9
49	Present your case effectively in an interview	13.10
50	Use words describing performance — not personal worth	14.1
52	Recognize the symptoms of underperformance and consult with mentor	14.3.1
53	If pertinent, use an interview with chair or mentor to identify possible cause of underperformance	14.4; 14.3.2
54	Use the life-change chart to identify personal level of stress	Table 14.1
55	Manage stress well	14.7
56	If pertinent, address cause of underperformance following the principles of Chapter 7	14.5 to 14.10

Administrator's checklist

Item		Chapter
1	Complete the first 17 activities on the individual's checklist	1, 2, 3
2	Learn their goals	9.1
3	Guide in helping them set up personal goals, criteria	9.1
4	Within what you can control create an environment where good teaching is valued; help them see how the mission, vision and culture can support their activities	9.2
5	Competence feeling; praise, celebrations	9.3.1
6	Annual interview	9.3.1
7	Interview to decide how Department can help individuals	9.3.1
8	Tell them about resources to improve competence	9.3.1
9	Provide autonomy	9.3.2
10	Provide relatedness, praise, good communication	9.3.3
11	High esprit des corps	9.3.3
12	Social events	9.3.3
13	Support from spouses	9.3.3
14	Praise and celebrations	9.4.1
15	Talk it up	9.4.2
16	Encourage informal support groups	9.4.3
17	Build trust	9.5.1
18	Clear, published, high expectations	9.5.2
19	Encourage all to do vitality list	9.5.2
20	Fair equitable teaching load / research facilities	9.5.3
21	Promise only what's within your control	9.5.4
22	Give feedback empathetically	9.5.5
23	Be a role model	9.6
24	Learn details about research-in-teaching to intrinsically motivate others	9.7
Please send me an e-mail saying that you have completed all the above in Chapter 9. <woodsdr@mcmaster.ca>		
25	Apply principles of Assessment	10.1
26	Use external criteria as appropriate for your M&V	10.2
27	Select a model where research-in-teaching has the most credibility for your University	11
28	Publish a motto	12.2.1
29	Create well-crafted M&V	12.2.2
30	Publish program outcomes	12.2.3
31	Publish performance indicators — basic data	12.3.1
32	Gather and publish performance data related to learning	12.3.2
33	Create institutional plan	12.3.3
34	Relate funding to plan and M&V	12.3.4
35	Policy re P&T and annual review follows principles of assessment	12.4.1
36	For P&T and annual review select at least seven options for assessing excellence in teaching	12.4.1
37	For P&T and annual review make service accountable; select at least four options for documenting and assessing excellence in service	12.4.1

... continue

Item		Chapter
38	For P&T and annual review make citizenship accountable; select at least four options for documenting and assessing excellence in "citizenship"	12.4.1
39	For P&T and annual review, explicitly address the issue of research-in-teaching by incorporating a model where research-in-teaching has credibility	12.4.1
40	Distinguish between excellence in teaching and excellence in research-in-teaching	12.4.1
41	Learn details about research-in-teaching to apply policies equitably	12.4.1
42	Learn the quality refereed journals that publish articles in research-in-teaching	12.4.1
43	For P&T and annual review gradually include the five skills as part of the expectations for both P&T and annual performance	12.4.1
44	Disconnect salary and rank	12.4.2
45	Annual performance review follows principles of assessment; Dean's activity	12.4.3
46	Annual performance review follows principles of assessment; Chair's activity	12.4.3
47	Hiring practice include "teaching" activity	12.4.4
48	Monitor practice re P&T and annual performance review	12.5
49	Resources — Allocate funds for operating budget to help improve student learning	12.6.1
50	Resources — Funds Centers for Teaching	12.6.1
51	Resources — Provide internal grants	12.6.1
52	Run workshops for outsiders to generate internal funds	12.6.1
53	Create Teaching Fellows	12.6.1
54	Provide relief time	12.6.1
55	Create a book account to support writing of textbooks	12.6.1
56	Research services for those doing research-in-teaching	12.6.2
57	Ask for Departmental Performance dossiers	12.7
58	Nominate others for external awards	12.8.1
59	Create internal awards	12.8.1
60	Help individuals understand and use the culture	12.9.1
61	Help new faculty get started	12.9.2
62	Use words that focus on performance and not personal worth	14.1
63	Contact HR for cases of unsatisfactory performance	14.1
64	Work effectively with difficult behaviors	14.2
65	Recognize symptoms of underperformance	14.3.1
66	Use OARS and listening in interviewing	14.4
67	Through interview can identify cause of underperformance	14.4
68	Use the life-change chart to identify personal level of stress	14.3.2
69	If pertinent, present case for dismissal based on post tenure review	14.5
70	If pertinent, reignite the spark of intrinsic motivation via facilitated motivational interviewing	14.6
71	If pertinent, help identify the stressors from work and change those within your control	14.7
72	If pertinent, guide colleague about resources to develop stress management	14.7
73	If pertinent, assist colleagues find positions elsewhere that match their new goals or interests in life	14.9
74	If pertinent, empathetically explore options for those with health problems	14.10

List of Illustrations

Figures

Tables

Motivating and Rewarding
University Teachers
to Improve Student Learning

A Guide for Faculty and Administrators

The context in which we work
On being an academic

The key idea is that to motivate faculty to improve students learning, we should understand the context in which academics work.

Traditionally an academic's expected duties are primarily research, teaching and service/administration. Teaching tends to focus on undergraduate education; external motivation through performance review tends to be primarily on research (because "we can't measure effectiveness in teaching"). Carolin Kreber's research and Boyer's work offer a new perspective on academia. Teaching embraces more than undergraduate activity and should include graduate, short courses and a wide variety of clients; research/ scholarship applies to all that faculty do (and in particular should include research of teaching and of our subject discipline). Besides the traditional three skills listed above, four important skills — that are not usually considered explicitly — are enthusiasm, integrity, skill in communication, problem solving, etc. and subject expertise.

As suggested in Table 1.3 (page 11), academics apply their skills to tasks for a variety of clients in such a way as to revise our traditional perceptions of teaching, research and administration. Such a new perspective forms an exciting basis for motivating faculty, motivating them especially to improve student learning.

At the social gathering Hector queried "What do you *really* do with all that spare time you have as an academic?"

One might define a university as a place for students to learn from those who create knowledge by research, discovery and invention. The three traditional responsibilities of an academic are to teach students, do research and provide service (Boyer, 1990; OCUA, 1994a). Some might add a fourth responsibility of consulting and clinical practice. In this opening Chapter we summarize the expectations of an academic and the amount of time devoted to these three traditional roles. Four commonly-held perspectives about the relative roles of "teaching" and "research" are given, and the impact of research funding on the university culture is explored briefly. With this background we extend Boyer's model (1990) and Kreber's research to identify seven key attributes expected of academics and to suggest a framework for recognizing, nurturing and rewarding good teaching in a university.

1.1   The "job description" of an academic

Although all academics understand that they are expected to contribute to research, teaching and service, rarely is a day-to-day job description published. Conditions for "promotion" and "tenure" (P&T), are published but those criteria are applied only four times in one's career — the initial hire, the promotion to associate professor, the granting of tenure and the promotion to full professor. For all the other times, the assumption is that academics are expected to be good teachers, good researchers and provide good service. What tends to be missing are the criteria and forms of evidence that are needed to assess performance and the necessary motivational components to provide incentives for excellent performance. Without clarification of the expectations, it is not surprising that stress levels and frustration are high among academics (Boyer, 1990; Gmelch, 1986). Nor is it surprising that much frustration is associated with performance assessment. When I became departmental chairperson, my predecessor warned me, "The task you are going to hate will be the annual recommendations for merit increase!" Probably more than any other single issue, the results from the annual performance reviews had the most dramatic impact on the faculty morale. Clarity about expectations, criteria, evidence and the assessment process are needed.

High expectations of excellence in all three roles makes superhuman expectations for us (Felder, 1994, Woods and Wood, 1996). One challenge for academics is to astutely distribute their time among the tasks of teaching, research and service.

1.2 The context — Time spent in the three roles

Per week, faculty typically work between 50 and 60 hours (OCUA, 1994a). Table 1.1 illustrates how that time is distributed among the three different functions based on surveys of faculty. The percentages vary depending upon how clearly the three functions were defined in the survey questionnaire. The results suggest:

- On average 40% to 54% of the time during the semester is spent on "teaching." Considering the lack of clarity for promotion, the missing job description, and the impression that research is more valued than teaching (Gray *et al.*, 1992), these average values are higher than might be expected.

- That committee work and service takes a large portion of time, with average values between 15% and 28%.

- That considering the research productivity of colleagues, it is surprising that so much can be accomplished in average values of 20% to 35% during the semester. Of course, most of the data are reported for a nine-month period.

Concerning the commitment to teaching, an alternative view is to consider the total time expected during the semester, instead of considering the contact time. Per nine-month teaching year, one model suggests that the usual total teaching component for all undergraduate and graduate classes is 550 hours. The 550 hours/nine months excludes graduate student supervision, weekly meetings and research group seminars. The time includes preparation time (including revisions, and updating of content and methods of facilitating learning), in-class "contact time," office hours, and marking. At this 550 hours, about 60 hours are expected for the revision of at least two courses per year (Woods, 1983). These numbers are consistent with the data in Table 1.1.

1.3 The context —
Models of the relationship between teaching and research

Although faculty are expected to provide all three duties, most attention is paid to the teaching and research activities. The relationship between these two represents deep-felt attitudes that affect the culture of the University. Four different models of the relationship between teaching and research have evolved that inherently underpin any discussion about academic responsibility and accountability. These four different models are:

Table 1.1
Distribution among the functions during the nine-month teaching semester
(from OCUA, 1994a; Rosenthal *et al.*, 1994; Bert, 1999; and Woods and Wood, 1996.)

Area	US Carnegie (for 9 month)	US NSOPF-88 (for 9 month)	US NCES 96 (for 9 month)	US Bert (1999) (for "typical week")	Canada CUPA/ OCGS (for 9 month)	Canada Woods and Wood (1996) (for 11 months)
Teaching	54 %	52 %	42 %	46 %	53 %	40 %
Research	27 %	20 %	30 %	35 %	23 %	30 %
Service	5 %	14 %	28 %	14 %	10 %	15 %
Administration	14 %	14 %			14 %	
Personal on-going education				5 %		
Hours per week	50	57		53.4	63.7	45–60

Footnote: These values are average. Faculty in some top-ten schools spend 50 to 75% of their time on research.

Model 1 — **Synergy**: *Teaching-research is a seamless, synergistic continuum.* In universities, the discovery of new information, interpretations, applications and procedures are central to all we do. Our function is to stimulate the intellectual growth of all our students so that each thinks critically, is curious, applies integrity in all he/she does and is scholarly.

Model 2 — **Independence**: *Teaching and research are independent endeavours.* "Promotion and tenure and hiring practices identify two distinct roles: teacher and researcher." Colleagues talk about separate endeavours. Teaching and research are assessed separately. Some institutions have separate streams, a teaching stream and a research stream. Some allow those with extensive research grants to "buy" their way out of teaching so that the researcher will be relieved of the unwanted "responsibility" of teaching a course. This idea of independence appears with different shadings: the two are different, the two compete (Model 3) and the research is valued more than teaching (Model 4).

Model 3 — **Competition**: *Research competes with teaching.* Some suggest that each person prioritizes his/her use of time between research and teaching. Since, "you can't do everything," one has to choose to be either an outstanding researcher or an outstanding teacher. This is often expressed as, "Teaching is a chore that I have to endure so that I can do the research that I really love." (OCUA, 1994b).

Model 4 — **Research superiority**: *Research is more valued than teaching.* Some make a judgment call about the merit of research compared with teaching. Bok (1990) argues that academics tend to value theory over practice; research over teaching. There tends to be more glamour, prestige, visibility and honor for outstanding research discoveries than for outstanding teaching. Research has more "Public Relations" value. Teaching is ho-hum. Teaching is a "second-class" activity.

In Chapter 2 and throughout the rest of this book we will meet President Jose, Dean Fred, Assistant Professors Nicole and Dianne and P&T Chair Dave whose actions seem directed by their belief in Models 3 or 4. In contrast, this book is based on Model 1 that teaching and research synergistically support one another. A university is an educational institution where the discovery of new knowledge and the learning and transmission of the knowledge are intimately mixed. Both are valued. Both are essential. Each supports the other.

1.4 The context —
Influences of research funding and alumni contributions

Any polarization between "teaching" and "research" can also be tracked to the budget of the university. For many universities, the total budget is strongly supported from the "research" enterprise. Monies from external "research" granting agencies can — depending on the conditions of the contract or grant — be used for:

- overheads (up to 50% of the external grants may be recovered for university "overhead")

- summer salary for principal investigators (applicable for universities that hire faculty on a nine-month basis)

- buy-out salaries to allow the principal investigator to spend more time on research and less on "teaching" and "service."

Some illustrative data of the amount of research funds relative to the other sources of funds are given in Table 1.2 for a typical research-intensive, provincially-funded Canadian University.

Hence, one way a university can generate more operating budget is to encourage faculty to bring in more "contract research funds," more external grants that allow overhead and faculty stipends to be charged as an expense and to increase the gifts by alumni. Noll (1996) suggests that alumni and wealthy donors are more willing to support prestigious universities — prestige that comes mainly from the research enterprise.

Table 1.2
Illustrative income for a typical research-intensive Canadian University

Source of funds	1993/94	1999/00	2003/04
1. Provincial government grants (including overheads from research and contracts when permissible)	40%	34%	29%
2. Tuition (undergraduate and graduate fees)	20.3%	21%	22.5%
3. Other: investment, alumni donations	6.5%	12%	14%
4. *Total operating funds*	*66.8%*	*67.0%*	*65.5%*
External research funds			
5. Government grants for research	22.7%		
6. Government contracts (that allow for overheads as expenses)	2.8%		
8. Industrial grants	4.3%		
9. Industrial contracts (that allow overhead as expenses)	0.9%		
10. Foreign grants/contracts	2.2%		
11. *Total*	*32.9%*	*33%*	*34.5%*
12. *Overall Total*, millions Canadian dollars	*$231*	*$300*	*$476*

In some of the faculties of Health Sciences, the "educational enterprise" is supported by clinical income. Pressures in such faculties are for the academics to spend more time on the wards and less time "teaching."

If the state and government subsidies for "education" are taken as fixed and for granted, then one attractive way to increase university income is to increase (and value) research and, in the case of Health Sciences, clinical practice. This increases the financial pressure into the teaching — research dilemma. Financial pressure intuitively supports Model 4: Research superiority.

1.5   The context — Seven attributes and a framework to encourage and reward good teaching: Extending Boyer's model

The foregoing discussion gives a simplistic view of academic responsibilities that creates boundaries and gulfs between the responsibilities and generates more questions than answers. For example, if a university's role is education, why is undergraduate education called "teaching" and graduate education called "research?" Where does a teacher's personal research fit into this classification? Is something called "research" only if it receives an external grant?

In an attempt to "break out of the tired old teaching versus research debate," Boyer (1990) suggested that faculty bring "research" to all that they do. Boyer suggested we redefine an academic's activities to be:

- scholarship of teaching (what was referred to above as "teaching")

- scholarship of discovery (what we referred to above as "research")

- scholarship of integration

- scholarship of application (what we referred to above as "service").

In other words, Boyer suggested that faculty bring "scholarship" to teaching, to the discovery of new information, to the integration of different ideas and concepts, and to the application of knowledge to solve problems.

His innovative views have prompted others to elaborate on these four views of scholarship. Rice (1992) and Paulsen and Feldman (1995) extended Boyer's view to include:

- scholarship of academic citizenship (what was referred to above as service)

- scholarship of service (again referred to above as service).

These classifications focus on the products that result from the scholarship of an academic. Kreber (1999) noted that whereas some academic activities produce products (grants, papers, skilled students, committee reports), other academic activities are process activities (mentoring colleagues, preparing for class, marking, keeping up to date) where direct products are more difficult to identify. She surveyed 58 experienced faculty who had received teaching awards. In a detailed study of 17 major process and product activities of academics she found that five significant factors clustered the typical activities in interesting combinations. These factors, Kf, with the activities listed in decreasing order of significance, were:

Kf 1 — "Learning and scholarship:" informal conversations with colleagues; networking with colleagues; learning about new developments in one's discipline; advising, mentoring and assisting colleagues; and learning about one's teaching.

Kf 2 — "Teaching:" advising students about assignments, projects and theses; formal instruction; counseling students on program and career issues; departmental and university committee work, and preparing and conducting evaluations of student's work.

Kf 3 — "Service beyond the university:" being a member/participant in professional associations, public talks, consulting and community service and off campus lectures, and conferences to professional societies.

Kf 4 — "Pre and post teaching activities:" reviewing and evaluating the work of colleagues (manuscripts, grant proposals), preparing for teaching, preparing and conducting evaluations of student's work.

Kf 5 — "Research:" conducting research; and writing books, articles, monographs and grant proposals. There is a difference between Kf 1 (Kreber's scholarship as learning about one's teaching) and Kf 5 (research as measuring the effectiveness of one's teaching).

Some noteworthy results from Kreber's research are:

- in factor 1, includes a set of "process" activities all related to keeping up-to-date. Such activities rarely are included in the traditional sense of "teaching," "research" and "service" nor are they included explicitly in Boyer's view of the four "scholarships."

- in factor 1, keeping up-to-date in both subject discipline and in teaching are related activities.

- in factor 2, activities related to both undergraduate and graduate student education are in the same factor.

- in factor 4, an interesting cluster of activities related to "teaching" and to "service" are juxtaposed.

- "preparing and conducting evaluations of student work" appears as a loading factor in both factors 2 and 4.

From the work of Boyer and Kreber a performance model can be created to establish policies and procedures to nurture and reward academics to perform their tasks well. Such a model is based on the following seven key skills expected of academics:

1. Enthusiasm about their profession. They have a sparkle in their eye for what they do.

2. Integrity and ethics; honesty and concern for students at all levels. No plagiarism, manipulation of the data, no deception, and no shirking or shortchanging their commitments. Building trust.

3. Skill in problem solving, teamwork, communication and self assessment that they use in solving problems in all contexts and for all clients.

4. Expertise in subject knowledge, and, for some situations, expertise about the culture, traditions, practices and policies of their university or professional association.

5. Skill in teaching with a focus on student learning. They are knowledgeable about what research says about learning and try to use that understanding to create effective learning environments for students at all levels and in all contexts.

6. Skill in research. Research is defined as the curiosity, perseverance, initiative, originality, critical appraisal and integrity one uses to create new understanding and practices and for self learning. As a sidenote, Boye and many others have helped us to see new facets to research by using the word scholarship. However, this has prompted a semantical jungle with the use of such terms as the scholarship of teaching and learning, SoTL, teaching as research, TAR. In this book the operative term I will use is research. Perhaps this is because my experience has been in a research-intensive university, because we have Vice-Presidents of research and because we have departments such as research services. Whether I apply my curiosity to questions related to student learning or to engineering, I use the same rigor, disseminate the findings through refereed journals, receive "research grants" and use the research services. Hence, I use the term research in this book. Also, I distinguish between "problem solving" and "research." The difference is subtle but important.

   > *For example, a teacher, Karen, might wish to solve the problem of "improving student ratings." Karen solves the problem by using active learning, learning the student's names, promptly returning marked assignments and getting frequent feedback from the students. She used problem solving. The result was 'The students liked it.' and 'I liked it.' Her student ratings improved. Problem solved! However, Karen did not take the extra steps to gather before and after data to measure which of the interventions was most effective. She was not curious. She tried something and it worked but she did not discover how well it worked or why it worked. She did not bring her skills in research to her teaching.*

7. Skill in planning and administration as exemplified by high standards of performance and conduct, being accountable, being aware of the context, challenging the conventional, anticipating the future, creating short and long term goals and developing plans to achieve these, skill in making decisions, interpersonal skill, skill in participating in and chairing meetings, enabling others to act and being trustworthy.

All activities done by academics use the first three skills. Solving problems for different clients draws on the remaining four skills to different extents. This is illustrated in Table 1.3.

Your ratings may differ from mine. Furthermore, for one particular client, the ratings will vary with the problem. For example, as an expert witness in one law case, you may need to do no research. You just share what you know. In another case, you need to do additional research about the application in this particular case. Hence,

Table 1.3
How academics use their skills when doing tasks for different "clients"

"Client"	Tasks academics do	Extent of application of skill in traditional areas of			Kf	Usual category
		teaching	research	service		
General public	explain discipline or research to the public	**	**	*	3	service
Community	committee work	—	*	**	3	service?
Advocacy groups	advise group	—	*	—		service
Local government	advise group	—	*	—		service
Law courts	serve as expert witness	—	*	—		service
Students	prepare to teach	***	***	**	4	teaching
Community students	give non-credit courses	***	*	*	teaching? †	
Undergraduate students	develop knowledge and intellectual skills; train professionals	***	*	*	2	teaching
Graduate students		***	***	*	2, 5	research
Post doctoral students		*	***	*	?	
Industry	give short courses	***	—	*		teaching? †
	consult	—	*		3	service ?
	do contract research	—	—	***	*	research, †
Professional organizations	present papers	*	***	*	3	research ?
	chair a session	—	**	***	3	service? †
	provide leadership as president, executive committee	—	*	***	3	service
	review grants and papers	—	***	*	4	research? †
	serve as editor	—	***	***		research?
	set exams for profession, serve on accreditation team, select scholarship winners	***	*	***		service?
Self	learn, keep up-to-date	***	***	*	1	
	attract potential graduate students, apply for grants in subject discipline	***	***	**	research?	
	do research	***	*		1, 5	research
	apply for grants, write papers in teaching, do research	***	***	*	1	research?
	research in administration	—	***	***		research ?
Colleagues	be a mentor, network	***	***	***	1	
University	serve on committees	**	**	***	2	service

*** means the skill is used extensively

*   means the skill is used a small amount

— means the skill is not used.

Kf. means the Kreber factor described earlier in this section.

†   means that this has been identified as a "service" role by OCUA (1999a).

different skills will be used to different degrees depending on the task. Also shown in the Table is the traditional coding according to teaching, research and service and, in column 7, the Kreber factor, Kf. Many of the activities could be in different categories and some are unclear. What is shown is that "research skill" is required in many different tasks; "teaching skill" is required in many.

In this book, we consider all of the **skills** of academics. In Chapter 3, factors 1 to 4 are explored. However, the major emphasis is on the traditional factors 4 to 7; these are shown in the vertical columns in Table 1.3. As suggested in this table, skill in teaching (column three) can be demonstrated in many different contexts. Evidence from all of these "clients" can, and we suggest should, be used to show excellence. Similarly, skill in research (column four) is used with a wide range of "clients." Traditionally, "research" has been considered only in the context of graduate education. We propose that this is too narrow a viewpoint. Evidence from all these activities could be used when assessing the performance of faculty. Indeed, until we use a model such as given in Table 1.3, the evidence used to support claims about excellence in teaching will be drawn from too limited a segment of our experience. We shortchange ourselves.

If we are to encourage and reward good teaching we need to include the full spectrum of our use of that skill in teaching. We need to provide evidence from all the tasks. Table 1.3 provides a model.

1.6   The context and culture are important

As described in this Chapter, the context in which we work includes attitudes about research in contrast with teaching, the role of research funding, models describing the role of academics and the relative times spend fulfilling each of the three traditional roles of teaching, research and service. The context is part of the culture which I describe as the environment determined by the collected actions, attitudes, standards, beliefs, decisions and practices about what is really important about the institution.

1.7   Outline of this book

If you try only one thing from this Chapter, Carolin Kreber's research provides neat insight about what we do as academics. Chapter 2 provides more about the context/culture in which university faculty function. Ten myths about universities are considered, especially in the context of improving student learning. The rest of the book is built around the framework suggested in Table 1.3, Kreber's research and the ten myths.

Then we consider, in turn, the seven Kreber factors that have been shown to be important in the life of an academic. In Chapter 3 we consider the first four factors (enthusiasm, integrity and trust building, higher order skills and keeping expertise up-to-date) and add an additional fifth factor — contribution to the vitality of the department. Usually these are not considered explicitly. Rather, the universities tend to consider teaching, research and administrative activities as the only measures of importance for assessing the performance of faculty.

Chapters 4, 5 and 6 define teaching, research and service, list criteria to measure excellence and list forms of evidence that might be used for assessing performance. In Chapter 5, the overall research process is detailed with elaboration for those interested in research-in-teaching. Clarification is given in Section 5.7 on what is research-in-teaching, why it is important, and the difference between excellence in teaching and excellence in research-in-teaching. Ideas are given as to why research-in-teaching rarely is recognized or rewarded.

The strongest motivation for faculty to improve their teaching is intrinsic motivation. That is, faculty work to improve teaching because they want to and because they get excited about the opportunity. Chapter 7 provides a seven-step process for intrinsic motivation. The follow-up Chapter 8 guides an individual through the seven-step process of intrinsic motivation. Chapter 9 suggests the actions administrators can take to nurture intrinsic motivation.

Chapter 10 describes options for extrinsic motivation for faculty to improve student learning.

One of the strongest extrinsic motivators is the criteria for promotion, tenure and annual performance review. One of the greatest challenge is to determine how to effectively credit, value and reward "research-in-teaching" (the discovery scholarship of teaching). Suggestions are given in Chapter 11 about Promotion and Tenure policy, P&T, and annual performance review.

Chapter 12 suggest actions that administrators can take to create the culture to motivate and reward faculty to improve student learning. Chapter 13 gives ideas for individuals. Chapter 14 considers suggestions for administrators for coping with faculty who underperform.

1.8   Reflection and self-rating of ideas

Most books end each chapter with a summary. I do not. Research has shown that reflection about what we have just heard or read, placing the ideas in the context of our past experience and discovering interesting connections improves our comprehension and performance (Kimbell *et al.*, 1991; Brookfield, 1990). Therefore, I encourage you to reflect on the ideas in this Chapter and create your own summary by reflecting and rating some of the ideas. Table 1.4 provides a place for such written reflection. Some already believe and are practicing some of these ideas. Some ideas may not suit your style. Some ideas deserve more investigation. To gain the most from this book, please reflect and rate the ideas in this Chapter.

Table 1.4
Reflection and self-rating of ideas about being an academic

Reflection: Some guiding questions to start your reflections might be "What interested you most in this Chapter?" "What ideas confused you the most?" "If you were writing this Chapter, what other issues might you include?"

_____

_____

_____

Rate the ideas presented in this Chapter

P&T means promotion and tenure	All published	P&T plus annual review	Only P&T	not available
Is a job description describing teaching, research, service available for your position?	O	O	O	O
Hours spent/week in all activities during teaching semesters	>60	50	40	<30
	O	O	O	O
During teaching semesters percent of time spent on	70%	50%	30%	10%
"teaching classes undergraduate and graduate"	O	O	O	O
"research including personal research"	O	O	O	O
"consulting, committees, grant reviews"	O	O	O	O
Total hours per two semesters dedicated to course preparation and delivery excluding graduate supervision	>1000	800	600	<400
	O	O	O	O
T means teaching; R means research	T and R seamless	T is separate from R	T vs R	R is better than T
My idea of the relationship between teaching and research	O	O	O	O
The University culture about teaching and research	O	O	O	O
	Agree	Somewhat agree	disagree	Disagree
Research contracts and funding are influential forces to the detriment of good teaching	O	O	O	O
	Agree	Somewhat agree	disagree	Disagree
Skills of an academic demonstrate:				
enthusiasm	O	O	O	O
integrity	O	O	O	O
skill in problem solving, communication, self-assessment	O	O	O	O
expertise in subject knowledge	O	O	O	O
vitality	O	O	O	O
skill in teaching at any level in any context	O	O	O	O
skill in research at any level in any context	O	O	O	O
skill in planning and administration	O	O	O	O

Adjustments to the scoring in Table 1.3. In Table 1.3 I used an *** rating to mean "used extensively." Reflect on the skills you use for different tasks and different clients and adjust the *-rating to better match your situation.

_____

_____

Other _____._____

My conclusion from these responses is _____

Some terminologies and acronyms used in this book

Administration — form of service involving administration over a unit, program faculty or university. This draws primarily on skills of planning, leadership, teamwork and administration.

ASQ — Approaches to Study Questionnaire, instrument for students to self-rate their approaches to learning; developed by Ramsden and Entwistle described in Section 4.5. Dr.Chris Knapper, Queen's University, altered the terminology to reflect North American practice. Instrument and scoring in Appendix B.

Basic skills of an academic — enthusiasm, integrity, ethics, trustworthy, has process skills and positively contributes to the vitality of the University.

BRI — Bridging Research Interests Questionnaire, instrument for students to rate the extent to which faculty integrate teaching and research in the classroom. Table 4.4, p. 92.

CPQ — Course Perceptions Questionnaire, instrument for students to rate the learning environment; the elements in the inventory were developed based on Ramsden and Entwistle's research on what promotes deep learning. Dr. Chris Knapper, Queen's University, altered the terminology to reflect North American practice. Example data in Section 4.3, p. 84. Instrument and scoring in Appendix A.

Culture/system — the environment determined by the collected actions, attitudes, standards, beliefs, decisions and practices about what is really important about the institution.

Dossier — a collection of papers giving detailed information about a particular person or subject. As in **Teaching Dossier** and **Private Teaching Dossier**. Related term — **Performance summary.**

Higher order skills — see Process skills.

Kreber factor — related to Carolin Kreber's research described in Section 1.5.

M&V — Mission and Vision statements of the University.

MRIQ — My Role Is questionnaire, instrument for teachers to self-rate their perception of their role in the educational process. Appendix E.

NSSE — National Survey of Student Engagement, available from the www.nsse.iub. edu.

P&T — Promotion and tenure.

PEEP — Peer Evaluation of Educational Programs, instrument for peers to rate and teacher's plans for a course. Instrument given in Appendix D; and described in Section 4.7.

Perry — attitude toward learning, described in Section 4.5. Instrument and scoring given in Appendix C.

Performance summary — Annual documentation of evidence of contributions to research, teaching and administration, for the purpose of annual performance assessment.

Portfolio — a set of pieces of creative work collected to be shown to potential customers or employers. Prefer to use the term "**Dossier.**"

Private Teaching Dossier — document to help us personally improve our teaching, p. 182; compared with *Teaching Dossier*.

Process skills — skills needed to function well. These skills include skill in problem solving, communication, listening, team work, self assessment, and lifelong learning. (Also referred to sometimes as "soft skills" or "higher order skills.")

Professional Dossier — document to help others assess our performance in teaching, research and service, see Performance summary.

Queen's exit survey, extracts from the exit survey developed by Queen's University, Kingston Ontario Canada Appendix F.

Scholarship — see Research.

Research — an organized and systematic way of finding answers to questions and thus discover new knowledge, skills or attitudes.

Service — activities that use primarily the academic's expertise. These include consulting, presenting seminars and workshops, serving on professional and/or community organizations, interfacing with industry, government and the community, open houses, events to improve relationships with high school, activities to improve recruitments of undergraduates, graduates and faculty.

Soft skills — see Process skills.

Syllabus — sometimes referred to as a course outline. Published material developed by the instructor and usually presented to the students at the first class. Usually includes the name of the course, details about the instructor, the major learning objectives, the required texts and statements about policy and assessment.

System — see Culture.

Teaching — facilitating learning of any subject or skill or attitude by any client.

Teaching Dossier — document to help others assess our performance in teaching; contrast with Private Teaching Dossier.

The Context
Myths and realities for motivating university teachers to improve student learning

The key idea is that ten myths about academia have a dramatic impact on individual's intrinsic and extrinsic motivation to improve teaching. Here are ten commonly-held myths and a critique of each.

"Promote him. He's a great researcher. He's got to be a great teacher too."

Since the mission of the University is education, why is low priority often given to effective teaching? If you go into most classrooms today, why are teachers using the same educational methods that were used in the 1950s? A survey of 45,000 faculty in 49 research universities has shown that most faculty and administrators disagree with the current emphasis on research as opposed to teaching (Gray *et al.*, 1992). More emphasis, motivation and reward should go to improving student learning. So why isn't that happening? Why aren't teachers demanding workshops to improve their teaching? Why aren't great things happening in the classrooms? Why aren't more faculty talking about their *teaching* in the faculty lounge — instead of the new grants they received and the papers they published? Perhaps this is because of strongly-held misconceptions or myths about teaching and how to improve teaching.

Let's consider some of the myths and realities about academic life, about assessment and the reward system, and about motivating faculty to improve teaching and how these might be influencing the *culture* of the university. Terenzini and Pascarella (1994) summarized five dysfunctional myths that permeate academia. Five additional myths are listed based on my 40 years of giving workshops on effective teaching, assessment and motivating faculty, being Departmental Chair and Program Director, being an expert witness and serving on tenure and promotion committees.

2.1 Myth #1 — Institutional prestige and reputation reflect educational quality

> *President Jose says, "Come to University X that has the largest number of Nobel Prize winners, the largest amount of research funding and that is ranked #2 in the country by the Gourman report (or by Maclean's magazine's annual scoring). Get the best education."*

Reality: This myth tends to be supported by those whose attitude is that research is more valuable than teaching (Model 4 in Section 1.3). Terenzini and Pascarella (1994) found that prestige, reputation and resources attributed to a university bear negligible relationship to the quality of the student learning. Jose is considering the wrong measures. The measures that relate to student learning that President Jose should be emphasizing are (Terenzini and Pascarella, 1994):

- the nature and cohesiveness of the student's curricular experiences,

- the student's course-taking patterns,

- the quality of teaching they receive and the extent to which the faculty involve students actively in the teaching-learning process,

- the frequency, purpose and quality of students' non-classroom interactions with the faculty,

- the nature of the student peer group interactions and extracurricular activities, and

- the extent to which institutional structures promote cohesive environments that value the life of the mind and high degrees of student academic and social involvement.

The National Survey of Student Engagement, NSSE, uses five indicators of effective educational practice. These are level of academic challenge, extent of active and collaborative learning, student-faculty interaction, enriching educational experiences available and supportive campus environment. (www.nsse.iub.edu)

How to address this myth is discussed in Chapters 4 and 12.

2.2 Myth #2 — Traditional methods of instruction provide proven, effective ways of teaching undergraduate students.

> *Professor Joan says, "I learned by the lecture method. It's easy for me. I can share my enthusiasm and expertise with my students. What else can I use with*

my class of 150 students? Besides, everyone else is using that method so it can't be that wrong!"

Reality: Terenzini and Pascarella (1994) note that Joan is correct. Faculty spend more than 80% of their time lecturing at students. However, Terenzini and Pascarella (1994) report that the traditional lecture with only "teacher talk" is not as effective as other options, especially learning environments that are individualized, active or cooperative. For example, individualized learning environments showed a learning advantage over the lecture of between 6 to 19 percentile points.

Two major studies illustrate methods that teachers can use to promote learning. Chickering and Gamson (1987) summarized an extensive review of the literature and 50 years of practice. They found that the top seven ways to improve student learning are:

1. Encourage contacts between students and faculty.

2. Develop reciprocity and cooperation — not competition.

3. Use active learning techniques. Do not have them passively receiving information in a lecture.

4. Give prompt feedback to students about their performance on learning tasks.

5. Emphasize "time-on-task;" help students use their time effectively. Students typically should spend 60 to 80 hours per week on their studies. This translates into about 120 hours per semester course to attend class, complete projects and assignments, do homework, study, prepare for the tests and exams and write the exams (Gibbs *et al.*, 1992).

6. Promote an environment that expects students to succeed.

7. Respect diverse talents and ways of learning.

Ramsden and Entwistle (1981) identified the statistically significant factors that caused students to spend time searching for meaning in what they learn, called deep learning, instead of the undesirable superficial memorization of facts without any effort to comprehend or connect facts, called surface learning. Surface learning is reflected in the student response "Tell me what I have to memorize, and I'll regurgitate it on a test." The two factors that encouraged the undesired surface learning are:

1. The use of formal lecturing as the teaching method.

2. High workload.

The six factors that nurtured the desired deep learning are:

1. Good teaching.

2. The teacher is open to the students.

3. Freedom for the students to select parts of their learning.

4. Clear goals and standards of student assessment.

5. Vocational relevance of the material.

6. Good social climate.

Teaching methods based on this research can improve student learning as we will see in greater detail in Chapter 4.

2.3   Myth #3 — The good teachers are good researchers

Meet Dean Fred. I met Dean Fred when I was giving a workshop on effective teaching. "Of course, all my top researchers are at your workshop. At this University, all my top researchers are top teachers."

Nicole is a new assistant professor seeking tenure. Meetings, grant proposals, more meetings, visitors from funding companies, invited seminars, informal Saturday morning meetings with her graduate students, conference presentations — when does she have time to improve her teaching? and why would she spend precious time to improve teaching? "I really don't need to spend my time working on my teaching. If I am an excellent researcher then I will be an excellent teacher."

Reality: This myth tends to be supported by those whose attitude is that research is more valuable than teaching (Model 4 in Section 1.3). Research has shown that there is no correlation between student ratings of teaching effectiveness and measures of research productivity (Feldman, 1987; Centra, 1983, Terenzini and Pascarella, 1994). For example, Figure 2.1 shows the student ratings from course evaluations (averaged over a four-year period) versus the publication of scholarly papers in refereed journals for the faculty members in one Department (Woods, 1999d). For the teacher effectiveness, the students were asked,

"Overall, what is your opinion of the effectiveness of the instructor as a teacher?" with options:

1, very poor; 2, poor; 3, 4, 5, acceptable; 6, 7, 8, good; 9, very good and 10, excellent.

For this period and for this Department, everyone had an average rating above 5, "acceptable." Most had average ratings in the 6 to 8 range, meaning "good," with

Figure 2.1

Teaching effectiveness and number of research publications for a Department

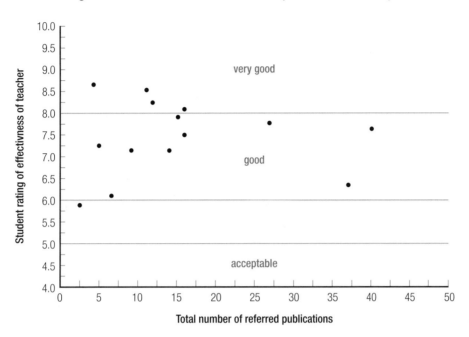

the total number of publications in refereed journals ranging from 2 to 39. There is no correlation between the number of publications and the rating. Faculty with many research publications can achieve high student ratings or they can have lower student ratings. So Nicole needs to focus on having high research productivity and high student ratings.

Until Dean Fred eliminates this persistent myth of good researcher = good teacher, good researchers in your faculty will continue to be excused for poor teaching, research on effective teaching will be ignored, good teachers will be denied tenure and the students in your faculty will be short changed. How to overcome this myth is explored in Chapters 5, 8 and 11.

2.4   Myth #4 — Faculty members influence student learning only in the classroom

> Charlotte says, "My job is to give lectures, have office hours and pose and mark assignments and exams. Don't ask me to go to 'Meet the Profs Night,'

invite students to my home, go to the coffee shop with them or attend student concerts. That's not my job! I have my own life to live."

Reality: Research cited by Terenzini and Pascarella (1994) and cited above by Chickering and Gamsen (1987) emphasize the importance of faculty and peer interaction outside the classroom. This could be such a small thing as greeting the student by name in the hallway, or taking time to ask about their weekend. It could include announcing, in class, new art exhibits, concerts, plays, seminars and then attending those events yourself. Chapters 4, 8 and 12 suggest actions to take.

2.5   Myth #5 — Student's academic and non-academic experiences are separate and unrelated areas of influence on learning

Andre says, "I don't want to get personal with my students. They have their life. I have mine. My role is to teach them 'biochemistry' and I do a good job at that."

Reality: Terenzini and Pascarella (1994) note that the university experience is about the whole person and not just their intellectual growth. The university community should value, provide and nurture a wide range of intellectual and social experiences. Faculty should encourage students to participate in the rich set of academic, interpersonal and extracurricular activities that university offers. Faculty should also willingly serve effectively on student-oriented campus committees such as "homecoming weekend," the various clubs and organizations (as faculty advisor), "Frosh week activities," and the athletic board. Furthermore, service through those committees should be rewarded and included as important evidence in tenure and promotion decisions as is discussed in Chapters 4, 6, 8 and 11.

2.6   Myth #6 — It's easy to be a scholar in teaching

This myth appears in three different forms.

Ahmed is concerned about his students. He attends workshops on effective teaching and then tries these in his class. "After I try something new I always check by giving the students a questionnaire. If they like what happens, I continue it next year. If they don't, I drop it and try something else." Ahmed has presented several papers at conferences on teaching in which he describes what he does in the classroom. He is disillusioned because he feels he is doing research in teaching, yet no one in the academic community will count this as real research. "Ahmed doesn't do research. He's the strong teacher in our Department." notes the Chair.

Like every teacher, Jessie sets exams. After 30 years of experience, she now feels she has a lot to share about "assessment" so she writes papers on how she does it. They are accepted and published in reviewed papers on effective teaching.

Stan has an outstanding record in discipline-specific research. He brings in large research grants; he publishes extensively in Physics of Fluids. *He applies for $5,000 from the Center for Teaching to provide some demonstrations to complement his lectures. His one-line request for "$5,000 to develop demonstrations for my class" is turned down. "I can't believe it. With my research record it should have been a shoo-in! I thought they were trying to encourage researchers to take teaching seriously. The first time I do, they turn me down."*

Reality: Research is research — whether it is in a subject discipline or in teaching as illustrated in Table 1.3. Ahmed's frustration is understandable. He is focusing his research efforts in education — that should be equally as valid as research in "Engineering." Ahmed's problem is that he is "diddlin' around" in education. He tries one thing. If it doesn't work out, he tries another. He attends teaching workshops, but he didn't include educational research in what he does. Table 2.1 compares research in "Engineering" with the generic term "research" and with "diddlin' around." In educational research, as in Engineering research, we create and test hypotheses. For example,

- for research in education, the stated hypothesis to be tested might be that "using active learning in the classroom will improve student's learning."

- for the Engineering research, the stated hypothesis to be tested might be "the limiting interfacial tension of an oil-water mixture processed with a hydrocyclone is 10 mN/m; above this value we get separation; below this value we get further emulsification."

In both of these situations, the process used to define the problem, plan the tests and analyze the data is monitored. The results are written up and submitted to peer-reviewed journals. The activity results in publications and financial funding for other projects and, occasionally, awards. In Ahmed's "diddlin' around," he has no stated hypothesis; he has a gut feeling about what to try. His assessment will be anecdotal. He mainly talks to others about what he tried; he tends to use "satisfaction" indicators such as "The students seemed to like my new approach." His publications are descriptive. The challenge for Ahmed is to change his "diddlin' around" into educational research.

Table 2.1

Research, Research-in-teaching and "Diddlin' Around"

Research	Research-in-teaching	"Diddlin' around"
Process: Create and test hypotheses	Create and test hypotheses	Playing around, trying, experimenting
Monitoring: Monitor the process	Monitor the process	No monitoring of the process
Validation: Validate via peer review of grants, awards and papers	Validate via peer review of grants, awards and papers	Mainly talk to others about what they are doing; use "satisfaction" measures.
Action: Accept that the research process can be applied to a subject discipline, to teaching and or to administration		**Action:** Consider shifting to research by improving the objectives, the assessment and the validation.

Jessie is "diddlin' around" as well. She is using her past experience only and has ignored the cognitive and educational literature in her area of claimed expertise. She wouldn't dare submit a research proposal in engineering without doing a thorough literature survey of the main stream literature. Yet, on the topic of assessment she doesn't bother. She "diddles around."

Stan, like Jessie, would not dare submit a grant application in Mechanical Engineering (his area of expertise) with no literature survey, no well-defined goal, no identified need and no plan to test the hypothesis. Yet, somehow, he expects agencies to give him money just because he asks. He wouldn't dare "diddle around" when he approaches a granting agency in Mechanical Engineering. Somehow, he thinks he can "diddle around" if it is in teaching or education.

More on how to be scholarly in teaching is given in Chapter 5. The difference between scholarly teaching and effective teaching is given in Chapter 5. Actions to be taken are discussed in Chapters 8, 11 and 12.

2.7   Myth #7 — To improve teaching we need to give more workshops on "how to teach." This is particularly true for new faculty.

Director Arnold says "We've got a lot of new faculty coming in. We need to get some funding to run a whole series of required workshops on effective teaching."

Dean Mary is frustrated. For the third time in a row Dave, a tenured faculty member, has a student rating of 2 to 3 out of 10 on each of the courses he teaches. This is well below the departmental average. Dave does acceptable research and is currently supervising four students. He works hard on the Faculty committees, but his teaching has gone down hill. Dean Mary interviews Dave and suggests that he should take some workshops on effective teaching from The Center for Teaching.

Reality: Giving workshops on teaching is an important option to improving teaching. However, conditions must be right for this option to be effective. Unfortunately, both Director Arnold and Dean Mary incorrectly have assumed that "attending workshops" will have the greatest impact! But they are wrong according to Wright's (1996) survey (of deans, chairs, directors and of directors of Centers for Teaching in 58 Canadian universities) to prioritize practices that would improve teaching. The 960 responses ranked #1 the *"recognition of teaching in tenure and promotion decisions."* The option "Giving workshops on teaching methods to targeted groups" was ranked #3 by deans and #5 by instructional developers. In other words, if teaching is not recognized and rewarded in tenure and promotion decisions, then terrific workshops on teaching methods may not be as effective as they might. Dean Mary is better advised to consider how teaching is recognized in the annual performance reviews. Requiring faculty to take workshops is unlikely to have a major impact unless teaching is valued.

For **all tenured faculty**, the reality is that the first priority is that good teaching must be recognized and rewarded. After that, then workshops on teaching may help.

The priorities for **new faculty** are different. Even if good teaching is recognized and rewarded, the practical realities are:

- it takes an immense effort to get a viable research program going.

- simple things that take a minimal effort can have a dramatic positive impact on teaching effectiveness.

Indeed, Brew and Boud (1995) and Candy (1996) suggest that faculty should concentrate on specific roles over time. Start with the role of primarily a researcher. Well-intentioned Director Arnold needs to be realistic. He needs to scrutinize the recognition of teaching in the college's tenure documents. They might read as follows: candidates

- must have about 10 to 15 refereed publications independent of your research supervisor.

- must have letters from outside experts attesting to your research reputation and skills.

- must have reasonable financial support for your subject research.

- must have "acceptable" teaching.

- must show "good" citizenship.

Since the evidence must be compiled for a decision after about six years, the practical realities point to the importance of the publications and grants. Indeed, 61% of young faculty surveyed see the most difficult requirement to obtain tenure is "obtaining research funding" (Bert, 1999). "Publishing" is rated the most difficult for 23% of the respondents and only 6% see "teaching" as the most difficult requirement. Even if teaching is highly valued and the methods of measuring it (outlined in Chapter 4) are accepted, the realities about research are:

- it takes a minimum of three years to get your first graduate student out the gate.

- it takes a total elapsed time of about five years to get the first three to five publications from that thesis into print in refereed publications.

- to get funding from current agencies you need extensive documentation and almost have to have completed the research before you get funded.

- young faculty need to submit numerous grant applications to get one funded.

On the other hand, for teaching, the key is to learn the simple things that make a major impact. The realities for teaching are:

- teacher attitude has probably the greatest impact on student learning. This is relatively easy to change and inexpensive. Focus on learning (not teaching), expect students to succeed, care about your students as individuals and learn their names (Woods, 1999a and Myths #3, 4 and 5).

- do simple things that have major impacts: use "ombudspersons" or one-minute papers to get feedback about how well your course is progressing (Woods, 1999a). "Ombudspersons" are class representatives who systematically and periodically give you feedback about how well the course is going. For one-minute papers, take one to two minutes at the end of some classes, and ask each student to anonymously write 1) the main ideas he/she learned and 2) the points that are unclear and confusing. Collect the responses and use this feedback to clear up misunderstandings, adjust deadlines, and spend more time working on identified difficulties.

- if you do anything different from the traditional lecture (and I hope you do), then give your interventions the best chance to succeed. See Chapter 8 for more details.

- learn how to reflect on your teaching, to document your efforts and,

- keep an idea file, attend a few conferences and workshops on teaching and keep yourself up-to-date about teaching (Stice *et al.*, 2000).

In addition, for young untenured faculty Director Arnold should minimize the expected teaching loads, provide mentors, provide some startup funding to his young faculty to get their research going, and ensure that the forms of evidence, criteria and expectations are well-understood. Hence, workshops on teaching methodology have their place, but for young faculty the priorities should be on helping them get their research established.

Actions for administrators to facilitate the development of good teaching are discussed in Chapter 12.

2.8   Myth #8 — To improve the quality of teaching include "effective teaching" in the mission and vision statements for the university

> *Mission:* "At our University our purpose is the discovery, communication and preservation of knowledge. In our teaching, research, we are committed to creativity, innovation and excellence. We value integrity, quality and teamwork in everything we do. We inspire critical thinking, personal growth and a passion for leaning. We serve the social, cultural and economic needs of our community and our society."

> *Vision:* "To achieve international distinction for creativity, innovation and excellence."

> *Dianne supports the university's Mission and Vision. "This particular year, I have so much to do. I'm committed to death, I am starting a new direction to my research. I have eight graduate students. Who really cares if my teaching is lousy this year? Besides, I have had terrific student ratings on all of my courses over the past five years. I can let things slip this year. The chair knows what I'm capable of."*

Reality: A popular action is to create mission and vision statements for the university as has been done above. Such statements provide explicit goals and expectations. The example university's mission and vision statements given above are excellent as far as they go. They emphasize the importance of teaching. However, the mission and vision must be a lived reality! If decisions are to be made based on these goals, then the goals must be well-stated, expressed as results not actions, expressed in observable terms, and tied to measurable criteria with published, agreed-upon forms of evidence. Some example criteria developed for this mission and vision statement are given in Table 2.2. Unless the goals are well-stated, every program will claim it is meeting the university's mission and vision. The first weakness in most mission and vision statements I have seen is that they are incomplete and not well-stated.

Table 2.2
Some example criteria and forms of evidence for this university's mission and vision statement

Dimension		Sample Criteria
M1. **Teaching** with international distinction	1.1 Creativity: unique set of knowledge, ways of learning/ assessing	Students win creative writing competition, entry in juried show, one person show, composition performed, play performed, design competition. Students or teams win regional championships.
	1.2 Innovation: transfer of a new idea into practice, development of unique learning environments, approaches to assessment	Awards to faculty for creativity and innovation: Faculty of Engineering Innovation in Education; President's Award Papers about the innovation Invitations to talk about your innovation Visitors to see your classes Emulation by others Ratings by Center for Teaching; Exit survey Praise from alumni Number of high quality undergraduate/graduate students who come to the university because of the innovative programs or approaches
	1.3 Excellence: quality of the knowledge, experience and learning environments used	Awards to faculty: 3M, OCUFA, Awards for papers, Student Union Awards; Graduate Supervisor Award Faculty Grants for educational development/Full Time Equivalent faculty (FTE) Papers on educational/FTE Numbers of textbooks published/FTE Invitations to speak about educational issues/FTE Visitors to learn about/FTE Emulation by others; Student ratings of courses External awards to undergraduate and graduate students; Exit survey Student response to the Quality of the learning environment (as measured by the validated Course Perceptions Questionnaire each year) Student response to the "deep" versus "surface" learning (as measured by the validated Ramsden-Entwistle survey) Student response to attitude toward learning (as measured by the Perry inventory) Program publishes "Program Outcomes" and criteria; gathers evidence and monitors progress and publishes benchmarks Rating by Center for Teaching No. of educational papers refereed/annum/FTE No. of educational grants reviewed/annum/FTE No. of external requests to referee P&T decision based on "teaching contributions" External rating among peer Departments to place the unit in the top 35% in Canada Number and quality of the undergraduate and graduate students who come to the university because of the excellence of the program [% Ontario scholars; % awards] Unsolicited $ donations to the Unit because of its teaching Membership on editorial boards of educational journals Writing columns in publications about education Requests to give "guest" lectures in other courses Requests to participate in TA day or in Teacher training program or to give courses on being an effective teacher

However, having well-stated mission and vision statements is a necessary but not a sufficient condition to improve teaching. The real key, as mentioned in Chapter 1 and in Myth #7, is to have a published job description, to make all faculty accountable annually and to base performance review (whether it be tenure, promotion or annual performance) on the fundamental principles of assessment.

Dianne sees her duties as research versus teaching (Model 3 discussed in Section 1.3). First of all, she doesn't consider her graduate supervision as "teaching." Secondly, lacking a published job description she feels that she is not accountable each year. Faculty are accountable for the ways they spend their time and for the contribution to the university enterprise. As accountable individuals, we set personal goals, gather data and self-assess our performance (as discussed in Chapters 7 and 8) . Administrators annually review the performance of colleagues (and give appropriate merit increases in salary). Periodically, peers decide issues of tenure and promotion.

The following principles of assessment apply:

Principle 1 — Assessment is about performance, not personalities.

Principle 2 — Assessment is based on evidence, not feelings.

Principle 3 — Assessment should be done for a purpose with clearly-defined performance conditions.

Principle 4 — Assessment should be done in the context of published goals, measurable criteria and pertinent agreed-upon forms of evidence.

Principle 5 — Assessment should be based on a wide range of evidence.

Having a university mission statement — without measurable criteria and published forms of evidence — violates Assessment Principle 4. Dianne is justifiably frustrated because the global university goals have not been given as individual expectations. However, she is accountable each year. She is hoping her performance will be judged on a recall of past performance and not on evidence — a violation of Assessment Principle 2. Actions to address this Myth are given in Chapters 8, 11 and 12.

2.9 Myth #9 — Excellence in research can be measured; excellence in teaching cannot be measured.

> *The divisional promotion committee Chair Dave says, "Good old Charlie. Annually he brings in over a million dollars in research funding and publishes six papers a year in the top journals. Teaching? The promotion requirement is "good teaching." We know his student ratings are low. Yes, it's the worst in the Department. But, Charlie teaches a challenging course! He doesn't pander to*

the students. That's why he gets such bad ratings from the students. Besides, what do student evaluations mean anyway? Measuring anything about teaching is touchy-feely. How can you evaluate something you can't measure? Charlie deserves to be promoted!"

Other variations on this theme include such statements as:

"Madeline is an outstanding teacher. Her student ratings are always above 7 out of 10."

Reality: This Myth tends to be supported by those whose attitude is that research is more valuable than teaching (Model 4 in Section 1.3). Excellence in teaching can be measured. The approach is to apply the principles of assessment (described in Myth #8).

Step 1 — create observable, unambiguous goals for excellence in teaching.

Step 2 — add consistent, measurable criteria.

Step 3 — identify forms of evidence that are consistent with the goals and criteria.

The process is illustrated in Chapters 3 to 5. The answer to the divisional promotion committee is that Charlie has not provided evidence that he is an effective teacher. Student ratings reveal that he is an ineffective teacher. The responsibility rests with Charlie to provide evidence of excellence in teaching. Promotion at this time should be denied. The committee violated Principle 1 of Assessment... "Charlie is a good guy. Promote him." Assessment is not about personalities; assessment is about performance. The committee violated Assessment Principle 2. They made the decision based on gut feelings. They did not seek and demand evidence. I have found that assessments are often a "sympathy vote." *"I feel sorry for the candidate. This decision to not grant tenure at this time will really hurt him. He has spent so much effort here getting his research program going."*

Consider student ratings. The committee calls into question research about the use and interpretation of student ratings, or "course evaluations." More details are given in Chapters 4 and 8. Suffice it to say here that research evidence shows that overall questions (such as "rate the overall effectiveness of the instructor") provide valid and useful evidence for the purpose of making decisions (Cashin, 1995). Furthermore, the committee is not familiar with the research findings that show that students rate highly those courses that they feel are difficult (Cashin, 1995). The committee has supported a myth that is contrary to research findings.

Madeline includes the high results from student ratings as the only evidence about her teaching effectiveness. However, student ratings alone are inadequate evidence about teaching (Cashin, 1995, McKeachie, 1999). More details are given in Chapter 4. Actions to overcome this myth are listed in Chapters 11 and 12.

2.10 Myth #10 — Faculty know how to present their cases for tenure, promotion and annual merit.

> *For his annual performance evaluation, John submits to the chair a list of his research papers, grants, the committees he served on and the selected results from his student evaluations for the courses he taught. "The chair knows what my contributions are to the department. I'm not going to inundate her with stuff."*

Reality: John makes five mistakes.

1. John doesn't understand the five principles of assessment described in Myth #8.

2. John hasn't taken the time to determine the expectations, the criteria or the forms of evidence. He submits what he thinks is needed. John has missed Principle 4.

3. John hasn't collected evidence in all three categories of teaching, research and service. His list of activities provides inferior evidence. He should at least provide some personal reflections and self-assessment of the impact of his annual contributions to the Department and the University. John has neither a *Teaching Dossier* nor a Performance Summary (discussed in Chapters 7 and 10 respectively).

4. John doesn't want to brag. Besides, he has forgotten much of what has happened this past year. He reviewed eleven grant proposals, but doesn't everyone do that? He gave three presentations in High Schools describing engineering. At the request of the Provost, he analyzed the results of the Exit Surveys for the students from the Nursing Program. He created a unique display and demonstration for the Open House. He helped the students with the Frosh week, even though he did not serve on the Frosh week committee.

    Assessment is not about bragging; it is about performance. John has missed Principle 2; assessment is based on evidence. Without written evidence peers cannot make a fair assessment. John has the evidence; he just didn't present it.

5. John really doesn't want to be branded a "teacher" especially in this university where the focus is on research. He responded to a survey of the "innovations in the classroom" but requested that his work on cooperative learning be described such that no one can identify this as his work. On four occasions faculty from other universities came to observe him in action teaching his class. John sees teaching as being inadequate compared with research (as discussed in Section 1.3). In reality, the Chair will be giving the same weight to teaching as to research contributions in her annual performance review. John needs to provide evidence.

Actions to overcome Myth #10 are suggested in Chapters 8 and 12.

2.11   Myths provide a framework for discussion

The myths, beliefs, attitudes and actions form the "*culture*" in which we work. Understanding your University's culture is critical because it affects what you do and how you are motivated and rewarded for what you do. The ten myths, together with the model based on Boyer and Kreber's research, provide a framework to discuss and explore how individuals and administrators can describe performance expectations, list measurable criteria and provide/use a wide variety of forms of evidence related to academic performance. Having agreed-upon forms of evidence leads to ways to intrinsically and extrinsically motivate us to improve student learning. These are considered in the next Chapters.

If you try two things from this Chapter

Apply the five Principles of Assessment (described in section 2.8). The university "culture" usually holds a number of *Myths*. Sort out your Myths about academia.

Reflect and rate the ideas

Create your own summary for this Chapter. Table 2.3 gives you an opportunity to reflect on the ideas in this Chapter and to rate their applicability to your situation. For each Myth, you are asked to 1) identify your personal perception and 2) indicate the University's acceptance.

Table 2.3
Reflection and self-rating about myths and realities

Reflection:

_____

_____

_____

_____

Rate the myths

		act supporting myth	believe myth	partly believe myth	act to disprove myth	doesn't affect me
Myth #1: Prestige = educational quality	My view	O	O	O	O	O
	University's culture	O	O	O	O	O
Myth #2: Traditional teaching methods	My view	O	O	O	O	O
	University's culture	O	O	O	O	O
Myth #3: Good researcher = good teacher	My view	O	O	O	O	O
	University's culture	O	O	O	O	O
Myth #4: Teachers influence only in the classroom	My view	O	O	O	O	O
	University's culture	O	O	O	O	O
Myth #5: Our business is not the "whole person"	My view	O	O	O	O	O
	University's culture	O	O	O	O	O
Myth #6: It's easy to be a scholar in teaching	My view	O	O	O	O	O
	University's culture	O	O	O	O	O
Myth #7: To improve teaching, "give workshops"	My view	O	O	O	O	O
	University's culture	O	O	O	O	O
Myth #8: To improve teaching, include teaching in Mission	My view	O	O	O	O	O
	University's culture	O	O	O	O	O
Myth #9: Can't measure excellence in teaching	My view	O	O	O	O	O
	University's culture	O	O	O	O	O
Myth #10: We know how to present evidence about performance	My view	O	O	O	O	O
	University's culture	O	O	O	O	O

Other: _____

My conclusion from these responses is _____

My view differs from the University culture in the following _____

3

The five basic skills that usually are not rewarded explicitly

The key idea is that four of the seven factors (identified as being important for academic success) are not normally used to assess performance — enthusiasm, integrity, skill in communication, problem solving, etc. and subject expertise. In addition, each academic should contribute explicitly to the vitality of the institution. These five are important in their own right because they can be thought of as being prerequisites for effective teaching, research and administration. For these five, research provides details of successful performance. This can be used for personal self-assessment and improvement and this suggests forms of evidence that might be used to assess performance.

"Research, teach and service — that's what an academic does, right?"

Of the seven key skills expected of academics, usually four are taken for granted. Although academics are expected to possess and use these, these four are not measured or rewarded explicitly. These four skills are 1) enthusiasm; 2) integrity; 3) skill in higher order skills of communication, problem solving, interacting and working with others and assessment; and 4) expert and up-to-date in subject discipline. The skills relate to behaviors between teacher-students and should also be displayed in all interactions with colleagues and the community. Complementing this work, Kelly summarizes characteristics of vital and peak performing professors. [1] Peak performers:

1. are enthusiastic, caring, dedicated, vigorous, creative, flexible, risk-taking and regenerative

2. love what they do

3. learn from the work they do and complete the work undertaken

4. focus on achievement

5. have a positive attitude that goals can be set and accomplished

6. are unsatisfied with past performance and believe capable of achieving much more

7. are effective in multiple roles

8. are curious and intellectually engaged

9. grow personally and professionally throughout their career

10. expand interests

11. acquire new knowledge and skills

12. are willing to explore and grow

13. are respected by colleagues

Kelly's list, in some ways, amplifies the four skills. One additional skill that is vital to a successful organization, and your success within it, is the skill of actively contributing to the vitality of the institution (and to the Department in particular).

Although these are not rewarded explicitly, these are prerequisites for the three other skills of teaching, research and service that are rewarded explicitly. Hence, it is useful to survey each of these five skills in turn. Each skill is described and illustrated. Some forms of evidence are suggested.

3.1   Enthusiasm

Enthusiasm might be expressed as a "sparkle in your eye." Award-winning teacher, Dr. Valentina Brashers, Professor of Nursing at University of Virginia, is known for her enthusiasm. She says, "I thrive on my daily interactions with my students. Nothing could take their place in my life. My students are brilliant, insightful, genuine and funny. They challenge me in so many ways, and honor me in so many more." How do the students respond? Students say that she shows infectious enthusiasm. She goes out of her way to encourage students individually. She never let me give up and she made me feel that I belonged. She shows a passion for teaching, makes students eager to learn more, noteworthy are her optimism and her wonderful way of cheering others up by a friendly smile or a word of encouragement. [2] Her credo and the response of her students set a high standard for us all. The ideas we can extract from her example include:

- shows respect for, concern for and has a positive belief in her students,

- has a passion for teaching,

- smiles and optimistic.

Enthusiasm appears in three contexts: a) We are fascinated by our subject matter; it is the most important one for the students to learn. [3] b) We love teaching; we are embarrassed when we get our pay check because we are being paid for doing our favorite thing. c) We consider each student as an individual, and our role is to help each identify special talents they possess and to make the very most of those talents. We want them to succeed in their career and in their life after graduation. These tend to be inner attitudes but these can be reflected by a range of positive verbal and non-verbal behaviors that communicate that enthusiasm to others, especially to our students. Consider each in turn.

Usually, we all are enthusiastic about the subject we teach. The questions is "How might we show that enthusiasm to our students?" One research study videotaped teachers and analyzed to identify specific behaviors that occurred over any 2 second intervals throughout thirty different 10 second intervals during the lecture. [4] For teachers rated as enthusiastic the percentage of 2 second intervals when the feature was displayed were:

- vocalization (variety in pitch, tone and volume), 91%

- eye contact, 77%

- gestures, 67%

- movement by circulating about the room, not standing in one location, 56%

- facial expressions, especially a smile, 15%

Enthusiasm for the subject can also be displayed by the type of assignments, exam questions and anecdotes introduced into the course. For example, Charles Urbanowicz, another teacher cited for his enthusiasm, brings current information from newspapers, journal articles or the Internet into every class. [5] Phil Wood, a 3M award winning teacher from McMaster University, assigned interesting and every-day problems (in a heat transfer course) such as estimating the wind chill factor, doing a beer cooling experiment. This is also related to Section 3.4 being an expert in the subject domain and keeping up-to-date.

Enthusiasm for teaching can be demonstrated outwardly by classroom teaching behaviors; others by the tone of their assignments, exams, grading and learning environment in the classroom. Important issues here include the learning environment, helping students see that assessment is about performance and not personal worth, fairness, integrity, establishing and enforcing the "no cheating" rule and building trust, giving students a clear rationale of "what's in it for them" in terms of knowledge, skills attitudes and learning environment and maintaining decorum, having applause in the classroom. This is also related to Section 3.2, integrity and trust.

Enthusiasm for caring for our students: We see our role as helping them as persons as opposed to teaching subjects. "From this course I learned subject knowledge and about life." Explicit ways that we can show this include knowing names and calling them by name; being interested in them as individuals, celebrating their successes and special events, doing a phone check if they are missing from class, expecting them to succeed, using self-improvement projects and personalizing the feedback on assignments, and showing concern for their long term success. Some examples include:

- provide extensive critique of student resumes,
- announce upcoming local social, theatrical, artistic, educational events,
- when we discover a lack of understanding of meaning of words, offer to give a 5 min/class time update on "power words,"
- brief in-class celebration of special student achievements,
- on marked assignments focus on giving at least 5 positives for every 2 areas to work on. Use positive descriptors and never negative ones.

In summary, enthusiasm for the subject, for learning and for students as individuals have an extremely positive impact on student learning. There are a variety of ways we can explicitly display that enthusiasm. Some forms of evidence that record such enthusiasm (other than anecdotal comments) include the published syllabus, the script on marked assignments, the Teacher's Dossier, the assignments, and attendance at student functions and events important to the students (such as graduation, students award ceremonies).

3.2 Integrity, ethics and building trust

Professors should show integrity, be trustworthy and create learning environments that are characterized by integrity and trust.[6] Trust is composed of three elements: integrity, benevolence and competence.

Integrity means being consistent so that others know what to expect, meeting commitments and doing what you say you'll do, clarifying expectations, being honest so that your word can be relied upon, being fair, being credulous in all communications, and being willing to see situations from other person's viewpoint. Integrity also means honoring the seven fundamental RIGHTS of personal interaction. These RIGHTS are:

R — the right to be Respected.

I — the right to Inform or to have an opinion and express it.

G — the right to have Goals and needs and express these.

H — the right to Have feelings and express them.

T — the right to have had Trouble and make mistakes and be forgiven.

S — the right to Select your response to other's expectations.

and the right to Claim these rights and honor these in others.

Benevolence means confidentiality, avoiding the abuse of team member's vulnerability, showing respect, is not rude, does not intentionally deceive, shows empathy by listening and trying to understand the other person and their interests and needs, acceptance of the other person's point of view; being concerned enough about the other's welfare that acts to advance but not impede; not saying bad about a person when they are not present.

Competence: performs task according to expected standards; you have the knowledge, skill and abilities to do what you claim to be able to do.

Table 3.1 provides an inventory to help individuals reflect on aspects of trust.

Although some of these overlap with topics 3.1 and 3.4, consider some items that characterize integrity, ethics and trust in the teacher-student; teacher-colleague and student-student environment. The learning environment must be perceived by the students as being fair and equitable.

1. Consistency — the exams and tests should be consistent with the published learning objectives; marking of assignments should be consistent (among students and with a grading script).

Table 3.1
Trust

Trust is having confidence that you can mutually reveal aspects of yourself and your work without fear of reprisals, embarrassment or publicity.

Trust works both ways: you trust them and they trust you. Trust is not developed overnight, trust takes time to develop. Trust can be destroyed by one incorrect act.

Check your current status

Building your trustworthiness — getting them to trust you	already do this	needs some work	need lots of work	unsure if this is for me
1. Do what you say you will do.	O	O	O	O
2. Be willing to self disclose: don't hide your shortcomings; share yourself honestly.	O	O	O	O
3. Listen carefully to others and reflect to validate your interpretation.	O	O	O	O
4. Understand what really matters to others; do your best to look out for their best interests.	O	O	O	O
5. Ask for feedback.	O	O	O	O
6. Don't push others to trust you more than you trust them.	O	O	O	O
7. Don't confuse "Being a buddy" with trustworthiness.	O	O	O	O
8. Tell the truth.	O	O	O	O
9. Keep confidences.	O	O	O	O
10. Honor and claim the 7 RIGHTS.	O	O	O	O
11. Don't embarrass them.	O	O	O	O
Checking your trustworthiness — do they trust you?	always	most times	sometimes	don't think applies
1. Do they disclose confidential information trusting that you will keep it confidential?	O	O	O	O
2. Do they assign you challenging tasks to do without frequently checking up on you?	O	O	O	O
3. Do they honor your RIGHTS?	O	O	O	O
4. Do they seem to look out for your best interests?	O	O	O	O
5. Honest and forthright.	O	O	O	O
6. Do not leave you feeling that they haven't told you everything about the situation; they seem to be holding back.	O	O	O	O

2. Consistency in handling copying, cheating and fabrication of data.

3. Clear establishment of the learning environment in the classroom — trust, decorum, academic integrity where competition is fair, integrity respected and cheating is punished.

4. Clear written statements of expectations, policies and defined standards about collaboration.

5. Fair and full assessment of all students' work.

6. Role models honesty and integrity.

7. Benevolence — no denigration of students behind their back or to colleagues.

8. Treatment of confidences with confidentiality.

9. Equitable availability of past exams, lab reports and major projects. Often clubs, sororities, and fraternities have an excellent collection of past exams. If professors use the similar exams, labs and projects every year, then students who do not belong to such clubs are at a major disadvantage. An easy way to remedy this is to post a file of past materials in the library or on the web.

10. Equitable availability to resources. In one PBL program, the students who first located the key articles tore the articles from the library bindings so that they alone had the information. Take steps to remove this temptation by, for example, having available multiple copies of the key articles; have sign out procedures so that damaged resources can be tied to student borrowers.

Regarding cheating. Surveys suggest that 50 to 75% of students cheat at least once in their program. [7] [8] "Why shouldn't I copy when student X copies and gets 95%; I do my own work and get a mark of 60%? Cheating pays," says a disgruntled student. Professor Rankin responds "Sure, I've caught students cheating, but if I report it, then I'll lose about a week of my time documenting, and attending the tribunal. It's not worth it to me."

Okay. So what might we do and what evidence might be used to demonstrate our commitment and performance in integrity? Prevent cheating and use a tiered process for responding promptly to any misdeeds.

Step 1 — Publish clear guidelines, rules, policies and penalties. Consider using a Class Honor Code that all sign.[9]

Step 2 — Demonstrate good practice in referencing and citing; show how easy it is to detect copying/cheating. For example, in a course on writing, hand out an example page of student work that includes original student writing and plagiarized sections. Ask them to read it and comment on the writing. They will quickly identify the plagiarized sections. Then lead an activity to build their confidence in how to handle the situation correctly.

Step 3 — Establish a Departmental (or personal, if the Departmental is inadequate) process that has various levels of penalty.

At the first level, half work, half marks. If Denise and Adam's assignments are the same, mark one assignment, divide the total marks in half and write on both "Half work, half marks, see the work of Denise. Please discuss with me if you wish." and vice versa. My experience has been that in over 3/4 of the cases no one sees me. In 1/4 of the cases, one will admit to copying, receive 0 marks.

At the next level, appointment with documentation. A personal interview is scheduled. The interview should include a written memo summarizing the situation, evidence and decision. This is signed by both the student and the faculty member. The memo is sent to the student's file and to the Departmental chair.

Other, more formal criteria and levels are given, for example, by the University of Guelph.[10]

Some examples of evidence related to our approach to integrity and trust include:

- syllabus, with its explicit outline of policies, how to handle copying, description of the learning environment, expectations. An example is given in Table 3.2,

- marking scripts and example marking of assignments,

- consistency between published learning objectives and tests and exams,

- letters from alumni,

- comparison of exams, projects from year to year,

- Teaching Dossier explaining policy used for handling lack of integrity,

- use of a Class Honour Code.

Activity 3.1

Analyze the syllabus in Table 3.2 and identify elements related to trust and integrity.

In summary, integrity, ethics and trust are expected of all. The three components of trust are integrity, benevolence and competence. Some written forms of evidence are suggested.

Table 3.2

An example syllabus

Chemical Engineering 4N4

McMaster University

HAMILTON, ON

Engineering Economics and Problem Solving

Course Outline

Instructors: D. R. Woods, JHE 117, ⟨woodsdr@mcmaster.ca⟩

Teaching Assistant: Santiago Faucher ⟨fauchesr@mcmaster.ca⟩ x 27322

Schedule: lectures, 11:30 to 12:20; 12: 30 to 1:20 Tues; 11:30 to 12: 20 Thurs; tutorial; 2:30 to 4:20; JHE 326H

Calendar description: Making decisions about the design and operation of engineering systems, with the analysis emphasizing safety, economics, equipment performance, uncertainty, flexibility and monitoring including trouble shooting. Students will work individually and in groups on problem-based projects.

Overall program objectives:

The graduates from our Department will:

- be technically sophisticated with an emphasis on the fundamentals;
- be not only computer literate but also able to program effectively and efficiently and would be familiar with a wide range of process flowsheeting programs, such as HYSIM;
- be skilled in lifetime learning skills;
- have good communication, problem-solving, interpersonal and group skills;
- know how to create hypotheses, perform experiments and draw valid conclusions;
- have enriched experiences through senior electives drawn from our Department's research expertise.

Rationale and where this course fits in:

What does this course do to contribute to the overall program objectives? Most of the engineering fundamentals you will have mastered in your previous courses. The purpose of this course is to integrate those fundamentals, illustrate how you apply them and introduce you to a variety of criteria you use in applying the fundamentals. Five main themes are 1) engineering economics, 2) process operability and safety, 3) trouble shooting, 4) ethics and 5) the development of the career skills of chairperson, lifelong learning, self confidence, personal uniqueness with continued enrichment of skills in communication, problem solving, self assessment, interpersonal skills and group skills that you are developing in the MPS program. Group skills will be enriched when you work in groups for the boiler house project and the small group, self-directed, self-assessed problem-based learning.

Engineering economics will be the focus for the four cycles of PBL and include the Goals, Teach and Assess meetings. You will be assigned to a group of 5 to 6; one you will serve as chair for each meeting and will be assessed on performance as chair. Each person will be assessed on the quality of their teaching and assessing. Other activities related to engineering economics include your personal investment project and the application to process operability. MPS 36.

Ideas related to **process operability and safety** will be developed through a Socratic discussion of the deprop-debutanizer P&ID, through the boiler house projects and through the trouble shooting activities. The activities will include individual, diads, small group and triad activities. MPS 39.

Skill in trouble shooting will be developed through cycles through a triad activity of expert system, observer, and trouble shooter. The first cycle is on fluid mechanics problems, the second cycle is fluids plus heat exchange and the third cycle considers cases

... continue

involving fluids, heat exchange and distillation. MPS 34.

Attitude related to **professional ethics** will be developed through small group assessment of ethical dilemmas in the context of PEO ethics and misconduct guidelines. C8.

Chairperson skills: you will chair 2 to 3 different meetings, receive feedback, set goals for improvement and self-assess skill development. MPS 29.

Lifelong learning skills: given a problem to solve, you will identify what you need to know, contract with each other to teach the needed knowledge, share teaching-learning-decision-making styles, identify pertinent and valid resources, learn the knowledge and teach — not report — the information to others. You will assess the degree to which you and the group have learned the new knowledge. Both Mr Faucher and I are pleased to be resources to help with your learning needs. MPS 36.

Communication: All required assignments are due before the beginning of the class on the due date. Assignments handed in late receive zero marks. All assignments must have a covering letter or memo that describes what the task was, what answer you obtained and some judgment as to the accuracy and whether the reader should put much credence to your answer. For any assignment, we may read and evaluate the complete assignment based on the brief, one page memo or covering letter **only**. MPS 48. Evidence includes resume, reports, self-assessments.

Self-assessment/self confidence: a variety of inventories will be used to help you identify and value the unique you. In your feedback and self-assessment you are expected to apply the principles of MPS 3 on self-assessment.

How? Teaching and learning is a two-way street. I want you to do well and succeed in the course and in your career. Here is what you can expect from me: clear indication of the objectives, support and encouragement, sharing of experience, prompt feedback, respect and trust, response to your suggestions, caring environment in class. Here is what I expect from you: participation and success in all activities, feedback on how best I can help you, helping to create a caring environment in class, respect and trust in me and your colleagues.

In this class I use ombudspersons to provide input about how best I can create the best learning environment for you.

We assume that you are working for us in a company; this is no longer "academia." Your performance will be judged as though we are your supervisors. **The learning environment** will have few, if any 50 min lectures of "teacher talk." Straight teacher-talk lectures are the least effective way to facilitate your learning. Most class activities with be active. The Socratic method will be used to help you acquire some of the goals for MPS 39 on operability. Because much of what is learned is through participation in class or tutorial, you are expected to attend and participate in all classes. For the MPS Unit 36 on self-directed learning (small group, self-directed, self-assessed PBL), failure to attend and do your share of the activities for all of the sessions (unless the group members are aware and agree to your actions) will result in removal from the group and failure in MPS 36. You will be expected the learn the subject knowledge through independent learning.

With the many self-assessment reporting activities, and the open-endedness of some assignments, the homework load may appear, to some, to be unusually heavy. At first glance, most of the assignments seem to ask for a more complicated answer than is humanly possible in the time available. Part of the learning experience in this course is for you to learn how to redefine the problem so that the optimum solution is produced in the time available.

The assessment of your performance will be based on at least five different forms such as resume, reports, individual tasks, feedback forms, performance evidence from PBL, questions you pose. Wherever possible, the assignments are evaluated in terms of what would be expected in engineering practice. This applies to the format and clarity used in presenting your results, and to the practicality and reasonableness of your answer. You may contract for the percentage weighting for the final grade or marks in the course. The details are as follows. The final assessment in this course is the highest combination of a 40% – 60% weighting for term work and for the final exam. You may elect

... continue

to have any other weighting between 10% term work to 90% term work. Your personal choice should be made in writing to us before Nov 3. The final exam is an open book exam. Up to 30% on self-assessment may be included in the term work mark. Because much of what is learned is through participation in class or tutorial, you are expected to attend and participate in all classes. For the Unit on self-directed learning, failure to attend and do your share of the activities for all of the sessions will result in a failure in that Unit. [This is repeated from earlier in the outline to ensure that there is no misunderstanding.]

Calculator requirement for tests and examinations: Any calculator can be used on tests and examinations.

Resources:

Required materials:

1. Safety shoes for the Boiler house project.
2. Woods, D.R. (2005) MPS Phase IV course material, 4n4, McMaster University Bookstore.

Others:

Woods, D.R. (2005) "Rules of Thumb in Engineering Practice" Notes and book from Wiley and sons,

Woods, D.R. (2005) "Successful Trouble Shooting for Process Engineers" John Wiley and sons

Woods, D.R. (1995) "Process Design and Engineering Practice" Prentice Hall, Englewood Cliffs, NJ.

Woods, D.R. (1994) " Problem-based Learning: How to Gain the Most from PBL" Woods, Waterdown, distributed by McMaster University Bookstore, Hamilton ON. The Chapters that are most pertinent are Chapter 1 and Chapter 7.

Woods, D.R., (1995) "Data for Process Design and Engineering Practice" Prentice Hall, Englewood Cliffs, NJ.

Seider, W., J.D. Seader and D.R. Lewin (2004) "Product and Process Design Principles" 2nd ed. John Wiley and sons

For this course, the Library is your textbook. We will consider many different topics. Some will be in depth; others very briefly. The content varies from year to year. The focus is on helping you to see how to function as a professional.

Policy Reminders:

The Faculty of Engineering is concerned with ensuring an environment that is free of all adverse discrimination. If there is a problem that cannot be resolved by discussion among the persons concerned, individuals are reminded that they should contact the Department Chair, the Sexual Harassment Officer or the Human Rights Consultant, as soon as possible.

Students are reminded that they should read and comply with the Statement on Academic Ethics and the Senate Resolution on Academic Dishonesty as found in the Senate Policy Statements distributed at registration and available at the Senate Office.

3.3 Possess "process" skills

Professors are expected to be skilled in communication, speaking, writing and listening, problem solving, critical thinking, interpersonal and group work, and assessment. Again, these are not attributes that are usually considered explicitly when the performance of faculty is assessed. However, these are required, underpinning skills that are needed for our professional roles. In this Section, each is considered in turn.

3.3.1 Communication

Our major role is communicating our knowledge, skills and attitudes to others. We need to be skilled in speaking, writing and listening.

Communication is speaking and writing that 1) correctly identifies multiple *audiences*, answers their needs and questions; 2) has *content* that includes evidence to support conclusions, 3) is well *organized* with summary and advanced organizers, 4) uses a *style* that is coherent and interesting, defines jargon or unfamiliar words, and 5) includes a *format* that is grammatically correct and follows the expected format and style. These five elements should characterize every communication. Table 3.3 lists target skills for the writing process used by effective communicators. This can be used to monitor and reflect on our skills.

Listening includes focusing attention on the talker, avoiding distracting behaviors, showing respect and frequently acknowledging through appropriate body language and "ahums" and reflecting statements. Table 3.4 lists evidence-based target behaviors for listening. Good listening skills are essential for our interaction with others, especially students.

Activity 3.2

You are having a hectic day; you have a grant proposal to finish, a review to complete and a meeting with undergraduates. Your graduate student, Tanya, pokes her head in the door and said, "I really have to talk to you"... and then quickly launches her story of her frustration with the latest experiment. You realize this is crucial, so you drop everything and listen. "I started to run the new tests we designed but the concentrations increase instead of decrease as we expected. The temperature controller doesn't seem to be functioning as well as it should and the GC is broken. What am I going to do?"

Which of the following might you use to show Tanya that you are listening to her?

a. "Ahum."

b. "Ok, please continue."

c. "As I understand it, the experimental tests are showing an increase, rather than our expected decrease, the control of the temperature is not working as well as you expected and the analyzer we are counting on is not working. Is that correct?"

d. "How best can I help you, Tanya?"

e. "I'm listening."

f. Other.

Table 3.3
Communication — The writing process

Evidence-based targets for goals

Evidence-based targets	Progress toward internalizing these targets				
	20%	40%	60%	80%	100%
• Audience-based, not writer-based. The content answers the needs of the audience (instead of a dump of all the information known by the writer).					
• Organization is hierarchical (not chronological or historical).					
• Consider writing to be linked with clear thinking and problem solving (instead of a talent you either have and don't have).					
• Are willing to work through many drafts and revisions with a process that jumps around from stage to stage (instead of a linear writing of a single draft).					
• Select the organization and content to answer the questions and needs of the audience (instead of one magic format or sample to be followed).					
• Welcome confusion because this helps them identify why the audience might be confused and provides a check on their own thinking (instead of confusion is bad and to be avoided).					
• Let the ideas flow. Over-editing kills the thinking process (instead of fussing over each sentence before moving on to the next).					
• Have a coherent plan; spends a lot of time planning (instead of planning in his/her head or using a brief outline).					
• Spend most of the time planning and revising (instead of spending 10% on planning and revising with most of the time writing).					
• Realize that the greatest challenge is to conceptualize the audience's expectations and in organizing (instead of the greatest challenge being to get the grammar right).					
• Are very selective in content (instead of providing information overload).					
• Are willing to discard sections already written (instead of being unwilling to discard anything that has been written and trying to use it somewhere).					
• In revising, they focus first on the macrostructure, organization, reasoning, purpose, goal. Willing to rethink the whole task (instead of focus at the sentence level on grammar and style).					

Based on novice vs expert research by L. Flower. *Problem solving strategies for writers* McGraw Hill, NY 1984; N. L. Stein "Knowledge and process in the acquisition of writing skills," *Review of Research in Education*.

Table 3.4
Listening

Evidence-based targets for goals

Evidence-based targets	Progress toward internalizing these targets				
	20%	40%	60%	80%	100%
• Attention is focused on the talker.					
• Attend well by focusing on the talker, avoiding displaying distractive behaviors.					
• Track/follow well by providing minimal encouragement *(Tell me more, ahum, Then...)*; using infrequent questions (*What* rather than *Why* questions) and attentive silences.					
• Use astutely-phrased reflecting statements: concise and accurate restatement of content and feelings in the listener's own words. *As I understand it.*					
• Realize that listening is about four times slower than thinking and use appropriate focusing and reflecting actions to cope effectively.					
• Are skilled at sensing the message and realize that about 55% of the message is communicated by body language, 38% by tone and 7% by the words themselves.					

Activity 3.3

You are working in your office helping undergraduate student, Ahmed, understand how to solve one of the homework problems assigned. Your concentration is interrupted by the telephone. Ahmed looks at you. Your response is:

a. Say "Excuse me while I answer the phone."

b. Say, "Let it ring. This is your time; now for this problem..."

c. You answer the phone and ask them to call back.

d. You answer the phone and respond to the caller over the phone. They have as much right for your time as Ahmed.

e. You use this as an opportunity to say "Ahmed, I'm sorry but this is homework. I must be fair to everyone. You are expected to solve this homework problem on your own without my help."

f. Other.

Forms of evidence related to our communication skill might include our grant proposals, papers, written enrichment notes, feedback from alumni, feedback about seminars given, awards for our publications, citations of our publications, the use of our text as a required text by others, and feedback from peers about administrative responsibilities.

3.3.2   Problem solving

We are expected to be skilled in the process of problem solving. Table 3.5 defines this skill and provides a long list of behaviors of skilled problem solvers. This list can be used for self monitoring and reflection. Related skills are creativity, Table 3.6, and critical thinking, Table 3.7.

Table 3.5

Problem solving

Problem solving is the generic mental and attitudinal process by which we effectively and efficiently obtain a "best" answer for a goal/decision/objective and that satisfies constraints. The skill is generic in that the skill is needed by people in all disciplines and in all contexts. However, skill in problem solving needs to be matched with knowledge about the subject and context. A chemist draws on her knowledge of chemistry to solve problems in chemistry.

Contrast problem solving with exercise solving. Professionals with years of experience have solved many problems and have mentally stored these as sample solutions. They draw on their experience to solve current problem-situations they encounter, they usually can use and adapt a sample solution and do not need to use generic problem solving skills. We call this exercise solving.

Evidence-based targets for problem solving

Evidence-based targets	Progress toward internalizing these targets				
	20%	40%	60%	80%	100%
• Overall: Are skilled in describing aloud their thoughts as they solve problems.					
• Overall: Their problem solving skill improves if they pause and reflect about the process and about what they are doing. Example reflective statements include: *"What have I done so far? What have I learned?"*					
• Overall: Successful problem solvers monitor their thought processes about once per minute while solving problems. Example monitoring statements include: *"If I do this... what will I achieve?" Am I finished with this stage? Why am I doing this? What do I do next?*					
• Overall: Each has his/her own particular style that works for them; others have a different preferred style.					
• Overall: Problem solving is done in short term memory; STM: they are active, write things down to help overcome the space limitations of STM.					
• Overall: Focus on accuracy and not on speed.					
• Overall: Problem solving is often a social process; they interact with others.					
• Overall: They solve their mental image of the problem; such a mental image is called the internal representation of the problem.					

... continue

Evidence-based targets	Progress toward internalizing these targets				
	20%	40%	60%	80%	100%
• Overall: Creativity is required anytime in the process of solving problems. For details see Table 3.6.					
• Overall: Know that problem solving skill interacts with subject knowledge (needed to solve the problem) and with the sample solutions (from past solved problems).					
• Overall: Differentiate between exercise solving and problem solving. In the classroom, most teachers demonstrate exercise solving (because they know too much and have solved most of the problems in the course already and, even if they try to role play problem solving, they don't wish to show the mistakes one makes when one problem solves because the students might judge them to be incompetent).					
• Overall: Unsuccessful problem solvers tend to memorize and try to recall equations and solutions that match the situation instead of defining the real problem and identifying key fundamentals. They try to exercise solve instead of the required problem solve.					
• Overall: Unsuccessful problem solvers tend to search for an equation that uses up all of the given variables. whereas successful problem solvers focus on an organized strategy that focuses on defining the real problem.					
• Overall: Unsuccessful problem solvers tend to take a trial and error approach; successful problem solves use a systematic strategy. Use a strategy to help them to be systematic and organized.					
• Overall: be systematic and organized. Use a strategy. An example, validated strategy is a series of about 6 stages(11). Each stage uses different thinking and feelings. This strategy is not used serially (following rigidly one step after another). Rather it is used flexibly; applied many times while solving a single problem with frequent recycling from one stage to another. The suggested stages are Engage, Define, Explore, Plan, Do it, Look back.					
• Define the problem well; do not solve the wrong problem. Be willing to spend up to half the available time in the first three-stages to define the real problem: Engage, Define and Explore. Most mistakes made by unsuccessful problem solvers are made in the define stages.					
• Engage: Manage distress well when problem situations are first encountered and throughout the problem solving process. They say, *"I want to and I can." "I have a proven, organized strategy that works for me."*					
• Engage: Spend time reading the problem statement. (Up to three times longer than unsuccessful problem solvers).					

... continue

Evidence-based targets	Progress toward internalizing these targets				
	20%	40%	60%	80%	100%
• Defining a stated problem: This is stage 2. Focus on the given problem statement only and classify the given information into the goal, constraints, criteria and the "situation."					
• In the Define stage, successful problem solvers can correctly differentiate between constraints, criteria, possible solutions and procedures.					
• Define: Use skill in classification, Classification is for a purpose. Change the purpose and you change the classification.					
• Define: For classification, at each level of classification, there should be a single basis or criterion for the classification.					
• Define: For classification, use tables, charts, pictures, checklists, diagrams to help systematically organize and to overcome the limitations of STM. Unsuccessful problem solvers do not use accurate and detailed bookkeeping procedures throughout.					
• Define: Extract and classify the information carefully. (Unsuccessful problem solvers omit given information, misread the words, unknowingly replace missing information with unstated assumptions).					
• Define: Can identify assumptions and hypothetical information in the given scenario.					
• Define: Systematically classify the input data and identify the goal as it was given in the problem statement. Refrain from replacing it with a possible solution (*"determine the offset in a control situation"* is not replaced with *"to solve a second-order differential equation"*), translating it into a symbol (*"solve for the force"* is not replaced with *"solve for F"*).					
• Explore: Keep their options open in the Explore stage. Unsuccessful problem solvers fail to keep options open, become quickly fixed upon an incorrect path, are impatient, jump into the problem with an immediate answer.					
• Explore: Patiently create a rich internal representation of the problem and then identify the real problem (via such activities as boundary exploration, simplification, What if? and Why? Why? Why?).					
• Look back: Manage exhilarating stress generated because of the successful solution to the problem; patiently and systematically check that the correct problem was solved; the constraints and criteria were satisfied; the solution was elaborated to provide a range a problem situations where a similar solution would apply.					

Table 3.6

Creativity

Evidence-based targets for goals

Evidence-based targets	Progress toward internalizing these targets				
	20%	40%	60%	80%	100%
• Ideas are stored in memory in patterns, so called d-lines, that relate similar ideas. For creativity, use triggers to enter our memory through unfamiliar and surprising routes.					
• For creativity, to maintain a positive self-image, each of us has an internal monitor that keeps us from saying foolish or crazy things. In brainstorming, we create an environment where it is acceptable to say such things.					
• For creativity, defer judgment; don't criticize ideas.					
• For creativity, be succinct; don't rationalize, elaborate on or justify an idea. Just state it. 50 ideas in 5 minutes is a reasonable criterion.					
• For creativity, write down the ideas.					
• For creativity, build on ideas; don't worry about repetition.					
• For creativity, control their negative feelings and silences by: rereading the problem statement or by introducing a trigger.					
• In any brainstorming session, over 80% of the ideas generated in the last 5 minutes are useless. However, among the remaining 20% are often the most interesting and unique.					
• For creativity, crazy ideas can be converted into feasible ideas by relating the individual characteristics of the crazy ideas to the goal situation.					
• For creativity, practice using each of the dozen or so triggers and discover which ones work best for them.					
• Inevitably, they will need to brainstorm as an individual; acquire skill and confidence to brainstorm on their own.					
• Different persons apply their creativity in different venues: some work within the constraints (the Adaptors); some try to change the constraints (the Inventors). Kirton's KAI is a validated instrument to help identify preference.					

Some forms of evidence for skill in problem solving include our grant proposals, our published research papers, the reviews we do of grants and papers, the awards received for our publications, the citations of our papers and peer feedback about our administration. Tables 3.5 and 3.6 can be used to monitor our progress for improvement; this could be included as part of our Private Professional Dossier.

3.3.3   Critical thinking

A definition of critical thinking is given in Table 3.7 together with a summary of research evidence about how skilled critical thinkers behave. This provides a convenient place to reflect and monitor skill.

Critical thinking is a basic skill; we demonstrate it ourselves and should help our students acquire the skill. For undergraduate students we might develop the skill through inquiry type classroom activities. For graduate students we might include sessions on "how to critique a paper." Forms of evidence might include our grant proposals, our published research papers, and the reviews that we do of grants and papers and awards for our publications.

3.3.4   Interpersonal and group skills

In academia we function as a team: a learning team with groups of undergraduate students, a one-on-one team with graduate students and post docs; a discovery team with researchers nationally and internationally; a decision-making team with colleagues within department, college and university and within professional associations; a problem-solving team with industrial colleagues and a sharing team with the tax-paying public and potential students. In these interactions the valued skills include interpersonal skills and team skills. The interpersonal skills overlap with some attributes discussed in Section 3.2 but are listed in Table 3.8. This provides a convenient format for reflection and monitoring growth. Table 3.9 lists the target behaviors for team work.

The major forms of evidence related to these skills are usually applicable to the service and administration sections of an academic's responsibility.

Table 3.7

Critical thinking

Critical thinking is gathering and validating information, checking for consistency, classifying information, recognizing patterns, reasoning and drawing valid conclusions.

Evidence-based targets for critical thinking

Evidence-based targets	Progress toward internalizing these targets				
	20%	40%	60%	80%	100%
• Acknowledge that we think in terms of our past experience.					
• Acknowledge that we accept new ideas because of logic (logos), of emotions (pathos) and of credibility of the source (ethos).					
• Logical reasoning can be deductive (if... then) whereby we accept a general conclusion and then accept a specific instance.					
• Logical reasoning can be inductive where facts are gathered and then we accept a generalization.					
• Can identify and combat about two dozen commonly-used fallacies in logic.					
• Can identify and combat about a half dozen commonly-used emotional appeals.					
• Can identify and combat about a half dozen, commonly-used ethos appeals.					
• Can list and apply a 10-step process for critical thinking, 1. context; 2. definitions; 3. identify conclusions; 4. check the evidence; 5. identify the point of view or assumptions; 6. diagram the argument; 7. identify whether inductive or deductive and rate quality of evidence; 8. assess counterarguments; 9. assess consequence and implications; 10. evaluate.					
• Can define and classify information into primary facts, event facts, reasoned facts, opinions and opinionated facts.					
• Can locate the data by using such words as *because, for, since, Table shows, if, as shown by, as indicated by, the reasons are, this is inferred by, the evidence is, assuming that, based on, whereas, it follows from.*					
• Can correctly identify the stated conclusions by locating such trigger words as *and so, I conclude, in conclusion, it is clear that, hence, thus, then, consequently, for these reasons, shows that, therefore.*					
• Can check the validity of the data via statistical analysis (for cause-effect identification or to identify a relationship) or check the premises (for arguments and reasoning).					
• Can correctly diagram the structure of an argument.					
• Can evaluate the acceptability of premises/data.					
• Can evaluate the credibility of the sources.					
• Can correctly identify assumptions, implied assumptions and hypothetical information in the given scenario.					

... continue

Evidence-based targets	Progress toward internalizing these targets				
	20%	40%	60%	80%	100%
• For deductive reasoning, can astutely analyze linear orders, syllogisms and "if..then" statements.					
• For inductive reasoning, can astutely use statistical methods.					
• For statistical methods, recognize the need to isolate and control variables in order to make strong causal claims.					
• For statistical methods, can check for adequate sample size and unbiased sampling when a generalization is made.					
• For statistical methods, able to describe a relationship between any two variables as being positive, negative or unrelated.					
• For statistical methods, can check for and understand the need for control groups.					
• Can consider missing components by assuming a different perspective.					
• Can assess the overall strength of an argument.					

Table 3.8

Interpersonal skills

Evidence-based targets	Progress toward internalizing these targets				
	20%	40%	60%	80%	100%
• Aware of their own uniqueness and personal style, and how they might differ from the style of others.					
• Honor the seven fundamental rights of individuals, RIGHTS. R, to be Respected; I, Inform or to have an opinion and express it; G, have Goals and needs; H, have feelings and express them; T, trouble and make mistakes and be forgiven, S, select our response to the expectations of others and claim these rights and honor these in others.					
• Can avoid the four destroyer behaviors that destroy relationships: Contempt, Criticism, Defensiveness and Withdrawal/stonewalling.					
• Can build trust by keeping commitments to themselves and others; clarifying expectations that they have of themselves and of others; showing personal integrity, honesty and loyalty to others, especially when they are not present; apologizing promptly and sincerely when they know they are wrong; honoring the fundamental RIGHTS listed above and avoiding the destroyers; listening and understanding another's perspective; being truthful; and accepting others "warts and all."					
• To improve and grow people need feedback about performance. Give feedback to others to encourage and help them; not for them to get their kicks and put them down. Focus on five strengths for every two areas to improve on.					
• Are skilled at responding assertively. "When you... I feel .. adjust by..."					

Table 3.9
Group and team skills

Evidence-based targets for group skills.

Evidence-based targets	Progress toward internalizing these targets				
	20%	40%	60%	80%	100%
• Performance improves when they have goals. [12]					
• Assessment must be related to the goals. [13]					
• Both Task (getting the job done) and Morale (feeling good about the group work and about how they have interacted with the other group members) are important. [14]					
• Any group functions better with a chairperson. [15]					
• Chairperson and leadership are different; different people may become leaders at different times. [15]					
• Group evolution tends to follow a pattern described as by such descriptors as "forming, storming, norming and performing." [14] Schutz's instrument FIRO-B seems to provide reliable insight as to the personal style of individuals towards other group members during three of these phases. [16] [17]					
• Can list the roles needed in both Task and Morale to make an effective group. [14]					
• When each person has a clear idea of roles and group norms, the group functions better. [14]					
• When groups are functioning effectively, about 75% of the time is spent on the task; 15% on morale building activities and 15% of task process activities (how the problem solving process is going; summarizing ideas, guiding the process). [18]					
• The products from groups or teams is improved when members have different "styles" (for example, in Jungian terminology some members are dominant S, and some, dominant N). The products from groups tend to be inferior when all the members "think and behave alike." [14] [15] [19] [20]					
• The quality of decisions, product, task is improved if group members offer different perspectives, disagree and seem to introduce conflict into the process. The trick is to manage the apparent conflict well. Teams have accepted methods for resolving conflicts. [14] [19] [20]					
• The characteristics of "meetings of individuals," "effective groups" and "teams" fall on a spectrum with sufficient differences that it is useful to differentiate based on those characteristics.					
• In a team, each accepts the team goals and willingly foregoes personal and constituent goals for the benefit of the team.					
• In a team, decisions are made by consensus.					
• In a decision-making mode, after 20 minutes of discussion on any one topic, few new ideas are presented and repetition of previously-stated ideas occurs. [21]					

3.3.5   Assessment

We define assessment as a judgment based on the degree to which the goals have been achieved using measurable criteria and pertinent evidence. We are expected to peer review papers and grants, to assess the work of undergraduate and graduate students, write letters of recommendation, do performance reviews of colleagues, technicians, administrators and secretaries. For all of these we apply the five fundamental principles of assessment. These principles are:

Principle 1 — Assessment is a judgment based on performance, not personalities. We need to help a person realize that a poor mark or performance review does not mean he/she is a bad person. The judgment is made about performance in completing a task. It has nothing to do with his/her value as an individual. This is an issue, especially for people with attitudes characterized by Perry's level 2. More details about Perry's levels and their implications to teaching and learning are given elsewhere. [22]

Principle 2 — Assessment is a judgment based on evidence, not feelings. We might intuitively feel that a person is skilled at team work. However, we need to replace that intuitive feeling with physical written evidence.

Principle 3 — Assessment should be done for a purpose with clearly-defined performance conditions.

Principle 4 — Assessment is a judgment done in the context of published goals, measurable criteria and pertinent, agreed-upon forms of evidence.

Principle 5 — Assessment should be based on multidimensional evidence: static and dynamic situations; small assignments and lengthy projects; academic, social and personal contexts; under a variety of performance conditions (exams and homework, written and oral, performance as an individual and as a member of a group), formative and summative data and with different persons being the assessors (self, peer, teacher and trained external observers).

To remove ambiguity from the assessment, the following *six issues in practice* should be addressed.[22–24]

1. Goals — What is being assessed? Knowledge in the subject discipline? Skills? Attitudes? Have the goals been expressed unambiguously in observable terms? Who creates the goals? Are the goals explicit and published?

2. Criteria — Do the criteria relate to the goals? Can each criterion be measured? Who creates the criteria? Are the criteria explicit and published?

3. Form of evidence — Is evidence consistent with the criteria? Do both the assessor and the person know that this form of evidence is acceptable?

4. Resources — Are the goals and the collection of the evidence possible to achieve in the time provided and with the resources available?

5. Assessment process — What is the purpose of the assessment? Under what conditions is the person's performance assessed? Who assesses? What type of feedback is given by the assessor? (For example, Pass/fail? A grade? A list of the five strengths and two areas to work on?) What is the form of feedback? Verbal? Written? What is the timing of feedback? Who delivers the feedback?

6. Training in the assessment process — Have both the person and the assessor received training in assessment?

Table 3.10 provides a feedback form that can be used to reflect on the assessment process. For faculty, the forms of evidence that can be used related to skill in assessment include:

- learning objectives — well defined in observable terms with measurable criteria?

- consistency between learning objectives and exams?

- performance expectations for colleagues and staff in the department — well defined in observable terms with measurable criteria?

- is the assessment done with integrity (as explored in section 3.2)?

- syllabus — describe the assessment process, criteria, conditions?

3.3.6 Summary

Skills important for a successful academic include skill in communication and listening, problem solving, critical thinking, interpersonal interaction and team work and assessment. Traditionally, many of these are not considered explicitly in evaluating an academic's performance. However, evidence-based descriptors of the skills are given in a format to aid in self monitoring. Some forms of evidence are available. Many of the skills overlap.

3.4 Expertise in subject

We are expected to be expert in our field; we are up-to-date. A first element of keeping up-to-date (or to be a lifelong learner) is to be information literate. Being information literature combines skill and attitude. Such a person recognizes the need for information and determines the nature and extent of the information needed; accesses

Table 3.10
Feedback about assessment

Goals: Content is well identified, goals are challenging and achievable, goals are written in observable terms, goals are unambiguous, the "given" conditions are specified.

None of these behaviors		Few of these behaviors but major omissions		Most features demonstrated		All of these behaviors
○ 1	○ 2	○ 3	○ 4	○ 5	○ 6	○ 7

Criteria: Criteria are consistent with the goals and are measurable and practical. The criteria are challenging and achievable.

None of these behaviors		Few of these behaviors but major omissions		Most features demonstrated		All of these behaviors
○ 1	○ 2	○ 3	○ 4	○ 5	○ 6	○ 7

Evidence: The type and quality of evidence gathered is consistent with the goals and criteria. The evidence has been gathered conscientiously over a long enough period of time. The evidence is well organized. The quality and extent of evidence is sufficient to allow me to judge the extent to which the goals have been achieved.

None of these behaviors		Few of these behaviors but major omissions		Most features demonstrated		All of these behaviors
○ 1	○ 2	○ 3	○ 4	○ 5	○ 6	○ 7

Process: The assessment process has been applied and as an independent assessor I concur with the decision as to the degree to which the goals have been achieved.

None of these behaviors		Few of these behaviors but major omissions		Most features demonstrated		All of these behaviors
○ 1	○ 2	○ 3	○ 4	○ 5	○ 6	○ 7

Strengths _____ Areas to work on _____

from D. R. Woods, *How to Gain the Most from Problem-based Learning* (1994)

needed information effectively and efficiently; evaluates information and its source critically and incorporates selected information into their knowledge base and value system; classifies, stores, manipulates and redrafts information collected or generated; expands, reframes or creates new knowledge by integrating prior knowledge and new understandings individually or as a member of a group; understands the cultural, economic, legal and social issues surrounding the use of information and accesses and uses information ethically, legally and respectfully; recognizes that lifelong learning and participative citizenship requires information literacy.

Lifelong learning might be defined as assuming responsibility for identifying what we need to know, creating learning goals and criteria, identifying pertinent and accessible resources, engaging in learning the knowledge especially the difficult parts, integrating the new knowledge with past knowledge and experience, using the knowledge to solve the need and assessing the degree of comprehension. We will use people and peers as resources. There are two approaches to lifelong learning — reactive and proactive. In reactive lifelong learning, we keep up-to-date on a need-to-know basis. We are externally motivated by the problem situation to learn new knowledge and skills. Usually there is a time constraint. That is, we suddenly realize that we don't understand the material required for the next lecture; we quickly locate the required information, check it for validity, internalize it and put it in the context of what we knew before.

In proactive lifelong learning we are motivated internally by a desire to keep up-to-date and learn knowledge that might be needed in the future. We do not wait for a sudden need-to-know as described in reactive lifelong learning. We prioritize and set aside time for the task. We may subscribe to specialized resources to aid. However, the skills of goal setting, resource identification, utilizing peers, validating evidence, self assessment, reflection and elaboration, that are needed for reactive lifelong learning, are also needed for proactive lifelong learning. Attitude toward lifelong learning is important.

The Self Directed Learning Readiness Survey (SDLRS) suggests that the following eight attitudes are important: [26] [27]

1. tolerance of risk, ambiguity and complexity in learning;

2. creativity;

3. view of learning as a lifelong beneficial process;

4. self concept as an effective, independent learner;

5. initiative and independence of learning;

6. love of learning;

7. self understanding;

8. acceptance of responsibility for one's own learning.

For most of these dimensions inventories are available to help identify these. Table 3.11 provides a convenient opportunity to self-rate.

The forms of evidence that might be used relating to proactive lifelong learning include requests to be a reviewer of papers or grants; number of journals viewed and workshops or conferences attended, invitations to present seminars, number of hits on website, invitations to write papers or be on panels on the topics "the future...," "the latest advances in" and being referred to as a pioneer.

3.5   Actively contribute to the vitality of the institution

A major theme throughout this guidebook is that great things happen in "vital" institutions. Vitality cannot be created by the administration alone. Vitality requires the input from each and every member of the Department/Institution.

What is vitality? Vitality is the capacity to live, grow and develop energetically and enthusiastically. Such a department promotes self motivation, self awareness and self confidence. Such departments are characterized by high support and encouragement, cohesiveness and trust, and pride in the accomplishments of students, support staff and faculty; frequent get-togethers and celebrations. They work hard and play hard. They enjoy each other's company.

What can individuals contribute? This is much more than being a "good citizen" who completes the tasks assigned. Beyond being a good citizen, those who contribute to the vitality of the department or unit through an application of the enthusiasm, integrity, and trust to the context in which we work. This includes being proud of the department and the people who make up the department; positively being aware of, congratulating and celebrating the achievements of others; encouraging and supporting each other in their work and social life, participating in student events, in departmental social events and in student-faculty events. We can contribute by being good listeners.

Table 3.11
Attitudes related to proactive Lifelong Learning

Attitude	Descriptors	Rate yourself
1. Level in learning: tolerance of risk, ambiguity and complexity [2] [33] [35] [36]	+ are stimulated by the challenge of sorting out ambiguous and ill-defined sets of information. Willing to sort out tough and difficult concepts and want to relate to previous knowledge.	
	− prefer a syllabus with clear instructions and deadlines. Do what is required and they hope never need to use the topics that are difficult to comprehend.	
2. Acceptance of responsibility for their own learning [9] [28] [30] [32] [36]	+ willingly accept own responsibility.	
	− are pleased when others define the learning expected.	
3. Motivation for learning [4] [7] [36]	+ believe on-going learning is beneficial and needed for personal enjoyment and growth; intrinsic motivation; enjoy the challenge; want to learn.	
	− did their learning at school and learn any additional knowledge/skills required to maintain licence and position; extrinsic motivation; what's in it for me?	
4. Self concept about learning [5] [28] [29] [32] [36]	+ see themselves as an effective independent learners; see teachers as being resources.	
	− see themselves as good learners in a well-defined environment. Prefer teacher as source.	
5. Initiative and independence of learning [6] [30] [31] [36]	+ have confidence in setting personal goals, developing and implementing independent plans for learning. Believe they can aggressively take charge of their learning.	
	− prefer to select from well-defined "courses" where the objectives, and recommended texts are supplied; enjoy a dependent or interdependent environment for learning. The needs for learning will be apparent to them and they will respond as needed.	
6. Self understanding and self concept [8] [29] [33] [34] [35] [36]	+ are aware of personal preferences for learning and for making decisions, self confident and work mainly at Mazlow's self-actualization level. Able to adjust to account for deficiencies in learning style.	
	− are unaware of personal style and how it might differ from teacher's, text author's and other learner's. Self confidence is developing. Cope with the learning style they have.	
7. Principles of learning [27] [38] [39]	+ believe such concepts as active learning, reflection, elaboration, learning plans, learning journals, self assessment can improve learning.	
	− believe that these concepts take too much time away from actual learning.	
8. Ability to manage personal change [38]	+ are aware of the typical stress and grieving process when change is thrust upon them; have confidence that they can proactively move through the process.	
	− are unaware and lack confidence in handling change.	
9. Problem solving [30] [31] [37]	+ have confidence in skill in problem solving; willing to engage in solving challenging and difficult problems.	
	− lack confidence in skill and prefer to avoid tackling difficult problems.	
10. Creativity [40]	+ believe in the benefits of deferring judgment, using many viewpoints, managing negative feelings and using "crazy ideas".	
	− prefer to judge; thinking up crazy ideas is a waste of time. the key useful options come to them promptly.	

3.6 Implications for performance in teaching, scholarship and administration

From our survey of these four factors presented in this Chapter we realize that we can set goals, identify criteria and suggest evidence that can be used to assess performance. Table 3.12 summarizes these and identifies the area T, teaching, R, research and S, for service where these might be most important and evidenced.

Table 3.12

Matching these attributes with the traditional areas of teaching, research and administration

Goal	Criteria	Forms of evidence	T, R, S,
1. Enthusiasm for subject	> 3 intriguing and current problems	assignments, projects exam	T
		letters from alumni	T
1. Enthusiasm for teaching	Positive reflective comments and activities related to student learning	Teaching Dossier	T
		letters from alumni	T
1 Enthusiasm for students	Attend > 80% of student functions during the semester		T
	Attend graduation		T
	Zero "put down" comments as judged by independent assessor	marked assignments	T
		letters from alumni	T
2. Trust: clear expectations	Clear expectations, published unambiguous learning objectives, statements about integrity, statements about collaborative work statements about assessment	syllabus, learning objectives, statements about integrity, policy about assessment, learning objectives for graduate students, assigned text and students notes	T
		self-rating form, Table 3.1	
2. Integrity	100% consistency between learning objectives and exam questions as judged by person skilled in development of learning objectives and subject discipline	published learning objectives; exams	T
	Equitable marking 100% consistency between marking script and marks on all assignments	marking script; marked student assignments	T
	Personal statements about trust and integrity are consistent with published calendar and University policy	syllabus; University Calendar/website	T
	Exams, projects and tests do not use the same questions year to year over a 5 year period	exams and projects over the years	T

... continue

	Goal	Criteria	Forms of evidence	T, R, S,
3.	Communication skill		grant proposals	R
			papers	R
			enrichment notes	T
			feedback about seminars given	S
			awards for their publications	R
			citations of their publications	R
			use of their text as a required text by others	R
			feedback from alumni	T, R
			self-rating form, Tables 3.2 and 3.3	
3.	Critical thinking		grant proposals	R
			papers	R
			feedback about seminars given	R, S
			awards for their publications	R
			citations of their publications	R
			reviews they write of papers and grant proposals	R
			self-rating form Table 3.7	T, R, S
3.	Problem solving		self-rating form, Table 3.6	T, R, S
4.	Team skills	people want to be on their team, class attendance is > 80%, meeting attendance is > 80%	renewal of position, invitations to assume leadership,	T, S, R
		agendas for meeting circulated in advance and include location and time, attendees, purpose, background expectations, decisions, and timing and as assessed by specialist and attendees	agendas	S
3.	Assessment skill	Published learning objectives are unambiguous, observable with measurable criteria as judged by person skilled in development of learning objectives and subject discipline	learning objectives	T
		Published process, criteria and conditions about assessment shall be judged to be consistent with assessment fundamentals and shall include multidimensional formative and summative components	syllabus	T
		Consistency between learning objectives and test items	learning objectives and exams or tests	T
			self-rating Table 3.10	T, R, S
		Integrity in assessment: equitable marking: 100% consistency between marking script and marks on all assignments	marking script; marked student assignments	T

... continue

	Goal	Criteria	Forms of evidence	T, R, S,
4.	Proactive lifelong learner	Asked to be a reviewer of papers or grants > 15 per year	annual list of activities	T, R
		Subscribe to > 5 journals (hard copy or on-line)	list of activities to "keep up to date"	T, R
		Attend > 2 workshops and conferences annually		T, R
		> 5 invitations to present seminars		T, R
		Hits on website, > 300 hits/ month		T, R
		Invitations to write papers, be on panels on the topics "the future...," the latest advances in...	Titles of papers, panels, seminars, invitations (whether accepted or not)	T, R
			Self-rating form, Table 3.11	
		Anticipates new areas of research, referred to as a pioneer	citations that use the word "pioneer," "classic paper;" letters from peers	T, R
5.	Contributing to the vitality	Attend > 80% of student functions during the semester	attendance dossier	T
		Attend and contribute to > 90% of Departmental and Faculty meetings	dossier minutes of meetings subcommittee reports	S
		Attend student graduation	attendance	
		Attend > 80% of departmental social get-togethers		
		Send personal letters of congratulations		
		Can describe details of the research progress being made by >80% colleagues, graduate students and post docs in the department		
		Can describe details of the teaching approaches and innovations being used by 100% of colleagues		
		Enthusiastically share details of the teaching and research work of colleagues when on visits to other departments or attending conferences.	Feedback from others outside the University	
		Develop trust	Meet commitments do what they say they will do Don't denigrate colleagues	
		Greet each other warmly		
		Attend celebrations for achievements by students, staff and faculty colleagues	Attendance; guest book entry	

It you try only one thing from this Chapter

As an individual, acknowledge and enrich your five unrecognized and unrewarded skills needed by an academic: be enthusiastic, show integrity, possess well-developed process skills, be a lifelong learner and add to the vitality of the institution. As an administrator, nudge the system to value these five skills explicitly.

 Reflections and self-rating

Since none of these attributes seem to be currently used to assess performance, why is this Chapter included? First, these elements are included because research has shown that all are important. Secondly, because they are important and we should try, in our various institutions, to include these explicitly in performance assessment. As individuals, we can use the information in this Chapter to set goals and monitor our personal progress in polishing these skills.

In this Chapter, the five basic skills are defined and evidence-based performance characteristics are listed. Some suggested forms of evidence have been given. Use Table 3.13 for reflection and self-rating. Identify the most important idea you gained from this Chapter.

Table 3.13
Reflect and rate the ideas

Rate:

	Already do this	Would work	Might work	Not my style
Enthusiasm				
Show it for the subject	○	○	○	○
Show it for student learning	○	○	○	○
Show it for caring for students	○	○	○	○
Integrity				
Create learning environment of trust and decorum	○	○	○	○
Publish policies for integrity, cheating, availability of resources	○	○	○	○
Tests and task are consistent with learning objectives	○	○	○	○
Implement policies re cheating	○	○	○	○
Show confidentiality and benevolence toward students	○	○	○	○

	Very useful	Useful	Not Useful	Not my style
Self-rating of target behaviors				
Trust	○	○	○	○
Writing/ communication	○	○	○	○
Listening	○	○	○	○
Problem solving	○	○	○	○
Creativity	○	○	○	○
Critical thinking	○	○	○	○
Interpersonal interactions	○	○	○	○
Team work	○	○	○	○
Assessment	○	○	○	○
Proactive lifelong learning	○	○	○	○
Contribute to the vitality	○	○	○	○

	Already document	Might document	Unlikely to document	Not my style
Forms of evidence				
Topics for assignment, projects, exams	○	○	○	○
Marked assignments, projects, exams	○	○	○	○
Learning objectives and exams	○	○	○	○
Attendance at important student events	○	○	○	○
Syllabus	○	○	○	○
Papers, grant proposals	○	○	○	○
Reviews of papers and grants	○	○	○	○
Awards	○	○	○	○
Citations	○	○	○	○
Invitations	○	○	○	○
Journal subscriptions	○	○	○	○
Conference attendance	○	○	○	○
Enrichment notes posted on web or written	○	○	○	○
Adoption of your text by others	○	○	○	○
Attendance at departmental meetings, celebrations	○	○	○	○
Attendance at departmental social events	○	○	○	○
Known for reliability, trustworthiness	○	○	○	○
Outsiders know details of departmental activities because of you	○	○	○	○

The most useful idea from this Chapter is _____

References

In all the Chapters in this text, the references are cited as "author (date)" and are listed at the end of the book. For this Chapter, such coding is awkward because of the extensive evidence-based data given in the Tables. Hence, a numerical citation system is used only in this Chapter and the references are as follows.

1. Kelly, Diana, "Reviving the Deadwood: how to create an institutional climate to encourage the professional growth and revitalization of mid-career faculty in a community college." Download from web. (1990)

2. UVA online. http://www.virginia.edu/insideuva/2000/16/teaching.html. (January 2007)

3. Mester, C. S. and R. T. Tauber, "Acting lessons for teachers using performance skills in the classroom." http://www.physchologicalscience.org/observer. (January 2007)

4. http://wik.ed.uiuc.edu/index.php/Teacher_Enthusiasm_Research. (January 2007)

5. The Enthusiasm of Teaching. http://www.csuchico.edu/pub/inside/archive/97_10_23/enthusiasm.html. (January 2007)

6. Ten Principles of Academic Integrity. D. L. McCabe and G. Pavela. http://www.collegepubs.com/ref/10prinAcaInt. (January 2007)

7. Christensen Hughes, Julia and D. L. McCabe, "Academic misconduct within higher education in Canada." *The Canadian Journal of Higher Education*, 36(2), 1–21. (2006)

8. D. L. McCabe, "Cheating among college and university students: A North American perspective." *International Journal for Educational Integrity*, 1(1). (2005). Retrieved from http://www.ojs.unisa.edu.au/journals/index.php/IJEI/article/view/14. (May 20, 2006)

9. Sample Class Honour Code. http://www.yorku.ca/academicintegrity/tas/honourcode3.htm. (February 2007) and D. L. McCabe and L Klebe Trevino (2002) *Academe*, 88, no. 1 p. 37.

10. Penalties and criteria. http://www.uoguelph.ca/undergrad_calendar/c08. (February 2007)

11. Woods, D. R., "An Evidence-based Strategy for Problem Solving," *The Journal of Engineering Education*, 89, 4, 443–460. (2000)

12. Locke, E. N., *et al.,* "Goal setting and task performance, 1969–1980," *Psychological Bulletin*, 90, a, 125–152. (1981)

13. Alverno College, *Assessment at Alverno*, Alverno College, Milwaukee, WI (1985).

14. Fisher, B. A., *Small Group Decision Making*, Second edition, McGraw Hill (1980).

15. Dimock, H. G., *Factors in Working in Groups. How to Observe your Group. How to analyze and evaluate group growth. Planning Group Development.* Concordia University Bookstore, Montreal (1970).

16. Schutz, W. C., *FIRO-B: A three dimensional theory of interpersonal behavior.* Holt, Rinehart and Winston (1958).

17. Whetten, D. A., and K. S. Cameron, *Developing Management Skills.* Scott, Foresman and Co., Glenview IL (1984).

18. Reddy, W. B., *Intervention Skills: process consultation for small groups and teams.* Pfeiffer and co, San Diego, CA (1994).

19. Hoffman, R. L., E. Harburg and N. R. F. Maier, "Differences and Disagreement as Factors in Creative Group problem-solving," *Journal of Abnormal and Social Psychology*, 64 , 206–214 (1962).

20. Boulding, E., "Further reflections on Conflict Management," in *Power and conflict in organizations.* R. L. Kahn and E. Boulding, eds., Basic Books, New York (1964).

21. Sandler, B., *Personal communication* (1988).

22. Woods, D. R., *Problem-based Learning: how to gain the most from PBL.* Woods, Waterdown (1994).

23. Alverno College, *Assessment at Alverno College*, Alverno College Publications, 3401 39th St., Box 343922, Milwaukee, WI. 53234-3922 (1985).

24. Alverno College, *Assessment at Alverno College*, Alverno College Publications, 3401 39th St., Box 343922, Milwaukee, WI. 53234-3922 (1994).

25. Boud, D., *Enhancing Learning through Self-Assessment.* Kogan Page, London (1993).

26. Guglielmino, Lucy. Self-Directed Learning Readiness Survey.

27. Brockett, R. G. and R. Hiemstra (1991). Self Direction in Learning. Download, for example from http://www-distance.syr.edu/ndacesdindex.html. March, 2007.

28. Rotter's locus of control; see Heppner control < 12

29. Kellner-Sheffield; negative self image < 8

30. Heppner's PSI: Control < 12; total < 70

31. Billings-Moos: PS > 8; avoid < 3

32. Perry inventory (ref. 22, PBL chpt 1) > 4

33. KAI-risk; Risk > 100

34. MBTI or Jungian typology; Kiersey -Bates

35. LASQ: deep > 13

36. Self Directed Learning Readiness Survey, SDLRS: > 240

37. PS inventory (ref. 22, PBL Chpt 3)

38. Ref 22, PBL chpts 1, 7

39. Heflin, John "Facilitating Lifelong learning," usafp.org/Fac-Dev/Teaching topics/Lifelong%20Learning/. March 2007.

40. Basadur, M., and C. T. Finkbeiner, "Measuring Preference for Ideation in Creative problem Solving Training" *J. Appl. Beh. Sci*, 21, no. 1, 37–49 (1985); Ideation > 24; Judgment < 20.

4

Excellence in teaching: Measuring and gathering evidence

The key idea is that to motivate faculty to improve teaching we should reward effective teaching.

Contrary to folklore, we can measure effectiveness in teaching. Many past errors, myths and misconceptions have clouded the issue. Among these are poorly-designed student course evaluations and overdependence on such evidence; practices that reward primarily research coupled with administrators who fail to apply the many research advances in teaching and learning; and faculty who mess up in documenting their case for effective teaching.

Dean Kitcher looks at you incredulously and says "You can't really measure good teaching! Oh, we might get some idea from student evaluations, but that is just a popularity contest."

Excellent teacher? A survey of the mission statements or, where these are missing, statements by the Presidents of most of the top-ranked public and private universities reveals "teaching" as a primary mission of a university. Yet, as suggested in Myth # 9, Section 2.9, many seem to believe that we cannot measure excellence in teaching. Other decision makers rely solely on undergraduate student course evaluations — and my survey of a dozen such evaluations for a law case showed only one evaluation to be well-designed. Furthermore, many faculty are unclear as to what constitutes evidence and how to present a case for excellence in teaching. What constitutes teaching? What is "good" teaching? How might we measure excellence in teaching? How might we present a case for excellence in teaching? What could be used as evidence?

In this Chapter, we offer a definition of teaching and relate this to the various activities in which we engage. Twelve criteria for effective teaching are described with a tabular summary (in Table 4.2) of options for measuring and example forms of evidence. Sixteen forms of evidence are described and illustrated. Consider each in turn.

4.1   What is teaching?

Teaching we define as "*the facilitation of learning.*" Although many institutions focus on undergraduate classroom activity as "teaching," we use skill in teaching in many different situations. Teaching includes all the activities shown column three of Table 4.1 where skill in teaching is required. Learning could be in an undergraduate course to 200 students, a graduate course to ten, a distance learning course to adults, project supervision with undergraduates, supervision of Masters, PhD and post doctoral fellows or short courses in industry. We should gather evidence about our use of the teaching skill in these many domains.

Teaching is more than how effectively we perform in class but rather how well our students achieve the learning goals for the course. Good teaching produces good student learning.

Research has identified those factors that enhance student learning: some relate to course planning or design and others to the delivery and climate for learning (Feldman, 1976; Chickering and Gamson, 1987; Stone, 1991; Piper, 1977; Perry, 1969; Elbe, 1970, Woods 1999a, Ramsden and Entwistle, 1981; Terenzini and Pascarella, 1994). This research identifies 12 major goals for "excellence in teaching."

Table 4.1

Academic tasks with an emphasis on "skill in teaching"

"Client"	Tasks academics do	Extent of application of skills in the traditional areas of			Kf	Usual category
		teaching	research	service		
General public	explain discipline or research to the public	**	**	*	3	service
Community	committee work		*	**	3	service?
Advocacy groups	advise group		*			service
Local government	advise group		*			service
Law courts	serve as expert witness		*			service
Students	prepare to teach	***	***	**	4	teaching
Community students	give non-credit courses	***	*	*		teaching? †
Undergraduate students	develop knowledge and intellectual skills; train professionals	***	*	*	2	teaching
Graduate students		***	***	*	2, 5	research
Post doctoral students		*	***	*		?
Industry	give short courses	***		*		teaching? †
	consult			*	3	service ?
	do contract research		***	*		research †
Professional organizations	present papers	*	***	*	3	research ?
	chair a session		**	***	3	service ? †
	provide leadership as president, executive committee		*	***	3	service
	review grants & papers		***	*	4	research? †
	serve as editor		***	***		research?
	set exams for profession, serve on accreditation team, select scholarship winners	***	*	***		service?
Self	learn, keep up-to-date	***	***	*	1	
	attract potential graduate students, apply for grants in subject discipline	***	***	**		research?
	do research		***	*	1, 5	research
	apply for grants, write papers in teaching, do research	***	***	*	1	research?
	research in administration		***	***		research ?
Colleagues	be a mentor, network	***	***	***	1	
University	serve on committees	**	**	***	2	service

Five relate to the course planning and design, one relates to activities to improve and share, five goals relate to the delivery or attitude, and one goal relates to the results or quality of the learning.

The five goals for course planning or design to enhance student learning are:

1. **Course in continuum.** The course (or component in the graduate student's experience) should be appropriately located in a continuum of accomplishment. Within a formal program, the course will be seen as helping students achieve some of the program outcomes. For example, if graduates of the program are to be team players, then the course will build or develop team skills. Students expect that the prerequisite for each course has been correctly stated. They will not require background knowledge that they do not possess. If this is a prerequisite course for a subsequent course A, they also expect this course to provide them with the sound foundation needed for course A.

2. **Clear goals and criteria.** Within the specific course (or graduate/post doctorate research), the goals for learning will be public, expressed in observable and unambiguous terms and coupled with measurable criteria.

3. **Appropriate assessment.** Student assessment for the course (or Masters or PhD program) should be consistent with the course goals, should assess deep (as opposed to superficial) learning and should include a wide variety of evidence (as opposed to a single written final examination, or final oral defense).

4. **The learning environment should promote learning.** Activities should be carefully selected to promote learning; for example, the teacher should not depend predominantly on the lecture (Myth #2, Section 2.2). The research supervisor should not treat the researcher as a technician, or as someone completing a contract for a funding agency.

5. **Continual evaluation of learning effectiveness.** The teacher should evaluate the effectiveness of the learning environment. This includes the in-class activities, the course design, the project selection and the research supervision. This can involve getting feedback throughout the semester through the "one-minute paper" (described in Section 2.7) or as complex as doing control studies to assess the effectiveness of your intervention in the classroom. It can be more involved, for example, asking peers to assess your examination. For graduate work, it could be monitoring the candidates progress so that, for example in engineering, a PhD candidate would "graduate" in four years with five refereed publications.

In addition to the five design goals, the teacher should work to improve and share the teaching experiences with colleagues.

6. **Reflect on and share experience.** Teachers might share their experiences by writing papers, by presenting workshops, by co-supervising graduate students, by informally mentoring others or they can share experiences by means of "communities of learning" (Boyer, 1990; Brent *et al.*, 1999). The teacher could create a *Private Teaching Dossier* in which he/she sets goals, creates criteria and identifies forms of evidence.

These six goals relate to the creation of a course and what happens within that course. Five additional goals consider the attitudes and skills of the teacher. These are:

7. **Expertise.** The teacher is a subject expert in the subject students are learning. He/she is up-to-date as described in Section 3.4. The teacher is enthusiastic about the subject — as an application of Section 3.1.

8. **The teacher's attitude** should nurture a climate for learning. All students trust that the teacher is concerned about them as individuals and that the teacher will help students try to succeed. A learning community is created. The teacher creates an environment of integrity, fairness. The teacher is enthusiastic about student's learning and about them as an individual. The latter are applications of enthusiasm and integrity (from Sections 3.1 and 3.2).

9. **Address the whole person.** Teachers should develop the "whole person." There should be high quality and frequent teacher–student interaction outside the classroom (Chickering and Gamson, 1987 and issues raised in Myths #4, teacher's influence is only in the classroom, and #5, our business is not the whole person; Sections 2.4 and 2.5 respectively).

10. **Integrate teaching and research.** The learning experience should integrate "teaching" with "research." Research from focus groups of students (Jenkins, 1998; Lindsay, 1999) suggests faculty branded as "researchers" are seen by undergraduate students as 1) being less accessible, 2) having their priorities distorted away from teaching toward research and 3) being tempted to downplay the relevance of teaching. On the other hand, the same research shows that students want to be in departments where their teachers actively do research. They see teachers with strong research programs as being 1) enthusiastic, 2) at the cutting-edge of the discipline and 3) able to bring the subject alive. What students ask is that faculty share their enthusiasm and research results with their classes. Keep undergraduates informed about the research and consulting challenges they are addressing. This relates to Sections 3.1 and 3.4.

11. **Basic skills.** The teacher demonstrates integrity, is trustworthy and is skilled in communication, problem solving, critical thinking, listening and assessment as addressed in Section 3.3.

A final goal is about the quality of the learning:

12. **Learning goals achieved**. The students should achieve the learning goals outlined in items 1 and 2 above.

4.2 Criteria for skilled teaching and student learning

As noted in the **Principles of Assessment** (described in Myth #8, Section 2.8 and Section 3.3.5), effective assessment depends on published goals, such as the 12 listed above, measurable criteria and pertinent evidence that demonstrates how well teachers have applied their skill in teaching. Table 4.2 summarizes the 12 goals, options for criteria and suggests some options for evidence. Evidence can come from:

- students (via course ratings and questionnaires),
- graduating students (via exit surveys [Queen's University, 2008, Appendix F]),
- peers (through an assessment of the syllabus, the learning objectives, the quality of student work, student performance in subsequent courses and examinations and by observing classes),
- you through self assessment and reflection (mainly via the Teaching Dossier),
- alumni,
- employers of your graduates,
- people in the community,
- patients and clients, and
- participants in workshops and short courses.

The evidence should address the four categories of criteria:

- evidence about course design and planning,
- evidence about improvement, reflection and sharing,
- evidence about the personal context and delivery,
- evidence about effectiveness.

Although most of the forms of evidence are self explanatory, consider briefly some of these forms of evidence: student ratings, the Course Perceptions Questionnaire (CPQ), the syllabus, The Peer Evaluation of Educational Programs (PEEP), the learning objectives, sample examinations and products of student work, the Bridging Research Interest questionnaire (BRI), published papers, self assessment of contributions to the "whole person" and the *Teaching Dossier*. Details for the forms of evidence given as acronyms and jargon terms (PEEP, CPQ, BRI, Kreber factor, ASQ, Perry data) are given later in this Chapter.

Consider now, 16 forms of evidence.

Table 4.2
Criteria for excellence in teaching
(Chickering and Gamson, 1987; Ramsden and Entwistle, 1981; Woods, 1999; Stone, 1991;
Terenzini and Pascarella, 1994)

Goal	Example criteria. Who assesses and to what standard?	Example forms of evidence to be used. What is submitted by the candidate. What is used for the assessment.
1. Course in continuum: Course content fits clearly into the continuum of the development of the knowledge and skills given as the published outcomes of the overall program; course content is up-to-date; content is consistent with pre and post requisites.	Peers judge that 90% of published syllabus items relate to published program outcomes. Peer Evaluation of Educational Programs, PEEP, rating <4; Course Perceptions Questionnaire, CPQ vocational relevance > 7.	Syllabus and program outcomes. PEEP. Research proposal of students. Course Perceptions Questionnaire, CPQ.
	Exit survey results for both the Quality of the Learning experience and Contribution to skills and development > 50% rate positive.	Exit survey results. Letters from alumni.
	200 pages of enrichment notes per annum prepared by the instructor; 1/3 of course is updated and revised every four years as judged by the chair. Peers with expertise in the area will rate the content in enrichment notes and the outline as being "current."	Enrichment notes. Contract with Department chair to update 1/3 of a course each year. Letter from Chair. Letter from Peer. Letter from outside guests visiting class.
	Students report that no unexpected background knowledge was required. On a pretest in subsequent courses, the students' average mark is >75%.	End of course student ratings of subsequent course. Pretest in subsequent course. Written evidence from instructor in subsequent course.
2. Learning goals and objectives are well done.	Peers are 90% satisfied that the published objectives are expressed behaviorally, unambiguously and are complete. Measurable criteria are given for each objective. PEEP rating <4; CPQ clear goals and assessment >7. (For Problem-based learning, the students create the learning objectives for the subject knowledge based on the cases. The cases are designed and cued such that the student groups of five consistently list 80% of the tutor's learning issues.) The teacher creates the objectives in process skills such as problem solving, self-assessment, group work, goal setting, self-directed learning and teaching.	PEEP. Syllabus Written expectations in a PhD program. Teaching Dossier. Self assessment of approach to prepare to teach (Kreber factor 4). CPQ. In PBL student-generated learning issues are compared with the tutor's.

... continue

Goal	Example criteria. Who assesses and to what standard?	Example forms of evidence to be used. What is submitted by the candidate. What is used for the assessment.
3. Assessment of student's performance is fair, valid and reliable. Assessment is consistent with the learning objectives and promotes deep learning.	Peers judge there is 100% consistency between objectives and assessment tasks. The average mark for a dedicated class is >60%. PEEP rating <4. CPQ clear goals and assessment > 7. Published process, criteria and conditions about assessment shall be judged to be consistent with assessment fundamentals and shall include multidimensional formative and summative components. Integrity in assessment: equitable marking: 100% consistency between marking script and marks on all assignments.	PEEP. Course objectives and copies of tests and exams. Letters from outside specialists. Element in the CPQ. Self assessment of approach to evaluation (Kreber factors 2 and 4). Response to examinations set for professional practice (eg., Professional Engineers). ASQ, Perry. Syllabus. Marking script and marked student assignments.
4. Learning environment is effective and appropriate	PEEP rating <4; The average mark for a dedicated class is >60%. The ratio of the rote to strategic + meaning measure on the ASQ should decrease. Overall CPQ value should be >20. CPQ formal methods <6; Perry inventory >4. Integrity: Clear expectations. Published unambiguous learning objectives, statements about integrity. Statements about collaborative work Statements about assessment Personal statements about trust and integrity are consistent with published calendar and University policy. Exams, projects and tests do not use the same questions year to year over a 5 year period.	PEEP. ASQ before and after class. CPQ. End-of-course student rating >5/10. Teaching Dossier. Perry results. Student ratings on critical thinking. Syllabus. Learning objectives. Statements about integrity. Policy about assessment. Learning objectives for graduate students. Assigned text and students notes. Exams and projects over the years.
5. Efforts to monitor and evaluate the learning environment and their effectiveness.	PEEP rating <4. Peers will assess Teaching Dossier and the Performance Summary.	PEEP. Teaching Dossier; Performance Summary. Awards. Visitors. Self assessment of own professional development and research in learning and keeping up-to-date (Kreber factor 1). Response to activities to explain discipline to the public. Response to industrial short courses. Letters from colleagues they mentored in "teaching".

... continue

Goal	Example criteria. Who assesses and to what standard?	Example forms of evidence to be used. What is submitted by the candidate. What is used for the assessment.
6. Improve and Share.	Publish two refereed papers every three years. Present one invited workshop or seminar per annum. >3 people use their teaching approach elsewhere. >1 request to serve as external evaluator for a case for promotion and tenure. >$1,000/annum of unsolicited donation identified for "teaching" sent to the Department from companies or alumni.	Papers. Notices of and any feedback from workshops and seminars. Teaching Dossier. Awards. Published articles citing their approach.
7. Expert in subject.	Peer assessment through interview and/or assessment of materials developed, texts chosen, syllabus and examinations that the instructor is a subject expert. Peers in subsequent courses rate that the instructor is a subject expert. Peers from Center for Teaching assess that comprehension of teaching skill is "good." Concerning proactive lifelong learning, peers will describe them as a leader, cutting edge, pioneer, latest advances in. Annually subscribe to > 5 journals; attend >2 conferences, review > 15 papers or grants; > 5 invitations to give seminars; obtain > 300 hits/month on website.	Letters from peers. Letter from Center for Teaching. Self assessment in Teaching Dossier. Summary of activities to keep up-to-date in subject and in teaching. Peer review of papers. Titles of papers, panels or seminars; citations that use the words pioneer, classic. List of activities to keep up-to-date.
8. Attitude: Sense of a "learning community"; mutual trust (as opposed to "do/learn what I tell you.")	80% of the students in class, or the students being supervised, will rate that the teacher took an interest in them as a person and wants them to succeed. PEEP rating <4 ; CPQ social climate >7.	Course Perceptions Questionnaire, CPQ. End of course student ratings. [PEEP, although rarely does the instructor include such details in the syllabus].
9. Address the "whole person."	Active on committees and student activities. Attends at least 3 student functions/semester.	Committees related to student and campus activities. Teaching Dossier. Exit survey. Self-assessment.
10. Integrate "teaching" and "research" and develop skill in "research."	>4 on creativity and critical thinking on the Bridging Research Interest Questionnaire (see Table 4.4).	BRI inventory. Teaching Dossier. Exit survey. Self-assessment, student ratings.

… continue

Goal	Example criteria. Who assesses and to what standard?	Example forms of evidence to be used. What is submitted by the candidate. What is used for the assessment.
11. Basic skills.	Subject experts will judge the enrichment notes, the texts written, the examinations as being characterized by excellent skill in communication, problem solving, critical thinking and assessment.	Enrichment notes, exams, textbooks, syllabus.
12. Learning goals achieved.	Peers assess that 100% of the examination questions are consistent with the Learning objectives. Student's marks leaving the course are within ± 5% of those entering the course. 95% student retention. Increase in ASQ for strategic plus deep. Increase in Perry. Peer assesses the quality of the student work to be "good." External evaluator of thesis rates it > "good" for contribution to knowledge. >5 positive citations of students paper within five years. 90% of the students looking for employment are employed in related work within three months of graduation. 10% of students receive awards for their work or for their grades. 2 letters per year from alumni or from recruiters about the quality of education. Peers in subsequent courses say "student well prepared." Alumni donations dedicated to your department. Sons and daughters of alumni register in your university.	Peer reports. Student marks. Student awards. Letters from alumni and recruiters. External evaluator's report. ASQ and Perry data. Retention data. Career placement service data. Citations. Peer reports from subsequent courses.

Footnotes for abbreviations:

BRI, Bridging Research Interests Questionnaire, see Table 4.4.

CPQ: Course Perceptions Questionnaire, described with example data in Section 4.4 and Appendix A.

Kreber factor, related to Kreber's research described in Section 1.5.

ASQ, Lancaster Approaches to Study Questionnaire, described in Section 4.5 and Appendix B.

PEEP, Peer Evaluation of Educational Programs, questionnaire given in Appendix D and described in Section 4.7.

Perry, attitude toward learning, described in Section 4.5 and Appendix C.

4.3   Forms of evidence — Student ratings

Student ratings provide valuable evidence for decision-making. Data from only certain questions about the *overall effectiveness* of the course have proven valid for promotion, tenure and merit decisions. Cashin's (1995) summary of research shows the statistically valid questions to ask students are:

- the overall effectiveness of the instructor,

- the overall value of the course to you,

- the overall amount learned.

These questions ask about "absolute" measures (where the students establish an internal set of criteria) instead of "relative" measures (comparing this course with other courses).

Each rating option should have a word descriptor. For example, we obtain less reliability if the student is to select a rating from 0 to 10 with 0 = very poor and 10 = excellent than if each rating is described: 0 = very poor; 1 = poor, 2 = inadequate, etc.

The environment used for gathering the data should include student anonymity, absence of the instructor from the room, the rationale and the use of a well-designed, standard set of instructions with descriptors for each rating option. The ratings should be interpreted in the context of a variety of courses, for two or more courses for every semester for at least two years, totaling at least five courses. If, for any of the courses, fewer than 15 raters provided data, then data from additional classes should be gathered. For example, for instructors in small group, self-directed problem-based learning, PBL, where a tutor works with five students, the ratings should not be released to the instructor until data from three PBL courses at the same level are completed. This removes the sensitivity students have in objectively rating teachers when the small numbers in the class mean that anonymity might be lost. If the students know that their data will be pooled with two preceding classes, better ratings should be obtained. This same approach can be taken for graduate courses that have low enrolments.

Given the correct questions, the correct environment and the correct context for interpretation, then student ratings are valued evidence upon which to make decisions about promotion and merit (Aleamoni, 1979, Murray, 1980, Centra, 1983, Cashin, 1995 and McKeachie, 1999).

Cashin (1995) reports that over 1,500 research papers have been published on student evaluations of teaching. The literature is extensive and complex, and yet major pertinent conclusions can be drawn about student ratings.

1. Student (evaluations) ratings provide one form of **useful** feedback to improve teaching effectiveness.

2. Student ratings are incomplete measures of effective teaching. They supply **one** element of many that should be sought. (Over 15 other forms of evidence are given in this Chapter.)

3. Student ratings are reliable (provided there are more than 10 to 15 raters); stable over time; generalizable measures of a teacher's general teaching effectiveness (if care is taken in selecting the items on the form and in choosing the conditions for gathering the data as suggested above). Cashin's (1995) analysis includes issues such as age, gender, level, grade point average, personal learning preference of the student; class size, time of day, time during the year; teacher's age, gender, race, personality, teaching experience, research productivity; course subject, level, workload/difficulty.

4. Classes with higher student ratings tend to be ones where students earned higher grades on final examinations.

5. Classes with higher student ratings tend to be those where students felt the course was demanding and they had to work hard. Students want to believe that a high grade was earned. This is contrary to popular belief where skeptics incorrectly claim "*My student ratings are low because I give a hard and rigorous course. I don't pander to the students!*" Piffle! Research (Cashin, 1995) shows the opposite to be true.

6. If ratings are used as feedback to improve teaching, the test elements in the rating forms should be different from those used in ratings for performance review and decisions by peers. Rating forms to give feedback to improve teaching typically have four types of test elements:

    1) Overall effectiveness questions (as illustrated at the beginning of this section)

    2) Questions about the higher order thinking skills. (for example, "To what extent were you asked to use creative and critical thinking in this course?")

    3) Test elements about the instructor's organization, communication skill, ability to inspire and motivate, empathy and enthusiasm.

    4) Anecdotal comments written by the students.

    Element 1 can be used for decisions; element 2 might be useful input for decisions. Elements 3 and 4 should not be used for decisions. However, as described in Chapter 8 on intrinsic motivation, elements 3 and 4 provide extremely useful feedback about a teacher's enthusiasm (as described in Section 3.1) and feedback to improve student learning.

7. We have found that student course evaluations typically decrease when teachers change their method of teaching away from the traditional lecture. For example, when we first introduce "cooperative learning" our course evaluations will probably drop. Similarly, Entwistle (1992) suggests that course evaluations will also drop when instructors try to encourage students to take a "deep" approach (instead of a "surface" approach) to learning. He says, "Some students are reluctant to put the amount of intellectual effort into their studying which the deep approach demands, and therefore the students appreciate teaching that cuts down on their work, rather than increase it by challenging them to think for themselves and carry out further readings." This serves to warn administrators against too ready acceptance of student ratings alone.

An example student evaluation form is given in Appendix G.

4.4. Forms of evidence —
Student feedback about the learning environment: The CPQ

The CPQ, the Course Perceptions Questionnaire. (Sometimes called the Course Experience Questionnaire). Contrary to Myth #2, traditional methods are effective, Section 2.2, Ramsden and Enwistle (1981) found that the learning environment dramatically affects whether students spend time searching for meaning in what they learn or whether they memorize and regurgitate on an exam without really understanding what they have learned. The positive factors that enhance a search for meaning (or "deep learning") include good teaching, openness to students, the clarity of the goals and assessment, student's freedom in learning, the vocational relevance of the course and the social climate. The negative factors are the workload and the degree of formal didactic lectures. The CPQ and scoring instructions are available from Knapper (1994), Ramsden (1983) and are given in Appendix A. Some example data for the CPQ are shown in Table 4.3. All the items are of particular interest for excellent teaching with "Good Teaching" being an overall measure; Openness and Social climate provide data about attitude (criterion #8 in Table 4.2). Vocational relevance gives some insight into criterion #1 in Table 4.2. Clear goals and standards of assessment pertain to criteria #2 and 3 in Table 4.2 and small values for "Formal methods" helps with criterion #4 in Table 4.2. Students usually are expected to fill out the CPQ in the context of the learning environment either within the Department or for one particular instructor. In Table 4.3, the data are given for the Department and for the courses of Jacques.

> *Professor Jacques tried cooperative learning in his classes last year. Students reacted with frustration, and his student course evaluations dropped from 6 to 3 out of 10. Jacques decided to return to lecturing this year. His student ratings returned to 6.2.*

Comment: Jacques has relied on just student ratings as the basis for making his decision to return to lecturing. Fortunately he also has CPQ data for both last year and this year. The results, given in Table 4.3, suggest he should have kept the cooperative learning approach and modified how he introduced the change. In particular, cooperative learning typically increases the social climate value (and perhaps the openness to students) and decreases the use of formal methods. Jacques should have remembered that any time teachers try something new, usually the student ratings drop (unless the teacher carefully helps the class cope effectively with change). Students prefer the "same old song and dance" (Benvenuto, 1999). If Jacques had done a better job of introducing this new method, then his "good teaching" rating on the CPQ should have increased. The decrease suggests that the students misunderstand his role and why he introduced cooperative learning. Incidentally, data from the Perry instrument, discussed next, would have helped Jacques too.

Table 4.3

Course Perceptions Questionnaire for the Department and for Jacques' course

Item	Student's perception of the Department				Jacques' Year 4 course	
	Year 1	Year 2	Year 3	Year 4	lecture	coop learn
1. Good teaching: max 12	6.88	7.2	6.6	6.8	7.2	5.9
2. Openness to students: max 12	5.71	6.27	6.55	7.1	6.5	6.8
3. Freedom: max 12	6.47	5.43	4.5	5.35	5.2	5.8
4. Clear goals and standards of assessment: max 12	7.77	7.43	7.15	7.1	7.3	7.4
5. Vocational relevance: max 12	7.83	7.17	7.38	8.1	8.3	8.3
6. Social climate for learning: max 12	8.08	7.13	7.2	7.1	6.2	8.2
7. Workload: max 12	9.23	8.67	8.3	8.4	8.5	8.4
8. Formal methods: max 12	7.27	6.83	7.3	6	7.4	5.8
Total (72 max)	26.3	25.13	23.75	27.2	24.8	28.2

Note: This is illustrative so that the standard deviations are not reported for each item. In general, the standard deviation is 1.5 to 3 for the "Items" and 9 to 12 for the "Total."

4.5 Forms of evidence — Student feedback via Lancaster Approaches to Studying (ASQ) and Perry

When our goals are to develop higher order thinking, two inventories or questionnaires are useful: The Lancaster Approaches to Studying Questionnaire, ASQ, and Perry's inventory.

The ASQ. Most teachers want to promote "deep" rather than "surface" learning. Teachers want to create learning environments to promote "deep" learning. Instruments to measure these dimensions include the Lancaster Approaches to Study Questionnaire, ASQ, (Ramsden, 1983). The ASQ helps identify the student's preference from among three different approaches:

- "deep learning" whereby students search for meaning and relate ideas together to construct new ideas,

- "surface learning" whereby students focus on memorizing details,

- "strategic or flexible learning" whereby students work hard and use whatever approach to learning is required to succeed.

An overall measure of the preference suggested by Ramsden is the "total" sum of strategic plus deep minus surface with values in the range -24 to 48.

The ASQ helps identify **preference**. The questionnaire is available from Knapper (1994) and from Ramsden (1983) and is given in Appendix B. Research has shown that using learning environments that have high ratings on CPQ will encourage students to shift from surface to deep learning.

How can the ASQ be used as evidence? Coles (1985) used ASQ for evidence before and after conventional lecture versus problem-based learning, PBL, learning environments for medical students. He reports that a cohort of students experiencing traditional lecture courses show, after one year, a significant shift toward poorer studying approaches: greater "surface learning" and lower "deep" and "strategic" approaches. Another cohort of medical students (with the same entry values for ASQ) learned via problem-based learning, PBL. After one year, the students in PBL maintained their entry level of "deep" and "strategic" approaches and showed a decrease in "surface" approaches. Regan-Smith *et al.* (1994) report similar findings. Our experience has been, with a program that has some elements of PBL, that the "total" sum of strategic plus deep is statistically higher ($p<0.02$) after three years in the program (Woods *et al.*, 1997; Woods *et al.*, 2000).

Perry. Another instrument that provides insight about the student's approaches to learning is the Perry inventory (Perry, 1968). Perry's Model of Intellectual Development (or equivalent model such as King and Kitchener's (1994) Model of Reflective Judgment) classifies student's attitudes about the learning environment into four major levels. The attitudes are about *knowledge*, the *roles* of the student and the teacher and about *assessment*.

The Perry levels are:

- *Level 1 & 2* — Every point of view is either right or wrong. All knowledge is known and obtainable from teachers and texts, and the student's task is to absorb what the teacher presents and demonstrate having done so by repeating it back. Confusion occurs if the text and the teacher do not agree. Students want facts and formulas and do not like theories or abstract models, open-ended questions, or active or cooperative learning. If they receive bad marks, they feel they are bad persons. They have not, as yet, understood assessment principle 1, that assessment is about performance and not about personal worth. (as was discussed in assessment, Sections 3.3.5).

- *Level 3* — Most information is known but there are some fuzzy areas with questions that still have no answers but eventually will. The teacher's role is both to convey the known answers and to tell students how to learn. Students start using supporting evidence to resolve issues rather than relying completely on what authorities say, but they count preconceptions and prejudices as acceptable evidence and once they have reached a solution they have little inclination to examine alternatives. They feel that they should get good grades if they work hard.

- *Level 4* — Some knowledge is known but some is not and probably never will be. Students feel that almost everything is a matter of opinion and their answers are as good as the teacher's. The teacher's task is to present known information and to serve as a role model that can be discounted. Independent thought is valued, even if it is not substantiated by evidence, and good grades should be given to students who think for themselves, even if they are wrong.

- *Level 5* — Students see that knowledge and values depend on context and individual perspective rather than being externally and objectively based, as Level 2–4 students believe them to be. Using real evidence to reach and support conclusions becomes habitual and not just something professors want them to do. Different knowledge is needed in different contexts, there is no absolute truth with good answers existing once the conditions are known. The student's task is to identify the conditions and to choose the best ideas, with the teacher serving as a resource. Students at this level seek both positive and corrective feedback.

In general, students often are at level 2 or 3 on this Perry scale. We might hope they would graduate at level five. The student's Perry level before and after a course could provide evidence about the development of intellectual growth. Published instruments and scoring instructions are available (Woods, 1994) and in Appendix C.

Other measures that can be used for intellectual growth are available (Woods, 1999b, Chapter E downloadable from the WWW and Felder and Brent, 2005).

4.6   Forms of evidence —
Peer assessment of the syllabus/course outline

The course outline or syllabus provides excellence evidence. First, it is a document that must be produced in most institutions. Secondly, it provides evidence about teaching skills. The assessment can be made by colleagues from the Center for Teaching or from subject specialists. Regrettably, few academics create excellent syllabi. Littlefield (1999) analyzed 37 syllabi. Usually they were about two to five pages in length and included only 20 out of 57 key types of information. None linked the particular course with the Department or College sets of published outcomes. Rarely did any instructor provide information about teaching philosophy, teaching methods or rationale for those choices. Here are some guidelines of what should be included:

- *Basic information* — course number, course name, semester, skill or perspectives, prerequisites, location, day and time, day or evening class.

- *Information about the instructors* — professor's name, title, office location, accessibility, office phone, e-mail address, office hours, home phone, when to phone at home plus similar information for the Teaching Assistants.

- *Goals and methods* — overall general goals or outcomes from the overall program, goals for the course, calendar/catalogue description (or own description or any kind of description), teaching methods to be used, rationale, link to Departmental mission and link to College/Faculty Mission.

- *Assignments* — required books, schedule of readings, assignments described, projects described, project due dates, papers described, exam dates and exam content.

- *Policies* — student expectations, instructor expectations, disability information, attendance, consequences of no attendance, class participation, class participation described, missed tests or exams, individual or group work, missed or late assignment, consequences of late assignments, academic dishonesty, consequences of academic dishonesty, types of calculators accepted for exams, grading criteria and weighting of the final grade.

- *Caveat* — a statement indicating that the details are "subject to change" or "tentative."

- *Student services on campus* — information about such services and how to take advantage of them.

An example syllabus is given in Table 3.2, Chapter 3.

4.7. Forms of evidence — Peer assessment via PEEP

The Peer Evaluation of Educational Programs, PEEP, was developed by Stone (1991) and extended by Woods (1999) for peer evaluations of courses based primarily on the syllabus. The course could be presented as lectures, problem-based learning, cooperative learning or via any learning environment. The form is given in Appendix D. The priority should be driven by the Departmental outcomes and the University Mission and Vision statements. The criteria are slightly different from the listing given in Section 4.4. The criteria are:

- attitude of the instructor,
- overall course content and how this particular course fits into the larger context of the Mission of the Program, Department and Faculty,
- specific learning objectives of the course,
- methods of assessment to be used,
- learning environment and learning activities selected and rationale, and
- efforts by instructor to monitor and evaluate the effectiveness of the instruction.

Stone recommends three peers evaluate the course based on the syllabus and the learning objectives. This can be augmented by discussions with the teacher. An overall rating of three or less is the target. Courses with ratings above four should be revised before they are given. The form is flexible. For different programs, different priorities can be assigned to the elements used in the evaluation.

4.8 Forms of evidence — Peer assessment of course learning objectives and criteria

Whereas the overall goals and outcomes are described in the syllabus, the specific learning objectives are often published separately. The learning objectives use observable action verbs and give measurable criteria to tell how we will measure that the student has achieved the objective.

The objectives are the key part in the student assessment (as outlined in the five principles of assessment described in Myth #8, Section 2.8). The learning objectives may be included with the syllabus but 15 to 30 pages of objectives are not uncommon. Some instructors, for example Jim Stice, University of Texas at Austin, hands sets of objectives out for the different sections as the course progresses. In the McMaster Problem Solving program (MPS program), we have about eight general goals and ten learning objectives for each of 15 topics or units in a course (Woods *et al.*, 1997). The objectives are included with each unit.

Without clear, unambiguous learning objectives, student assessment is a game of chance, like a crapshoot. Suggestions on how to create effective objectives are given by Felder et al. (2000), Woods (1999a) and Popham and Baker (1970).

4.9 Forms of evidence — Peer assessment of tests, exams and sampling of student work

> *An outside expert on "strength of materials," Professor Jack, has rated your tests, exams and assignments in your course on "strength of materials" as "excellent" and of "high standard." Professor Jack neglects to look at your syllabus and learning objectives. "I don't need to see those. I know quality when I see it!"*

Sorry Professor Jack, but you failed to use the criteria needed to make a valid assessment. The exams, assignments and student work only have meaning in the context of the whole course. The key criterion that Professor Jack should have used was:

- the degree to which the assessment activities agree with the learning objectives and criteria.

Other criteria that should be used to assess tests and examinations include:

- *the clarity of instruction*, lack of typing mistakes, completeness of the instructions.

- *the consistency in the application* of the marking scheme, consistency between the syllabus and the exam, between the criteria and the exam and consistency across all student responses.

- *the clarity and reasonableness of the expectations*: an indication of the amount of time or the relative number of marks given to each question, project or assignment; the reasonableness of the time the teacher allowed the students to complete the task. For example, Stice (1997) recommends that the teacher allow students five times the amount of time it takes the teacher to answer the question. Wankat (1997) suggests four times.

- *the appropriateness of the intellectual challenge*. The tasks require a mix of thinking skills from "comprehension" to "higher order thinking" consistent with the goals of the course. The taxonomy for cognitive development proposed by Bloom *et al.* (1956) and updated/revised by Anderson *et al.*,

2001, provides a good way to assess the level of thinking skills. They identified the following levels of thinking skill expected:

Level 1 — **Definition/recall**: For example, "*Define the second law.*" "When did Columbus discover America?"

Level 2 — **Comprehend**: For example, "*Contrast interest with depreciation.*" "Describe, in your own words, the theme in "Les Miserables." The student is expected to explain ideas, theories and principles in the context of other information they know and to identify the conditions and assumptions embodied in the knowledge. They interpret, translate and extrapolate ideas.

Level 3 — **Apply**: For example, "*Given the following information, use Newton's second law to solve for the acceleration.*" "*List at least four medical reasons why a person might faint and become unconscious.*" The student is expected to "solve a well-defined problem" with equations, theories and principles that are easy for them to identify.

Level 4 — **Analyze**: For example, "*Analyze the following situation and estimate the force on the ramp.*" "*In the following excerpt, identify the underlying assumptions.*" The student is given extraneous information; the theory and principles to be used may not be clear. The students is expected to make reasonable assumptions, identify the "real" problem and select the pertinent theories.

Level 5: **Evaluate**: For example, "*Use the following criteria to select the best option.*"

Level 6: **Synthesize**: For example, "*Create a ten-minute test question that is consistent with the course objectives.*" Students are expected to create something new.

In general, examinations should be a mix of levels with perhaps five questions at Levels 1 and 2, three questions at Level 3, two questions at Level 4 and one question at Levels 5 and 6.

- *the complexity of the task (the string effect)*. This has two forms. Form one occurs where questions are posed that require the student to string together a series of concepts and equations. If the number in the string exceeds five, then Johnstone and El-Banna (1986) suggest that the exam is testing the student's ability to "chunk" information more than it is to show competence in the subject. Form two has a sequence of parts to the question but the student cannot complete a subsequent part if the precursor is wrong.

- *the appropriateness of the degree of explicitness or "tightness" in the task description*. A "loose" set of instructions asks the student to do a task without suggesting the steps to take, the criteria to apply or without suggestions or hints about "how to do the task." A "tight" set of instructions lists the steps the student is expected to take in solving the problem. Kimbell *et al.* (1991) found that providing "loose" descriptions gives a greater divergence in marks between poor and good students than if the task description is "tight."

4.10 Forms of evidence — Peer assessment of course materials

Peers can assess the enrichment notes prepared by the instructor to update and improve the text based on:

- the number of pages provided.

- the purpose of the enrichment notes: to update, to clarify difficult sections in the text, to express the text in the teacher's words, to link to the teacher's research, to provide worked examples, to provide a clearer understanding of the limitations or to highlight the knowledge structure and how this information relates to the "big picture."

- the quality of the citations and knowledge included.

- how well the notes were integrated with the required text: symbols the same? terminology the same?

- how well the research and consulting experience is integrated into the notes.

- coherence and communication skills.

- completeness of the references.

4.11 Forms of evidence — Student feedback about Bridging Research Interests into the classroom learning experience

The course material described in Section 4.10 might bridge the research and consulting into the classroom. Other evidence could be the student response to the Bridging Research Interest (BRI) questionnaire such as that given in Table 4.4.

4.12 Forms of evidence — Published papers

Once we reflect on what we have done in the classroom, we often want to share that excitement and achievement with others. We prepare papers and have them published. Typically the paper describes the context, what was done and our general satisfaction with the approach. We refer to such papers as *descriptive*, to distinguish them from scholarly (that will be discussed in Chapter 5).

Table 4.4

Feedback about Bridging Research Interests into the undergraduate learning experience.

Most of your instructors are strong researchers and consult with government and industry about their latest findings. We hope that your instructor brings the perspective of research and the latest, cutting-edge findings into your classroom. Please provide feedback to your professor about the degree to which he/she has been able to do that for you.

	strongly agree	slightly agree	slightly disagree	strongly disagree
1. I know my teacher's area of research and consulting expertise.	○	○	○	○
2. My teacher frequently relates his/her research findings and consulting work to the course.	○	○	○	○
3. My teacher elaborates for over 20 minutes on what he/she experienced when he/she attended a conference, presented a paper, gave a seminar or consulted with a client.	○	○	○	○
4. My teacher encourages creative and critical thinking in this course.	○	○	○	○

4.13 Forms of evidence —
Self-assessment of activities to enrich the "whole person"

Myths #4 and #5 summarized the misconceptions academics might have about the learning process. We know the development of the whole person, not just the intellect, is important. We can foster the development of the "whole person" by meeting with students informally at community events, attending student functions, guiding students and helping them acquire "skills for living" or taking a few minutes to chat briefly with a student in the hall. We foster the development, and improve the learning of the intellectual skills, by getting to know our students by name and as individuals. We learn of and talk to them about their interests, hobbies and aspirations. Contributions through certain committees (shown, for example, by an * in Table 6.3) should be included as evidence here. Activities with both undergraduates and graduates should be included.

Another source of evidence is the "acknowledgment section" of undergraduate project reports, Masters, and PhD theses. Academics, other than the supervisory committee, are often acknowledged for the encouragement they provide.

The evidence will come partly from the academic's description of his/her role and partly from a brief description of the types of events initiated, events attended, number and nature of student "drop ins" just to say "Hi" and the interactions with students outside of class. Thank you letters and acknowledgments in theses and papers also are evidence.

What is vital is that:

- such contributions are valued,

- such contributions are recorded,

- such contributions are correctly included as evidence for "excellence in teaching" and not hidden away in "service" or as "other things I do."

4.14 Forms of evidence —
Effectiveness with graduate student education

Six types of evidence are useful:

- the number of years it took to complete the degree (target 16 months for a Masters and four years for a PhD).

- the number of refereed publications resulting from the work (one for a Masters and five for a PhD).

- self reflection and enrichment notes on 1) helping students manage their time, 2) project planning activities and 3) how to read the literature critically.

- the number and quality of the reviews of grant proposals and papers completed by the PhD students.

- the external evaluator's judgment of the thesis.

- the number of positive citations of the published work.

4.15 Forms of evidence — Feedback from industrial and organizational
short courses and workshops

Since teaching skills are also used in presenting short courses and workshops, course evaluations, the number of repeat requests, follow-up by the client and personal letters of thanks from the participants are all useful forms of evidence.

4.16 Forms of evidence —
Self-assessment and reflection via the Teaching Dossier

Personal reflections and self-assessment of skill in teaching provides valuable evidence. A *Teaching Dossier* is a convenient summary document where we can summarize and synthesize this form of evidence.

A *Teaching Dossier* is prepared to help **others** make decisions about our performance. Because the *Teaching Dossier* is becoming acknowledged as an important form of evidence for the assessment of performance, a standard format is preferred so as to make assessment easier and more consistent. (Those authors who suggest that *Teaching Dossiers* be individualized, such as Seldin (1991), are describing a different document prepared for a completely different purpose: *Private Teaching Dossiers*, described in Chapter 8.)

In preparing the document, recall that you are summarizing evidence related to the criteria listed in Table 4.2. In deciding what to include, the focus is on your use of skill in teaching. Scan Table 4.1 and identify clients and tasks where skill in teaching dominated. Education of undergraduate and graduate students is expected. Are there any other areas that should be included?

In preparing your *Teaching Dossier* remember,

- only you know about some of the things you do as an effective teacher. You need to describe your contributions without bragging and without self consciousness.

- peers need written evidence, some of which is only available through self-assessment, so as to make judgments about your performance.

A recommended format for a *Teaching Dossier* might be as follows.

Preamble:

You might, for example, introduce the Dossier by clarifying your use of this format. "This Dossier is my reflections and self-assessment of my skill in teaching. Although I use this primarily in areas of undergraduate and graduate education, I also.... [add list of industrial short courses and other pertinent clients and tasks]. The focus is on this current year."

This helps the assessor realize that you will not be limiting yourself to "undergraduate teaching" which has been the mindset traditionally.

1. Summary of teaching responsibilities

List the courses, the class sizes, the level, the graduate students supervised and the time commitment you spent. Include courses beyond the university that use your skill in teaching. Provide brief comments about the way you teach each course. "I use workshops and reflective journal writing to develop student's confidence and skills in ..." You might include the courses taught over the past five years.

You want to demonstrate the range and levels of courses taught. This provides the context for what follows and gives some brief evidence related to criteria 1 to 6 in Table 4.2.

2. Course development and modification

What do you see is special about your course? Some might mistakenly believe they have nothing to write in this section. Each teacher creates something special in his/her course. It could be the choice of text, the superb organizational skill, the interesting exams, the use of discussion, the project topics, the extensive use of learning objectives, the plant tours, the visits to the wards, the demonstrations and videotapes, the enrichment notes.

What did you do differently? If you didn't change anything, then ask what is it about the material that works so well. Did you make special arrangements to accommodate special student's needs? See your course through the eyes of the students, through faculty conversations where you reflect on and appraise your practices, and through your personal reflections about your goals.

Innovations and changes, methods used to design your course, the types of materials you have developed, the use of a wide range of teaching and learning strategies, empowering students with parts of the assessment — these are some items to highlight.

This section gives evidence for criteria 1 to 5. Depending on the content, it might be easier to include the unique approaches with the descriptions in Section 1 and give a general description here in Section 2. Alternatively, you could describe in more detail one particular course or innovation in this section.

This could be described in general "In all courses I tend to create my own set of notes."

This could be specific, for example "I use the "Feedback Lecture" format in Course 402. I started using this format for 1/3 of the course..."

Self-assessment of your approach to graduate education.

... continue

3. Relationship between your courses and the outcomes of the program and of the vision and mission of the university

Describe the relationship between how-and-what you teach with the published outcomes of your Department or with the University Mission and Vision statements. For example, The work on team skills in course 209 helps achieve our program outcome "all graduates of this program will be skilled team players."

Or, "My innovative use of PBL in large classes provides evidence that the University's Mission of innovative education is being addressed in the courses I teach."

This addresses criterion #1. This section may not be pertinent if your program has no published outcomes and your University has no Mission or Vision statements or motto.

4. Reflective statement on teaching philosophy, practices and goals

What is your philosophy? Your classroom practices? Your goals for teaching? Your approaches to assessment? This might be difficult to write the first time. Treat this like a mini-research proposal. Your philosophy, your goals and what happens in the classroom need to be consistent.

Ask "what do I do in the classroom and why?" How does any of this relate to what I have read on effective teaching? (from such resources as Chickering and Gamson, 1987 and listed in Section 2.2, Stice *et al.*, 2000; McKeachie, 1999, Wankat and Oreovicz, 1993 and Woods, 1999a). Identify the suggestion by name. Write down the reference to an article that caught your attention. What does this say about what you think is important in teaching? Use the information from the previous sections to help you elucidate your philosophy.

In your reflective statement you might include philosophy, the practices you use, the goals and your method of student assessment. You might also include the approach you take to monitor and evaluate the effectiveness of your approach.

This section is probably the most difficult to write. It can address the first 11 criteria. It can focus on several.

5. Goals, achievements and major contributions

Self-assess your major contributions in teaching over the years.

This could satisfy any of the criteria depending on the contribution.

... continue

6. Activities to keep up-to-date in the subjects taught and with teaching and learning

Not all of us teach in our area of subject research. Describe how you keep up to date in both the subjects you teach and with teaching and learning. For graduate courses in your areas of research this is relatively easy. You are continually at the cutting edge. But what about the "service" courses you teach? The courses that are not right in your areas of immediate expertise?

Comment on your overall qualifications in teaching and learning. Provide a brief succinct summary of the long term short courses, seminars, specialized training that you have received.

Workshops you attended, papers you read and the people you contacted. Include your reflections about your networking (Kreber factor #1) and how you prepare for teaching (Kreber factor #4).

This addresses Kreber factors #1 and 4 and criteria 2, 3, 5 and 7.

7. Evidence about monitoring and evaluating effectiveness

Self assess your activities to systematically achieve student feedback, to benchmark, to continually monitor and improve the leaning environment and to meet the obligations of your contract with the Department to develop and improve courses.

This is related to criterion 5.

8. Evidence about the personal context

Self-assessment of activities to maintain an attitude toward learning, to help develop the "whole person" (described in Section 4.13) and to integrate teaching and research (given in Section 4.11).

A self-assessment of your efforts to focus on learning including an expectation that the students will succeed, empowering the students with parts of the learning, trying to promote deep (rather than surface) learning and trying to inspire and motivate students. Describe how you feel your service on certain committees enriches the university experience for students. Comment on your efforts to have strong teacher-student interaction.

This evidence relates to criteria 9 and 10.

... continue

9.   Evidence about the effectiveness

Summarize the results of student ratings and put these in the context of ratings for the same course over the past six years; self-assess the implications and what you might do differently next time. Highlight your strengths.

For the development of higher order thinking skills, summarize such data as ASQ, CPQ and Perry inventories. Assess the implications. Describe efforts made to use Bloom's taxonomy to characterize the level of expectation in examinations and assignments.

Assess the results from the Exit Survey.

Impact and feedback from others. Occasionally you receive letters or feedback from students or alumni (a card of thanks). An alumnus might write and claim he/she was successful in completing a task because of the skills/ course you taught. Save these and include excerpts in your Dossier. Include any letters and excerpts from calls from alumni or students in which they refer to your empathy or effectiveness or the role you played in their life.

Assess the impact through the use of your materials by others.

Criteria 6 and 12 are addressed in this section.

10.   Awards and recognition

Add information about nominations for and awards received. Include the citation or the criteria for the award. Indicate the pool of persons from which you have been selected.

Criterion 12.

Different portions of the Dossier apply to different criteria as listed in Table 4.2.

Above all, the Dossier itself should show:

- that the teacher took care in the reflection and the documentation,
- that the evidence gathered was analyzed and synthesized in the context of the teacher's plans and goals,
- that the evidence and statements are consistent.

An example *Teaching Dossier* is given in Table 4.5. As an aside, this recommended format does not include:

- Plans for professional development that belong in a Private Teaching Dossier, described in Chapter 8.

- Research in teaching that belongs with other material on Scholarship of Discovery (Research), described in Chapter 5.

The following excerpts illustrate a poorly-crafted *Teaching Dossier*.

"Teaching approach:

> *I want to use cooperative learning where I facilitate student learning. I no longer lecture. I focus on student learning.*

Actions taken:

> *In course 301, I used cooperative learning for the first three weeks with me doing no teaching. I did not think I was contributing, so I canceled the approach and returned to lecturing so that I could better fulfill my role as teacher."*

Comment: In this Dossier, the writer claims to be trying cooperative learning where his role is one of coach. However, the wording of the actions taken suggest that he still equates teaching to "lecturing." His focus is on "teaching" and not on student "learning." The actions are inconsistent with the approach. Consistency among all elements in the Dossier is expected.

As a side note, I have waded through Teaching Dossiers that included, for example, 50 to 150 pages of individual student ratings of the instructor (with no summary); letters that say "nice things" but do not clearly identify expertise in teaching. If this trend continues, then Dossiers will become so unwieldy, bulky and filled with trivia that they will lose their impact and usefulness. Indeed, these sentiments have been reported by both Bligh (1983) and by Gibbs (1983).

Knapper (2011) suggests that the length of the Teaching Dossier should be about 10 to 12 pages. He recommends the addition of Section 11. Future plans to improve teaching.

4.17 Other forms of evidence

Other forms of evidence, such as letters from employers, are pertinent. These are listed in Table 4.2. We do not elaborate on these because we feel these to be self-explanatory.

Table 4.5
Components of a Teaching Dossier

PREAMBLE

1. SUMMARY OF TEACHING RESPONSIBILITIES

    Courses

    Projects and project supervision

    Graduate student supervision

2. COURSE DEVELOPMENTS AND MODIFICATIONS

    Including special help to students lacking full pre-requisites

3. MY COURSES IN THE CONTEXT OF THE PROGRAM

    The published outcomes for the nursing program are:

    1. Demonstrate personal characteristics that reflect a developing professional manner:

        a) recognize the intrinsic dignity, worth and uniqueness of persons,

        b) demonstrate sensitivity and awareness of personal assets and limitations,

        c) demonstrate advocacy, empathy, tolerance, accountability,

        d) maintain ethical standards,

        e) think rigorously and critically,

        f) foster independent and collaborative practice,

        g) provide leadership for change.

    2. Accept responsibility for life-long learning and professional growth.

    3. Identify and understand internal and external influences on human health.

    4. Utilize knowledge of biological, physical, verbal, emotional and spiritual factors in nurse/client situations.

    5. Demonstrate knowledge of the impact of inter-professional interchange on nursing, other health disciplines professionals and the health care system.

    6. Demonstrate nursing practice that reflects knowledge of the processes of change, caring, coping, valuing, learning and critical appraisal.

    7. Demonstrate a comprehensive approach to nursing practice in a variety of settings.

    8. Support and promote a humanistic and scientific approach to the care of nursing clients.

    As tutor in the PBL units, I have focused on items 1a, b, e and f and 2. In particular I have asked students to reflect on these issues, set goals for growth and use peer and self-assessment for the results. This worked well. The students appreciated my linking this particular course to the Program Outcomes.

4. REFLECTIVE STATEMENT ABOUT TEACHING

    Philosophy

    I try to create a learning environment such that:

    Students learn better when the learning environment is open, warm and encourages them to succeed.

    Students need to feel it is important to come to class prepared and anticipating that they will learn.

    Students are valued and respected in their own right.

    Students are expected to be honest, truthful and accountable.

    I treat students the way I want to be treated.

... continue

A little bit of me lives on in all my students.

Keep confidences and be trustworthy.

Practices

Clearly and explicitly outline expectations before hand.

Try to provide prompt feedback; if students have been given 1 week to prepare an assignment, then I need to mark it and get it back to them within 1 week or else they all get 100% on the assignment.

Show a personal interest in the students as individuals (by celebrating their birthdays, their achievements in class)

Come to class prepared.

Share knowledge with my colleagues.

Continually monitor the quality of student learning and adjust my approaches accordingly.

Talk privately to students on personal and performance issues.

Goals

Develop my student's confidence and self-esteem in the context of being a professional.

Focus on student learning and not my delivery of the material.

Focus on student learning and not on "covering" material.

Explicitly develop my student's "process skills" (communication, interpersonal, problem solving, change and stress management) skills as well as develop their knowledge in Nursing.

Share knowledge with colleagues.

Contribute to a variety of significant educational roles.

Development of enrichment materials, of laboratory projects.

Revise courses and curriculum.

Respond to student ratings so as to continually improve the quality of the learning in my courses.

Don't embarrass students.

Assessment

Develop students skill and confidence in self-assessment.

Engage the students in the assessment process.

Assessment must be related to the published learning objectives and their criteria.

Assessment is only possible with published, explicit criteria.

5. GOALS, ACHIEVEMENTS AND MAJOR CONTRIBUTIONS

6. ACTIVITIES TO DEVELOPMENT MY SKILLS

    For both subject knowledge and teaching:

    Seminars and Workshops attended.

    Publications perused.

    Conferences attended.

    Peer assessment/mentor activities.

7. EVIDENCE OF MONITORING AND EVALUATION

    I use ombudspersons in all of my classes. We meet at least three times during each term so that together with the class we can improve the learning environment.

... continue

At the beginning of each course I identify any particular change I plan to make, identify criteria and forms of evidence that I might use to try to measure whether the change had an impact. For example, last year, I felt that the PBL groups could work more effectively if I assigned one person to be "chairperson/facilitator" for each session. Part way through the term and at the end of the term the students completed a rating form on the "effectiveness of our group." The results confirmed that the addition of a chairperson improved performance for this group.

8. EVIDENCE ABOUT PERSONAL CONTEXT

I use the My Role Is questionnaire (MRIQ) to sensitize me to my attitudes about my roles. The results suggested that I might do more to empower the students with the process.

9. EVIDENCE OF IMPACT

SUMMARY OF FEEDBACK

From students

From peers

From alumni

From others

Development of higher order thinking skills: The measures of the Course Perceptions Questionnaire (24 question version) were 38.2 with a standard deviation of 4.1. This is consistent with a learning environment that promotes a search for meaning.

10. HONOURS AND AWARDS

Note: based on ideas from the Teaching Dossier of Linda O'Mara and used with permission

If you try only three things from this Chapter

Excellence in teaching can be measured. Use the Course Perceptions Questionnaire. Critique the student/course evaluation form used by your Faculty.

Reflection and self-rating of ideas

Create your own summary for this Chapter. Table 4.6 gives you a chance to write reflections about the ideas given in this Chapter and to rate what you are doing already and what ideas might work for you. The ideas include those listed in Table 4.2. Those items that might be included in the *Teaching Dossier* are noted in the last column by an asterisk. The section of the *Teaching Dossier* where this evidence might be discussed is also identified. Some items that may be included in the *Teaching Dossier* are shown with a ?.

The variety of evidence that can be used to measure excellent teaching is overwhelming. Yes, some of the measures are extensive; some require much work of evaluation. My favorites, and ones that I believe to be strong evidence, include:

- well-designed student ratings;
- Course Perceptions Questionnaire;
- course learning objectives, and;
- syllabus.

The first two sample the student's response to the learning environment; it is relatively easy to gather and score this evidence. The last two are documents that faculty prepare for any course. There is a time commitment for peers to assess but this is a relatively small commitment compared to some of the other options.

Although a *Teaching Dossier* is a popular choice, the main elements describing a teacher's approach to learning should, in my opinion, be succinctly communicated to the students in the syllabus.

Table 4.6

Reflection and self-rating for measuring and providing evidence about excellence in teaching

Reflection:

The most interesting idea for you in this chapter was _____

_____

In this Chapter ideas were given about how to provide evidence for excellence in teaching

Rate the ideas

	already	would do this	might work	not my work style	in Teach Dossier
Evidence about course planning and design related to criteria #1 to 5 in Table 4.2					
Self reflection of teaching philosophy, strategies and objectives	O	O	O	O	* 4
Self-assessment of goals and achievements in "teaching"	O	O	O	O	* 5
Self-assessment of the way you design a course	O	O	O	O	* 2
Self-assessment of the innovations and changes you introduced	O	O	O	O	* 2
Self-assessment of plans to evaluate	O	O	O	O	* 7
Self-assessment of how your teaching meets Dept. outcomes	O	O	O	O	* 3
Self-assessment of your qualifications in teaching and learning	O	O	O	O	?
Self-assessment of how your teaching meets University Mission	O	O	O	O	* 3
Peer Evaluation of Educational Programs, PEEP by three peers	O	O	O	O	
Peer assessment of your in-class teaching by direct observation or from TV taping	O	O	O	O	
Peer assessment of your course syllabus	O	O	O	O	
Peer assessment of your learning objectives	O	O	O	O	
Peer assessment of your exams	O	O	O	O	
Peer assessment of Instructor grading of student performance on exams	O	O	O	O	
Peer assessment of your enrichment notes	O	O	O	O	
Peer assessment of examples of student work, projects, essays	O	O	O	O	
Chair assessment of your contributions to the Department	O	O	O	O	
Chair assessment of your enrichment notes	O	O	O	O	

... continue

	already	would do this	might work	not my work style	in Teach Dossier
Evidence about efforts to improve and share criterion #6					
Self-assessment of major contributions to "teaching"	O	O	O	O	* 5
Self-assessment of efforts to improve	O	O	O	O	* 6
Self-assessment of efforts to evaluate the effectiveness	O	O	O	O	* 7
Published papers describing your approach	O	O	O	O	
Peer comments at other universities that use your materials	O	O	O	O	
Evidence about the context related to criteria #7 to 10					
Self-assessment of your qualifications in teaching and learning	O	O	O	O	?
Self-assessment of approach to prepare to teach, Kreber # 4	O	O	O	O	* 6
Self-assessment of research in keeping up-to-date Kreber #1	O	O	O	O	* 6
Self-assessment of quantity and quality of teacher-student interaction	O	O	O	O	* 8
Self-assessment of efforts to integrate research with teaching	O	O	O	O	* 8
Self-assessment of efforts toward the education of the "whole person"	O	O	O	O	* 8
Data from the BRI inventory (Table 4.4)	O	O	O	O	* 8
Peer assessment of your expertise in subject areas	O	O	O	O	
Assessment by the Center of Teaching of expertise in teaching	O	O	O	O	
Chair assessment of service on committees related to student activities	O	O	O	O	?
Acknowledgements in theses for "encouragement" as non supervisor	O	O	O	O	?
Courses taken, membership in professional educational organizations	O	O	O	O	* 6
Teaching Dossier (an analysis of self reflection and self-assessment items in one document)	O	O	O	O	***

... continue

	already	would do this	might work	not my work style	in Teach Dossier
Evidence about effectiveness related to criterion #11					
- Student ratings based on the overall effectiveness	O	O	O	O	* 9
- Student ratings based on the subsequent course	O	O	O	O	?
- Student performance on pretest in subsequent course	O	O	O	O	?
- Exit survey for graduating seniors	O	O	O	O	* 9
- Statistics of student retention in the program	O	O	O	O	?
- Before and after scores of students	O	O	O	O	
Self assessment of faculty advising activities	O	O	O	O	?
Self assessment of approach to supervising graduate students	O	O	O	O	* 2
Peer assessment as faculty advisor	O	O	O	O	
Peer assessment of student's preparation for subsequent course	O	O	O	O	?
Number of visitors to observe class	O	O	O	O	
Awards for "teaching"	O	O	O	O	* 10
Award of graduate student supervision	O	O	O	O	* 10
Invitations to give seminars and workshops on "teaching"	O	O	O	O	
Enrichment material for graduate education, peer review of	O	O	O	O	
Number of publications of Masters and PhD students	O	O	O	O	
Completion time for Masters and PhD students	O	O	O	O	
Number and quality of grant and paper reviews by students	O	O	O	O	
Letters from alumni	O	O	O	O	
Survey of career paths of graduates	O	O	O	O	
List of awards students received	O	O	O	O	
List of awards for students' work	O	O	O	O	
Letters from recruiters or industry	O	O	O	O	
Response to public events to explain discipline: TV, radio, newspaper	O	O	O	O	
Response to examinations set for professional agencies	O	O	O	O	
Letters from colleagues you mentored in "teaching"	O	O	O	O	
Response to industrial short courses	O	O	O	O	

... continue

	already	would do this	might work	not my work style	in Teach Dossier
Development of higher order thinking skills:					
Course Perceptions Questionnaire for the course (Section 4.4)	○	○	○	○	* 9
ASQ in the context of other courses (Section 4.5)	○	○	○	○	* 9
Perry inventory or King and Kitchener (Section 4.5)	○	○	○	○	* 9
Student ratings on encouragement of critical & creative thinking	○	○	○	○	* 9
Assessment of Bloom's level of questions on exams	○	○	○	○	* 9
Other _____	○	○	○	○	

The conclusions I draw from my responses are _____

_____

_____

_____

_____

Excellence in research in teaching and subject knowledge: Measuring and gathering evidence

Excellence in research is relatively easy to measure and in most institutions the rewards for excellence in research motivate many to sacrifice teaching for research activities. The key idea is that research can be done in both teaching and subject specific domains.

All academics are familiar with the research process of identifying an area of interest; identifying the overall context; setting goals; establishing criteria; gathering resources, and evidence; reaching conclusions and sharing results. They use this process effectively for their specific subject discipline. Unfortunately, when it comes to research-in-teaching, many "diddle around." By trivializing the process when applied to teaching and claiming it to be research-in-teaching, this has damaged the reputation of research-in-teaching.

In this Chapter we elaborate on a definition of and a list of goals for research. Criteria and forms of evidence are given. Special attention is paid to measuring and documenting research-in-teaching. An example of Cindy's and Jose's approaches illustrates the difference between excellence in teaching and excellence in research-in-teaching.

> *"I'm trying something new this year. I ask the students to write a weekly learning journal. I'll collect a bunch of these. They'll make a good contribution to my scholarship in teaching," noted Victor. "How will you measure whether the journal writing did any good?" asked Janne. "Huhh?" responded a puzzled Victor.*

Research we characterize as the curiosity, perseverance, initiative, originality, critical appraisal and integrity one uses to create new understanding and practices. In Table 1.3 skill in research was used in many different contexts. Our focus here is primarily in the context of the subject discipline and in teaching. Some examples are shown in Table 5.1.

All faculty are expected to be curious, to show perseverance, initiative, originality, critical appraisal and integrity so as to create new understanding and practices. That is why research is expected of all faculty, even Victor. But Victor seems to be "diddlin' around" and claiming it is research-in-teaching. The term "diddlin' around" was defined in Myth #6, Chapter 2.

In this Chapter, first we define research, then we list the criteria and forms of evidence for research. Several forms of evidence are described in detail with the emphasis on research-in-teaching. Throughout examples are provided for research-in-teaching. Finally in Section 5.7 specific questions and issues related to research-in-teaching are addressed. An example is given of Cindy's and Jose's evidence to illustrate the difference between excellence in teaching and research-in-teaching.

5.1   What is research?

Scholars, regardless of the context to which they apply their skills, apply a process of inquiry and critical appraisal that includes the following elements. These can be used as criteria to assess the quality of the discovery scholarship or research (Natural Sciences and Engineering Research Council, Boud and Falchikov, 1989; Davidson and Ambrose, 1994 and Guyatt *et al.*, 1993–1994).

1. Identify an area of interest. Focus. A scholar identifies areas of expertise. The area is focused, manageable and is one where the scholar has made contributions in the past and identifies focus topics where he/she believes contributions can be made. In Chemical Engineering research, this might be "polymerization reaction kinetics and reactor design." In teaching, this might be "assessment." If they are starting to develop their expertise, then they should team up with those with expertise and/or bring in consultants. Expertise in various areas of teaching can often be found at or through their university's Center for Teaching. Just because they have set exams for

Table 5.1

Academic tasks with emphasis on "skill in research"

"Client"	Tasks academics do	Extent of application of skills in the traditional areas of			Kf	Usual category
		teaching	research	admin.		
General public	explain discipline or research to the public	**	**	*	3	service
Community	committee work		*	**	3	service?
Advocacy groups	advise group		*			service
Local government	advise group		*			service
Law courts	serve as expert witness		*			service
Students	prepare to teach	***	***	**	4	teaching
Community students	give non-credit courses	***	*	*		teaching? †
Undergraduate students	develop knowledge and intellectual skills; train professionals	***	*	*	2	teaching
Graduate students		***	***	*	2, 5	research
Post doctoral students		*	***	*		?
Industry	give short courses	***		*		teaching? †
	consult			*	3	service ?
	do contract research		***	*		research †
Professional organizations	present papers	*	***	*	3	research ?
	chair a session		**	***	3	service ? †
	provide leadership as president, executive committee		*	***	3	service
	review grants and papers		***	*	4	research? †
	serve as editor		***	***		research?
	set exams for profession, serve on accreditation team, select scholarship winners	***	*	***		service?
Self	learn, keep up-to-date	***	***	*	1	
	attract potential graduate students, apply for grants in subject discipline	***	***	**		research?
	do research		***	*	1, 5	research
	apply for grants, write papers in teaching, do research	***	***	*	1	research?
	research in administration		***	***		research ?
Colleagues	be a mentor, network	***	***	***	1	
University	serve on committees	**	**	***	2	service

20 years does not make them an expert in assessment. There is a rich set of pertinent scholarly research with which they should become familiar.

2. Maintain awareness of the context of the research. A scholar is well aware of the background literature. The works cited are mainstream and modern. The current research is critiqued in the context of the previous research. In Chemical Engineering research this is usually done well. In polymerization kinetics, the research work of Archie Hamielec, Joe Schork, Gary Poehlein, Don Sundberg, Kyu-Yong Choi and Harmon Ray are often cited. Unfortunately, in research-in-teaching, this aspect is often not well done. For example, in assessment, too often the author just writes about his/her own experiences and neglects to cite important work by such pioneers as David Boud, Marcia Mentkowski, Georgine Loacker, Patricia Cross, David Swanson or Cess van der Vleuten. The evidence often presented in Teaching Dossiers doesn't support a claim that the author understands the field.

3. Set goals, create a written hypothesis to test, or pose a question to answer. A scholar selects a research goal that is significant, not trivial; original and innovative, and that has potential for contributions. The goal should be well-framed with a clear statement of the scope. The scope should address all the relevant issues.

4. Create criteria for the measurement of progress toward the achievement of the goal. Identify the measurable criteria to be used throughout the study.

5. Gather resources. Obtain funding; graduate students, research space, computer facilities, purchase tests; identify labs to analyze samples; identify consultants. The budget must be consistent with the goals. For example, if the plan calls for the publication of articles, then a budget item for page cost should be included.

6. Gather evidence. Plan and run the experiments. Obtain data and analyze.

7. Reach conclusions. Conclusions are based on evidence and are put in the context of previous findings.

8. Share results and successfully defend conclusions to others. Publish papers, present seminars. Host guests. Answer queries. Receive awards.

9. Apply effectively the basic skills of communication, critical thinking, problem solving and assessment.

Now consider some options for criteria and forms of evidence for these nine elements of research.

5.2   Criteria and forms of evidence for research

Table 5.2 lists examples of measurable criteria and forms of evidence for research with illustrations especially for research-in-teaching. The forms of evidence include:

- grant proposals

- grants received

- published papers

- awards for research

- referee reports on their submissions

- Performance Summary

- Teaching Dossier for research-in-teaching

- referee documents they prepared when they reviewed submissions of others

- invitations for seminars

- membership on editorial boards of scholarly journals

- citations

- membership on approval boards for granting agencies

Here are some more details about some of the forms of evidence: grants, papers published and Dossiers.

5.3   Forms of evidence — Grant proposals/grants received

Grant proposals for research in Chemical Engineering research are usually well-crafted. The goal is well-stated and achievable and is placed in the context of a rich description of published, mainstream knowledge. The background expertise of the applicants is in the area. The plan and time line are consistent with the goals and are achievable. Plans for data analysis and evaluation and for disseminating the results are given. The budget is consistent with the plan. The same criteria apply for research-in-teaching. This can be seen from the grant applications.

Grant money available differs with the country and the agency and may differ for education grants versus subject domain grants. Consider the difference in country. In

Table 5.2

Criteria for Excellence in Research

Goal: did the scholar...	Example criteria	Examples forms of evidence.
1. Identify area of interest.	Acknowledged experts in the area will assess that the author (or team) has the experience needed in the identified area and that the identified area is worthy of investigation. Published papers are cited positively at least once/paper/annum by other authors.	Supporting letters from outside experts. Citations of the scholar's work by experts (excluding self-citation). Awards to author for work in subject area.
2. Show awareness of context of the research.	Experts will judge that major, mainstream, modern references and works have been cited. The current work is discussed in the context of that background.	Citations used in the publications, grant proposal, Teaching Dossier. Published papers and Teaching Dossier: the discussion of the results and the background sections. Performance Summary. Referee reports.
3. Set goals, create hypotheses; may include training of qualified personnel as a goal.	Experts judge that the goals are well-stated, non-trivial and can be achieved with the resources available. All pertinent issues are addressed. Judgment to be made by three independent peers with expertise in the subject area. For research-in-teaching, experts will judge that the research will have a significant impact on how we teach.	Written statement of overall scholarly goals in the Performance Summary. Published papers. Grant applications. Referee reports. Reports from personnel trained.
4. Create criteria related to the achievement of the goals?	Experts assess that the "gold standard" selected is clearly identified and pertinent. Assessment tools are well-designed, based on sound research, and they test the target behaviors. Scholar is knowledgeable about the range of assessment options available.	Published papers. Grant applications. Referee reports for papers.
5. Gather resources, funding, equipment, inventories, technicians, graduate students.	> $1,000/annum from internal grants for research-in-teaching. > $20,000/annum plus overheads and summer stipend as pertinent from external granting agencies.	Grants received. Performance Summary.

... continue

Goal: did the scholar...	Example criteria	Examples forms of evidence.
6. Plan experiments and tests; gather evidence.	Plans shall include both positive and negative tests. Where appropriate statistical analysis will be done. Experts assess that the numbers and types of student cohorts are well-defined and sufficient. Plan is organized, and systematic as assessed by peers. The conditions used optimize the chance of success, (such as preparing and motivating students about the task) as judged by three peers. Uses statistical methods, when appropriate, to quantify the results, as judged by referees or peers.	Peer reports. Grant applications. Performance Summary. Referee reports from papers submitted.
7. Reach conclusions.	Experts assess that conclusions are evidence-based. Experts assess that the scholar's conclusions have been critically analyzed in the context of the body of previous, pertinent work.	Referee's reports. Positive citations of the scholar's work. Candidate's self reflective analysis of his/her most significant contributions. Performance Summary.
8. Share results and successfully defend conclusions to others.	> 2 scholarly papers published per annum in refereed journals with each > 2 pages /article. Papers are judged by two peers as being "scholarly" as opposed to "descriptive." If papers are coauthored, then letters from the coauthors will indicate that the candidate's contribution was "significant." Feedback from workshops or seminars will show that > 50% of the respondents found that workshops to be "useful."	Papers. Peer reports. Performance Summary. Awards. Membership on boards of scholarly journals, grant review. Citations.
9. Apply the basic skills.	Subject experts will judge publications, grant proposals, referee comments as being characterized by excellent skill in communication, problem solving, critical thinking and assessment.	Publications, grant applications, papers or grants to be reviewed together with their reviews.

Note: Natural Sciences and Engineering Research Council, Boud and Falchikov, 1989; Davidson and Ambrose, 1994 and Guyatt et al., 1993–1994.

the United States, usually the grant is expected to cover 48% University overhead and the scholar's summer salary. Hence, an annual grant for $150,000 has about $30,000–40,000 for graduate student support, equipment and supplies, computing, travel and publication expenses. In Canada, however, the expenses for overheads and faculty summer salary are not allowed by federal granting agencies and hence the equivalent grant would be $30,000–40,000. For the purposes of this analysis, consider just this latter amount of $30,000–40,000/annum per project. For research in Engineering, depending on the project, graduate student support and equipment might consume a major chunk of this money. For research-in-teaching, the major expenses are supplies, perhaps summer student support, travel, computing, publication and costs for professionally-developed inventories and tests. Again, depending on the project, $20,000/annum per project should support a reasonably ambitious research program in teaching.

Internal grants for research-in-teaching, for $500 to $5,000/annum per project, are often available within most institutions, and some very meaningful research has been completed with this level of funding.

In summary, money is usually needed to do research-in-teaching. The amount of funding is not as large as that required for projects in Engineering. Such grants, and perhaps the proposal itself, provide evidence about research-in-teaching.

5.4   Forms of evidence — Papers published

In terms of publications, a challenge is to assess the "quality" of the journals because most subject-research oriented colleagues are unfamiliar with the journals and the quality of the referee system used for publications in teaching. Cabell's *Directory of Publishing Opportunities in Education* (annual) lists the refereeing methods used by different journals. Table 5.3 offers an example of some journals. The options are increasing but certainly are not as plentiful as in chemical engineering, for example. In this table, we have added our own coding system to share experience some have had with these journals. The rating ***** means the journal focuses on research, theory, employs three independent referees who are knowledgeable in the subject. This is analogous to *Chemical Engineering Science* and the *AIChE Journal*. The rating **** means that the journal accepts articles on research and some on professional practice ("how to articles"). The referees are still three, independent and knowledgeable in the subject discipline. The papers are accepted based on research components. The chemical engineering analogues might be *Industrial and Engineering Chemistry* and *Canadian Journal of Chemical Engineering*. The rating *** means that the journal

Table 5.3
Some journals in teaching and learning

Journal title	Quality of the refereeing	Pertinence to in-class teachers	Comments
Academe [American Association of University Professors, www.aaup.org]	**	*	Few articles on in-class teaching.
Academic Medicine [www.academicmedicine.org]	*****	**	Emphasis on statistical comparisons; difficult for non-medical authors to get published.
American Association for Higher Education: Bulletin, ceased publication in 2005	*	***	Interesting and very practical.
American Educational Research Journal (AERJ), one of many publications of AERA [www.jstor.org/journals]	****	*	Scholarly articles on teaching, learning and human development.
Assessment and Evaluation in Higher Education [www.tandf.co.uk/journals]	***	**	Focused on assessment, scholarly.
Canadian Journal of Higher Education [www.ingentaconnect.com]	****	*	Independent reviewers that comment on research. Teaching and learning is not the main focus. Favor data-driven articles.
Canadian Journal of Educational Communications; now the *Canadian Journal of Learning and Technology* [www.cjlt.ca]	***	*	Anonymous reviewers.
Change [www.heldref.org/change.php]	**	*	Journalistic interpretation of mainstream themes in teaching and learning written by leading experts. Very influential.
Chemical Engineering Education [Chemical Engineering Department, University of Florida, Gainesville FL 32611, USA; www.cee.che.ufl.edu]	**½	*****	Chemical Engineering plus teaching and learning. Mix of how to do it and scholarly papers.
Cognition and Instruction [www.leaonline.com]	*****	**	Educational research.

… continue

Journal title	Quality of the refereeing	Pertinence to in-class teachers	Comments
College Teaching [www.heldref.org/ct.php]	**	***	Widely read with focus on how to do it. Reviewing more on writing style than on content.
Education in Chemistry [www.rsc.org/education/EiC]	*	**	Widely read with general articles, and news.
Educational Leadership [www.ascd.org]	**	*	Widely read; shorter articles.
Educational Evaluation and Policy Analysis (AERA), one of many publications of AERA [www.jstor.org/journals]	****	*	Scholarly articles about program evaluation and policy.
Educational Researcher (AERA), one of many publications of AERA [www.jstor.org/journals]	****	*	Scholarly articles of general significance. Philosophically based. Emphasis on theoretical issues.
European Journal of Engineering Education [www.tandf.co.uk/journals]	**	**	
European Journal of Science Education, now the *International Journal of Science Education* [www.tandf.co.uk/journals]	***	**	Educational reforms and general development in Western and Eastern Europe.
Global Journal of Engineering Education [www.eng.monash.edu.au/uicce/gjee]	**½	*****	Engineering plus teaching and learning. Mix of how to do it and scholarly papers.
Higher Education in Research and Development (Australasia) [www.herdsa.org.au/journal.php]	****	***	Educational issues, scholarly. Much wider range than just Australasia.
Higher Education [www.nea.org/he]	***½		International outlook on teaching and learning.
Innovative Higher Education [www.uqa.edu/ihe]	***	**	In-class activities to improve teaching and learning.
Innovations in Education and Training International, UK [www.tandf.co.uk/journals]	***		Specializes in articles on educational technology.
Interdisciplinary Journal of Problem-based Learning [www.thepress.purdue.edu]	***	*	Focus is on PBL although some of the principles apply to other learning environments.
International Journal for Academic Development [www.tandf.co.uk/journals]	***		Instructional development with an international flavor.

... continue

Journal title	Quality of the refereeing	Pertinence to in-class teachers	Comments
International Journal of Engineering Education [www.ijee.dit.ie]	**	***	
International Journal of Science Education (formerly *European Journal of Science Education*) [www.tandf.co.uk/journals]	***	**	Educational reforms and general development in Western and Eastern Europe.
International Journal of Technology and Design Education [www.springer.com/west/home]	**	*	
Journal of Chemical Education [jchemed.chem.wisc.edu]	***	**	Chemistry flavor with good articles on teaching and learning.
Journal of College Science Teaching [www.nsta.org/journals]	**	***	Mix of science education.
Journal of Educational and Behavioral Statistics, one of many publications of AERA [www.jstor.org/journals]	****	*	Research papers on statistical methods.
Journal of Educational Development renamed *International Journal of Educational Development* [www.elsvier.com]	*		
Journal of Engineering Education [Jack R. Lohmann, College of Engineering, Georgia Institute of Technology, Atlanta, Georgia, 30332-0360, USA; www.asee.org/publications/jee]	** ½	***	Revision of *Engineering Education* but not up to the quality of refereeing in *Annals of Engineering Education*. Engineering with more global planning issues rather than in-class.
Journal on Excellence in College Teaching [www.celt.lib.muohio.edu/ject]	***½		Focus on instructional development.
Journal of General Education [www.psupress.psu.edu/journals]	***	***	Scholarly articles on the development of general skills such as skill in communication, problem solving, critical thinking.
The Journal of Higher Education [muse.jhu.edu/journals/journal_of_higher_education]	*****	*	Traditional focus on research in higher education, and policies with less emphasis on in-class suggestions.
Journal of Research in Science Teaching [ca.wiley.com/WileyCDA/WileyTitle]	****	**	Wide range including elementary and high schools.

... continue

Journal title	Quality of the refereeing	Pertinence to in-class teachers	Comments
Journal of Staff, Program, and Organization Development [www.newforums.com/prod03.htm]	**		
Journal of Teaching and Learning in Medicine, see *Teaching and Learning in Medicine*			
Prism publication of *ASEE* [www.prism-magazine.org]		**	Overview articles, news.
PRS-LSTN Journal [www.prs-ltsn.ac.uk]	**	*	
Research in Higher Education: Journal of the Association for Institutional Research [www.springerlink.com]	**½		Main theme is institutional research, effectiveness of institutions: curriculum and effectiveness, student characteristics, recruitment and admissions, campus climate (as opposed to classroom activities.)
Review of Research in Education, one of many publications of AERA [www.jstor.org/journals]	**	**	Critical essays, theme orientated.
Review of Educational Research, one of many publications of AERA [www.jstor.org/journals]	**	**	Critical reviews of the literature.
Studies in Higher Education [Petersham Hollow, 226]	****		Emphasis on day to day teaching issues with the requirement that the fundamental underpinnings be clear.
Teaching and Learning in Medicine [www.siumed.edu/tlm]	****	**	The title is misleading; contains articles that are very relevant for teaching and learning.
Thought and Action Journal [www2.nea.org/he/tanda.htm]	*	*	Overviews.

accepts articles based on writing style and research; the referees might be from an editorial board who may or may not be fully acquainted with this specialty. Articles on professional practice are encouraged. The chemical engineering analogue is *Chemical Engineering Progress*. The rating ** means that the journal features articles on professional practice; the publication may use some type of refereeing but the criteria are mainly writing style and usefulness. Perhaps *Hydrocarbon Processing* and *Chemical Engineering* are illustrative journals. The rating * means that there is little assessment done. The editor selects what he/she wishes. There is great variability in the standards and goals of each journal. The assessment given in Table 5.3 is a biased effort to suggest this variability based on the author's experience. Another source is www.elearning-reviews.org/journals. This does not rate the quality of the reviews; however, it is easy to scan the articles in a wide variety of journals related to e-learning.

Just as in the assessment of papers in the subject of chemical engineering, the quality rating of the journal is only a starting guideline. For example, both descriptive and scholarly papers appear in the same issue of **½ journals. The assessment should be done on the individual paper.

In summary, we can help others appreciate our contribution if we provide as evidence

- an analysis of our most significant contributions and how these contributions have influenced the field and the activities of others,

- excerpts from reviewer's comments,

- a list of persons requesting reprints, and

- citations by others.

5.5　Forms of evidence — Performance Summary

We use the generic term *Dossier* to describe a reflective critique and documentation of performance. In Chapter 8 we described a *Private Teaching Dossier* where the focus is on in-class teaching written primarily for self-motivation. Somewhere they should provide a similar reflective critique and documentation about their research in both subject discipline and teaching. They might elect to include the research-in-teaching in the *Teaching Dossier* as described in Section 4.16. Alternatively, they could create a *Performance Summary* that addresses all three criteria used to assess their performance: teaching (as discussed in Chapter 4), research and administrative/ professional/service (as outlined in Chapter 6). More details about a *Performance Summary* are given in Chapter 13. Regardless of the title of the Dossier, somewhere they should list papers published, presentations made and reflect on their research both in the profession/ faculty, such as Physics, and in teaching. Include reflections on their publications and contributions (as described in the previous Section 5.2). The Dossier provides an avenue for them to display their expertise and credentials. Include awards and honours they have received for their research. As a sidenote, put awards for in-class teaching in the *Teaching Dossier*; put awards for research in the *Performance Summary*. An example of a *Performance Summary* is given in Chapter 13.

5.6   Other forms of evidence

Table 5.2 reminds us of others forms of evidence related to our research that should be included.

5.7   Research-in-teaching

Here we consider what is research-in-teaching, why it is important, how research-in-teaching differs from teaching and what is the problem in recognizing and rewarding research-in-teaching?

5.7.1   What is it?

Research-in-teaching is the application of the research process to student learning. Usually we are asking questions related to proving how best to facilitate student learning.

5.7.2   Why is it important?

Our Mission involves student learning. Why do we continue to use the conventional 50 minutes lectures of teacher talking when evidence shows this to be the least effective way to improve student learning? Part of the answer is that most of us have enough trouble keeping up-to-date in our subject discipline that it is difficult to keep up-to-date in the research on learning. Namely, we are unclear about the options. However, if student learning is our business then we should, at least, try to use effective methods. Rather than just try the latest fad — let's try e-learning — we should take our innate research curiosity and skills and apply them to the learning situation. Most universities supply many resources to help make this happen.

5.7.3 How does excellence in *research-in-teaching* differ from excellence in teaching?

Can a person be an exceptional teacher but not bring research to what he/she does in the classroom? Yes. Can a person bring research to what he/she does in the classroom and be a lousy teacher? Yes. Teaching and research are two activities, with two different sets of criteria and supported by different forms of evidence (as illustrated in Tables 4.2 and 5.2). It is true that "published papers" and the "Teaching Dossier" may be used as evidence by both; but different elements from each distinguish teaching from research.

Here, for example, are my personal definition *"teaching."* Teaching includes:

- what happens in the classroom or via the teacher-student interaction,

- presenting a workshop to others,

- developing course materials,

- writing a textbook about the subject knowledge,

- preparing e-Learn materials,

- publishing refereed papers describing what was done in the classroom together with evaluations such as "I like it" and "the students like it."

"Research-in-teaching" requires the research components described in Section 5.1:

- an identified area of interest; for example "the use of active learning intervention after 20 minutes of teacher talk. The intervention is *"Turn to a neighbor and..."*

- awareness of the context; for example, three recent refereed papers in this area are....

- goals/hypothesis; for example, the active learning intervention should improve student learning compared with the 50 minutes of teacher talk.

- criteria for measurement; indirect measures could include the Course Perceptions Questionnaire. In the subject discipline a validated instrument such as Statics Concept Inventory (Steif *et al.*, 2005), the Force Concept Inventory (Hestenes *et al.*, 1992) or the Thermal and Transport Science Concept Inventory (Miller, 2008).

- funding and resources are available.

- data are gathered, analyzed and the hypothesis accepted or rejected.

- results are shared and published.

Table 5.4 presents the evidence from two colleagues Cindy and Jose. The evidence suggests that Cindy is an excellent teacher but not a scholar. Cindy "diddles around." Jose brings research to what he does in the classroom; he uses his classroom as his laboratory. However, the evidence suggests that he is not an excellent teacher. We present these examples to emphasize that we can measure and distinguish between in-class teaching and research-in-teaching based on evidence.

Table 5.4

Evidence in teaching and research provided by two colleagues, Cindy and Jose, provided mainly from their Teaching Dossiers

Evidence supplied about "teaching"	Evidence supplied about "research"
Cindy	Cindy
• student ratings for the same course over six years for question on "overall effectiveness of the instructor:" 7.2/10- with a Departmental average of 5.4/10. • CPQ overall score 32. Departmental average 27.2. • PEEP rating of course outline by three peers combined with interviews 2.3. • Major update in content for course on reactor design and reaction kinetics in contract with the Department. Written accountability for part load. • Produced 200 pages of enrichment notes for her course. • Completed supervision of one PhD candidate, "Metallocene catalysis," with time of completion 3 ½ years; 4 refereed publications. • Successfully introduced and used "cooperative learning" in the classroom based on student ratings, and Teaching Dossier. • nominated by students as "Teacher of the Year." • published a paper in ASEE Conference Proceedings on "Innovations in Teaching Reactor Design." • otherwise normal teaching and supervisory load for the Department. • attended workshops on Cooperative Learning.	• in her Teaching Dossier she identified her area of research as "teaching." • in her Teaching Dossier she makes little mention of the literature on "cooperative learning." • Teaching Dossier is inconsistent between "Philosophy" and "Action." • Teaching Dossier seems to have been hastily written. • received a grant from "Teaching Center" for $15,000 for "cooperative learning." • published paper described what she did. The evaluation was "They liked it. I liked it." No literature survey was included in the paper. • Teaching Dossier shows little reflection about what she did last year and what she plans to do this year. All the description seems positive with no failures encountered. • published a paper in ASEE Conference Proceedings on "Innovations in Teaching Reactor Design."

... continue

Evidence supplied about "teaching"	Evidence supplied about "research"
Jose	Jose
• student ratings for the same course over six years for question on "overall effectiveness of the instructor:" 3.2/10 with a Departmental average of 5.4/10.	• In the Teaching Dossier he identified his area of research as "Mastery Learning" This is a new area for him and he drew on expertise from the History Department and from Michigan Tech to help him in areas of weakness. Consultant's travel and fees were included in his grant proposal.
• CPQ overall score 18.5. Departmental average 27.2.	
• PEEP rating of course outline by three peers combined with interviews 5.8.	• in his Teaching Dossier and his publications he describes the research on recent mainstream workers in Mastery Learning. He compares his findings with theirs.
• Major change from lecture to Mastery Learning in contract with Department. Written accountability for part load.	
• Produced 5 pages describing Mastery Learning for his students. Handed in as evidence.	• Teaching Dossier is well written. We have a clear idea of what he wants to do, his goals, and the steps he has taken toward the goals.
• Completed supervision of one PhD candidate, "Hierarchical Process Control Strategies," with time of completion 6 years; 2 refereed publications.	• received a grant from "Teaching Center" for $15,000 for "Master Learning:" he and three students presented a seminar about his findings.
• Sought feedback from class by using ombudspersons (from Teaching Dossier.)	
• Attended workshops on Mastery Learning.	• his paper, published in "Cognition and Instruction," compared a lecture-presentation with the Mastery class. Both groups tried the same written exam. ASQ inventory showed statistically significant differences. This was the first time that deep vs rote dimensions had been explored in the context of Mastery Learning. The work also considered gender differences, Piagetian levels, and Perry levels on performance. Unique efforts to develop higher thinking levels were included in the approach.
• Published a paper on "Mastery Learning versus lecture-based learning in Process Control," in "Cognition and Instruction."	
	• Teaching Dossier shows extensive reflection especially about the difficulties he encountered in getting student acceptance of the new approach. "All wanted to be in the lecture section."

5.7.4 What is the problem in recognizing and rewarding *research-in-teaching*?

Five things:

1. Not everyone has a clear distinction between what happens in the classroom (as excellence in teaching) compared with the evaluation of what happens in the classroom (as excellence in research-in-teaching). Researchers in subject discipline (and faculty) often confuse teaching and research-in-teaching. I have given my definitions of "teaching" and "research-in-teaching." Definitions may differ in other institutions. The distinguishing definitions should be publicized for each University — individuals need to ensure that when they are claiming scholarship/research-in-teaching that it is not "teaching."

2. Bad reputation for "diddlin' around"; scholarship is a flavor of the month with many claiming to do scholarship in various aspects yet the activities (and products) do not meet the standards given in Chapter 5.

   Unfortunately, research-in-teaching has been tainted because those who are "diddlin' around" (a term defined and described in Chapter 2, Myth #6) claim to be doing research-in-teaching!

3. In the past, few outlets for the refereed publication of research-in-teaching. We have suffered in the past because there have been few journals with rigorous review systems where scholarly articles in teaching can be published.

4. Our colleagues are unfamiliar with the journals that are as rigorous in the refereeing as one experiences in subject discipline. For example, few engineering colleagues acknowledge the research caliber of the journals. *"You published in 'Assessment and Evaluation in Higher Education'? Oh, that's one of those teaching journals!"* discounts the Dean, who has no idea of the standards used by referees for that journal. Researchers in a subject discipline are unfamiliar with literature and journals in education.

5. In Canada, we also have had few awards or grants available to support research. That is changing for the better. NSF in the United States has been funding research-in-teaching since the early 1980s.

   Some possible actions to take include:

   - all documentation related to performance should clearly distinguish between "teaching" and "research-in-teaching."

- Deans, Chairs and members of the T&P committees should accept "research-in-teaching" as "research" and invest time learning which are the quality refereed journals for educational research. Members know such journals in their subject discipline, but may not be aware of them in the educational arena. Table 5.3 may provide a start.

Some further suggestions are given in Chapter 11 where models for P&T and performance review are discussed.

If you only try three things from this Chapter

Research is research (regardless of the context); clearly distinguish between excellence in teaching and excellence in research-in-teaching. Don't *diddle* around and call it research.

Reflection and rating

Table 5.5 provides space to write reflections about the ideas in this chapter and allows you to rate the applicability of the ideas to your situation.

Table 5.5

Reflection and self rating for measuring and gathering evidence about excellence in research

Reflection:

The most interesting idea in this Chapter was

_____

_____

I wish more was said about

_____

_____

In this Chapter, ideas were given about research and especially about research-in-teaching. Rate the ideas

	already do this	would work	might work	not my style
In general				
Provide evidence of expertise in identified area	O	O	O	O
Put your research in the context of the past work	O	O	O	O
Set goals, create measurable criteria	O	O	O	O
Gather resources: students, funding, space, time.	O	O	O	O
Gather evidence	O	O	O	O
Reach conclusions	O	O	O	O
Share and defend results	O	O	O	O
Evidence for research-in-teaching				
Peer letters assessing your work	O	O	O	O
Citations of your articles	O	O	O	O
Number of peer-reviewed papers	O	O	O	O
Awards for research	O	O	O	O
Grant proposals	O	O	O	O
Types and amounts of grants received	O	O	O	O
Peer assessment that a scholarly approach is taken and not "Diddlin' around"	O	O	O	O
Self-assessment of the most significant scholarly achievements	O	O	O	O
Self-assessment of overall scholarly goals	O	O	O	O
Performance Summary	O	O	O	O
Sections of the Teaching Dossier	O	O	O	O
Information, eg. Table 5.3, about the quality of the journals	O	O	O	O
Samples of reviewer's comments	O	O	O	O
Other	O	O	O	O

What conclusions can you draw from your responses? _____

_____

Excellence in administration and service: Measuring and gathering evidence

The key idea is that there is little motivation to provide service and administrative contributions. In particular, although service is expected and a list made of committees and services, little effort is made to gather evidence to assess one's skill.

In this Chapter we consider first service activities where we use our knowledge expertise; then, administrative activities that require leadership, teamwork and basic skills. Criteria and forms of evidence are given.

"Here's the list of the six committees I served on this year. What a great contribution I made," proudly declared Jakle. Rex thought, "I'd be surprised if Jakle showed up for one meeting."

Service and administration are a "catch-all" component of an academic's job that includes "Community Service" (OCUA, 1999a), "Practice" (Boyer, 1990), "Service and Academic Citizenship" (Paulsen and Feldman, 1995) and "duties related to University, Local, National and International Service." Yet none of these titles captures the wide array of responsibilities nor the range of skills an academic uses to perform these duties. From Chapter 1 we noted that this activity consumes about 15 to 20% of an academic's time, yet, books offering advice to academics usually neglect this academic role and discuss only the "teaching" and "research" components. In this Chapter are given 1) guidelines about classifying activities relating to service and administration and 2) criteria and forms of evidence that can be used in assessing individual performance.

6.1   Some dimensions of service and administration

Consider first how service and administration are viewed within the university and then elaborate on the wide range of activities that fall into this category.

How is this "service" and "administration" responsibility viewed within academia?

- The administrative and service functions have some role in the reward system. In tenure and promotion decisions, the question inevitably is asked "Is the candidate a good citizen?" No evidence is usually produced beyond, perhaps, a list of committee responsibilities. Here important career decisions are made essentially discounting the service dimension without gathering evidence.

  For annual performance reviews, the "service and administrative function" is usually given a weighting of about 20% (with 40% for "teaching" and 40% for "research"). The candidate usually lists activities. Often important salary decisions are made on inadequate evidence.

- Most faculty try to avoid these administrative responsibilities — except for personal consulting. University committee work, in general, is seen (to quote colleagues) as "a colossal waste of time" and "a thankless task" because "not everyone does their homework and most meetings are poorly run."

- A few individuals contribute immensely to the University community without being on any committees. They are asked to write position papers. Their advice is sought. They willingly answer questions, greet visitors and resolve difficulties on a one-on one basis. They are usually intimately aware of the

University culture and, when they see gaps, weaknesses, or missing elements, they write letters to the Provost or the President. They form informal action groups advocating change. These individuals provide great service to the University through individual altruistic activities that are rarely listed or documented.

Both within the University (where most decisions are made by committee) and outside the University (where the expertise of the university community can be used to better society) the administrative and service functions are of increasing importance. In fact, I believe that Universities are the greatest untapped resource of any country.

The wide range of activities that fall into the title of service and administration are illustrated in Table 6.1. Some of the activities draw primarily on the subject knowledge expertise of the faculty (columns 3 and 4 of Table 6.1), and others draw mainly on such basic skills as planning, leadership, teamwork. Those that draw on subject knowledge expertise and that positively advance the University's Mission and Vision and that bring credit and prestige to the University might be called service. Some examples of such activities are illustrated in Table 6.1. Consulting and clinical practice (for those in health sciences) also draw primarily on the subject knowledge expertise of the faculty. Although these can be an important component in an academic career, policies and rewards tend to be very specific to an institution. In this book, where we try to address general issues, we do not discuss these.

Those activities that draw primarily on basic skills of planning, leadership and administration (column 5 in Table 6.1) and that positively advance the University's Mission and Vision and that bring credit and prestige to the University might be called administrative service. Included in this category would be serving the university through altruistic initiatives and committees, and being session chair, conference organizer or as an officer in a professional organization. These are shown in Table 6.1.

Consider first "service" and then, in Section 6.3, "Administration."

6.2   Service — Use of expertise in the subject discipline

Service might be defined as the activities that use primarily the academic's expertise. The activities are for clients outside the university community and that positively advance the University's Mission and Vision and that bring credit and prestige to the University.

The goals could include:

- that expertise is used effectively,
- credit is brought to the university.

Table 6.1

Academic tasks with an emphasis on "sharing expertise" and "skill in administration"

"Client"	Tasks academics do	Extent of application of skills in the traditional areas of			Kf	Usual category
		teaching	research	admin.		
General public	explain discipline or research to the public	**	**	*	3	service
Community	committee work		*	**	3	service?
Advocacy groups	advise group		*			service
Local government	advise group		*			service
Law courts	serve as expert witness		*			service
Students	prepare to teach	***	***	**	4	teaching
Community students	give non-credit courses		***	*	*	teaching? †
Undergraduate students	develop knowledge and intellectual skills; train professionals	***	*	*	2	teaching
Graduate students		***	***	*	2, 5	research
Post doctoral students		*	***	*	?	
Industry	give short courses	***		*		teaching? †
	consult			*	3	service ?
	do contract research		***	*		research †
Professional organizations	present papers	*	***	*	3	research ?
	chair a session		**	***	3	service ? †
	provide leadership as president, executive committee		*	***	3	service
	review grants and papers		***	*	4	research? †
	serve as editor		***	***		research?
	set exams for profession, serve on accreditation team, select scholarship winners	***	*	***		service?
Self	learn, keep up-to-date	***	***	*	1	
	attract potential graduate students, apply for grants in subject discipline	***	***	**		research?
	do research		***	*	1, 5	research
	apply for grants, write papers in teaching, do research	***	***	*	1	research?
	research in administration		***	***		research ?
Colleagues	be a mentor, network	***	***	***	1	
University	serve on committees	**	**	***	2	service

Table 6.2 elaborates on these goals, lists criteria and offers forms of evidence that can be used to assess performance. In general, the sources of positive evidence come from the written reports, the transcripts of oral events, letters from the clients commending the work, peer assessment of published or public statements, the frequency of requests, the reputation (the number of recommendations and repeat business) and self-assessment of the contribution. The sources of negative evidence come from "letters to the editor," law suits, written complaints of "not finishing on time or within budget," embarrassment on behalf of the university community, and unwillingness to recommend the person as an expert.

6.2.1   Forms of evidence — Letters from clients

Probably the best evidence is the feedback and satisfaction from the client. Often the client does not formally comment on the consultant's work. They might ask the client to write a letter commenting on their contribution that they would like for their records.

6.2.2   Forms of evidence — Repeat calls for their expertise

Their trustworthiness, the value of the expertise and an informal evaluation of their contribution is shown through their current clients using them often, extending their interaction with them, and recommending them to others. Document the amount of repeat "business," the number of requests for advice, including the ones that they cannot accept because they are already overloaded. This will usually be in the form of self-assessment.

> *"This past year I advised the "Stop the Quarry" group by providing expertise about the sintering process, the number of employees needed and the resulting impact on the community. This involved 16 meetings with the group of concerned citizens and two presentations at public meetings attended by over 200 people."*

Comment: in this example, the type of expertise was identified, the number of meetings and the number of people involved are quantitatively given.

> *"As a result of my work with "Stop the Quarry" I was asked to provide expertise to four other advocacy groups. Because of the anticipated time commitments, I turned down these requests, but suggested they contact...."*

Comment: In this example, all the requests were turned down. However, this information provides evidence of the impact of the service contribution, the reputation and the quality of service provided. This should be included as evidence in the Performance Summary, discussed in Chapter 13.

Table 6.2

Criteria and example evidence for the application of expertise
beyond the University — "Service"

As a representative of the University, the academic has specialized, up-to-date expertise, has high standards of performance and conduct and has a prime commitment to provide service to the public.	
Goals and criteria or general characteristic.	Example forms of evidence.
• High quality results: As judged by an independent expert and by the client, the knowledge used was competent and up-to-date; used the best methods and technology available; gave credit to sources used; did not unethically use information owned by others. Quantitative: number of pages in the report, number of citations, dates of citations. Judgment done by an independent expert.	Written reports. Citations and awards for the quality of the "result." Personal citation as "Contributor of the year." Peer assessment. Client assessment.
• High quality results: As judged by an independent expert and by the client: answer is correct. Exhibits critical thinking, draws valid conclusions. Checked and double checked results to ensure that the results are correct. Critiques published data for accuracy and reliability.	Letters of commendation from the "clients." Peer assessment. No published retractions.
• Meets goals: As judged by the client, completed tasks on time and within budget; documented work well so that all can understand the assumptions, limitations and sources used. Quantitative: amount of time allowed, amount of budget.	Time and budget schedules. Projects completed on time. Letters of commendation. Others ask for the service of the expert. Number and frequency of clients (including both the number of clients accepted and the number turned down because the expert is too busy.) Repeat "business."
• Meets goals: As judged by an independent expert and by the client, the results are useful and timely. Showed willingness to work positively under uncertainty, aware of the limitations of the knowledge; willing to forego perfection so as to produce useful products. Willingness to make decisions. Error analysis is included; assumptions are listed and checked.	Written reports. Lack of delays. Client assessment. Peer assessment.
• Pertinence of results: Accountable to the public, to the University, to colleagues and to himself/herself. The prime accountability is to the public. Quantitative data: number of responses, number of public issues considered.	Written reports. Newspaper, magazine, TV, radio accounts. Responses to web pages. University does not issue "counter comments."
• Credit to the University: Trustworthy. Meets commitments; does not misrepresent self, peers, University community, data or answer. Listens. Speaks truthfully. Lack of lawsuits, complaints.	Letters from clients. Reputation based on letters and surveys.
• Credit to the University: Aware of the limitations of his/her own experience and skill and draws on and contributes effectively to team efforts to solve problems. Clearly identifies limitations and assumptions of answers. Lists and acknowledges input from others.	Written reports. Transcript of oral proceedings. Peer assessment.
• Credit to the University: Willing and able to explain and justify the impact of advice or expertise on society and the environment. Does not misrepresent the knowledge or mislead the public.	Self-assessment. Peer assessment.
• Skilled use of basic skills.	Written reports. Client feedback.

6.2.3   Forms of evidence — Other forms

Table 6.2 lists other forms of evidence related to our service that should be included. The greatest challenge for faculty is to gather the evidence over the year and to provide objective self-assessment.

6.3   Administration — Use of skill in administration and leadership

Administration might be defined as the activities using skill in leadership, planning and administration. The skill can be applied within the University Community or for clients outside the University (such as professional and community organizations).

The application within the University also requires knowledge of the subject discipline and usually knowledge of the structure and culture of the university. The activities should positively advance the University's Mission and Vision and bring credit and prestige to the University. Similarly, the application outside the University should positively advance the prestige of the organization. Although the focus in this section is on the application to the University context, the same principles, criteria and forms of evidence apply elsewhere.

Consensus is important in Universities. University decisions are made mostly through committees. This means that faculty are required to serve on many different committees. Some examples of the committees at the University, Faculty or School and Department levels are listed in Table 6.3. These are illustrative rather than exhaustive. Nor are these meant to be a model of how to set up the administrative consensus-building infrastructure. What this does suggest is that most faculty might be expected to serve on about two Departmental, two Faculty or School and one to two University committees. That represents a major commitment, especially if the meetings are without purpose and poorly run. Furthermore, the committee work might provide evidence more pertinent to teaching. Just because a faculty member is on a "committee" doe not mean that the contribution should be listed under "service." As described in Myth #5, a student's academic and non-academic experiences are separate (Chapter 2.5), an academic's service on committees that directly enrich the "whole person" should be provided as evidence of teaching as discussed in Section 4.13. Such example committees are shown with an * in Table 6.3.

Effective committees are essential to all well-run institutions. Although an academic's performance on committees is expected, valued, included in major decisions and rated in most performance reviews, the criteria and evidence used in the past are grossly inadequate. The criteria for an individual's contribution should consider the diversity, the depth, impact, experience or length of time of

Table 6.3
Some example University Committees where Faculty membership is expected

University
Board of Governors; Board of Regents
President's Senior Management Committee (presidents, vice presidents, deans)
President's Committee on Athletics
President's Committee on Teaching and Learning
President's Awards Selection Committee: faculty, staff
President's Committee on Native Students
President's Committee on Disabled
University Committee on Academic Integrity
University Animal Research Ethics Board
University Committee on Ethics in Human Experimentation
University Committee on Biohazards and Biosafety
University Museum of Art Board
University Health Physics Advisory Committee
University Intellectual Properties Board
University Pension Trust Committee
University Planning and Priorities Committee
University Resource Allocation Committee
University Undergraduate Student Awards Committee
University Capital Campaign Committee
* University Community Relations Committee
University Learning Technology Committee
University Grants for Teaching and Learning
University Library Users Committee
University Computer Purchasing Advisory Committee
University Tenure and Promotion Committees
University Traffic and Parking Committee
University Traffic and Parking Appeals Committee
University Campus Names Committee
University Budget and Priorities Committee
University International Students Committee
University Service Board
University Bookstore
University AV facilities
Research Boards: Startup funds: Science & Engineering; Arts
Research Ethics Board
Research Planning and Priorities
Institutional Review: internal

Senate
General meetings of the Senate (about seven per annum) with the following subcommittees:
Senate Executive Committee
Senate Committee on Faculty Appointments
Senate Committee on Honorary Degrees
Senate Committee on University Ceremonials and Insignia
Senate Committee on By-laws
Senate Committee on Human Rights
Senate Committee on Student Affairs
Senate Committee on Faculty Discipline
Senate Committee on Student Discipline
Board-Senate Hearing Panel for Research Misconduct
Board-Senate Hearing Panel for Sexual Harassment
Board-Senate for Student Appeals
Board-Senate for Faculty Tenure and Promotion Appeals

Undergraduate Studies
Undergraduate Council
* Welcoming Week Committee

Graduate Studies
Graduate Council
Graduate Curriculum and Calendar
Graduate PhD Defence Committee (Chair and External Examiners)

Continuing Education and Extension
Extension Council
Extension Curriculum and Calendar

Faculty or School
General Faculty Meetings (about five per annum)
Faculty Executive Committee
Faculty Undergraduate Recruiting, Open House and Admissions Committee
Faculty Undergraduate Examination and Marks Review Committee
Faculty Undergraduate Hearings Committee
Faculty Undergraduate Curriculum and Policy Committee
Faculty Undergraduate Student Awards Committee
Faculty Graduate Curriculum and Policy Committee
Faculty Graduate Admissions and Studies Committee
* Faculty Student and Professional Affairs Committee (chairs of various student organizations)
Faculty Committee on Computing
Faculty Health and Safety Committee
Faculty Women in Engineering Committee

Department (some are committees and some are individual responsibilities)
General Departmental Meetings (about twelve a year)
Departmental Undergraduate Recruitment
Departmental Graduate Recruitment
* Departmental Graduate Student Ombudsperson/advisor
Departmental Faculty Awards
Departmental Promotion, Tenure and Consulting Committee
Departmental Laboratory Equipment Committee
Departmental Website Committee
Departmental Curriculum Review Committee
* Departmental Faculty Liaison and Advisor for Student Groups (Example, AIChE Student Section)
Departmental Health and Safety Committee
Selection committees (at all levels)
* Faculty advisor to... various student organizations
University Faculty Club
University Faculty Union

similar service, reliability and the amount of leadership and initiative. A listing of responsibilities helps an assessor establish diversity and length of service.

However, this is not sufficient. Evidence about accountability and impact would include self and peer assessment together with an assessment of the process and the products.

The general goals for the work of the committee include such items as:

- high quality results — high standards of performance, decisions based on evidence and on published criteria with the inclusion of a wide range of perspectives and stakeholders.

- goals are met — satisfactory completion of annual goals and tasks, gets the job done.

- pertinence of the results — consistency of the decisions with the culture of the University (as opposed to local Departmental or Faculty needs and vendettas) and with the terms of reference and mandate of the committee.

- initiative and leadership — where appropriate brought in new perspectives, challenged the terms of reference, used benchmark data and experience from other universities and institutions and proactively considered long range perspectives,

- creates its own long range plans, goals, criteria and process of evaluation, and

- benchmarks its own performance and uses principles of Total Quality Management to continually improve as a consensus building component of the university system.

Evidence about an academic's altruistic contribution to the University comes from various groups on campus that have benefitted. For example, an assessor can telephone student liaison and ask "If you have a request to provide an unscheduled tour to a student group in Science, who would you phone?" or "If you have students "drop in" who wanted to find out about university life, who would you ask for help?" Many Departments receive unsolicited telephone requests for advice that usually are sent through to a Departmental secretary. To whom do they forward the request? For example, " I have a can of paint that has settled into two layers. Have you anyone in your Department that can help me figure out what to do?"

Table 6.4 lists some criteria and possible forms of evidence for assessing performance for administrative service. The criteria are given for:

- products of committee work,

- individual contribution to the committee,

- contribution as chair (for those serving this function),

- altruistic, non-committee contributions.

Table 6.4
Criteria and forms of evidence for committee and individual contribution to the
administrative service within the university

Criteria	Example forms of evidence
Results from a committee	
High quality results: decisions are made using published "must" and "want" criteria; views from all stakeholders considered. All members rates their satisfaction with the decision as >8 on a scale from 0 to 10 (with 10 being very satisfied; 0 very dissatisfied). Decisions are not reconsidered at subsequent meetings. Accountable for the usefulness and timeliness of the decisions: willing to work positively under uncertainty, aware of the limitations of the knowledge; willing to forego perfection so as to produce useful decisions.	Published criteria. Minutes of meetings. Agenda of meetings. Decision "satisfaction" data from committee members. Self-assessment. Annual report of the committee. List of assumptions. List of stakeholders consulted.
Meets goals: Complete the task: peer or person commissioning the committee reports that 100% of the initial goals are completed in the time frame.	Peer report. Senate, Chair or Dean report. Annual report of the Committee. Minutes of meetings. Self-assessment.
Pertinence: High Impact: important decisions addressed. Accountable to the students, public, faculty, staff and to himself/herself. The prime accountability is to the students. Impact of decisions on the students are documented. Students include full-time, part-time, on-site , off-site, undergraduate, graduate, postgraduate credit and non-credit.	Written decisions. Annual reports. Mission and vision statements. Published outcomes from programs. Self-assessment. Small number of law suits and appeals.
Pertinence: All decisions consistent with culture, terms of reference, mandate. Peer evaluation shows that 100% of the decisions are consistent with the terms of reference of the committee and with the Mission and Vision of the University.	Published terms of reference, annual report of committee, peer report. Decisions are approved at all levels without referral to "reconsider." Decisions praised in newspaper, press releases. Morale high among the stakeholders affected by the decision.
Initiative and leadership: Creates their own short and long term plans: express the target results in observable terms with consistent measurable criteria and lists of evidence. Includes resources, space and budget. Gathers benchmark data from comparable organizations. Gathers evidence and completes evaluation for the annual report.	Goal statements. Peer and self assessment. Annual report. Recommendations for change submitted.
Individual contribution to the committee	
Diversity: Member of >4 different types of committees.	List of committees with an explanation of their mandate.
Depth of service and Experience brought to the service: >3 years.	Number of years served on the same committee (and progression of responsibility).

... continue

Criteria	Example forms of evidence
Reliability: attends more than 80% of the meetings punctually. Brings key information to the meeting. Prepared for the meetings. Gathers data needed for the meeting from the stakeholders ahead of time.	Chair letter. Minutes and attachments to minutes. Self-assessment.
Trustworthiness: Meets commitments; does not misrepresent self, peers, data or answer. Listens. Speaks truthfully.	Chair letter.
Initiative: introduces new ideas and tasks. Completes tasks.	Chair letter. Self-assessment.
Leadership: challenges current approach. Aware of the Mission and Vision of the University and the "big context." Looks for opportunities in current and future. Explores long term view of the institution. Anticipates changes.	Chair letter. Self-assessment. Leadership Practices Inventory, LPI > 22.
Leadership: inspires a shared vision. Suggests new ways of working. Creates short and long term plans. Express them as goals and measurable criteria. Gets buy-in by stakeholders. Provides details on all perspectives: resources, space, budget. Benchmark data from comparable institutions given.	Recommendations for change. Chair letter. Peer and self-assessment. LPI > 20.
Leadership: empowers others to act and makes them accountable.	Chair letter. LPI > 23.
Leadership: models the way. Sets clear goals and milestones.	Chair letter. Excerpts where goals and milestones are presented. LPI > 22.
Leadership: encourages. Celebrates successes and progress of others. Writes thank you letters. Writes articles about success.	Articles. Awards given to others. LPI > 21.
Contribution as chair	
Excellence: creates and distributes detailed agendas. Starts and closes meetings on time. Facilitates the process. Focuses on both the task and morale. Encourages leadership. Decisions are made based on published criteria. Gives praise. Writes annual thank you letters to each committee member.	Peer assessment of agendas. Willingness of others to serve on future committees chaired by this person. Quality of the "thank you" letters and of the annual report of the work of the committee. Self-assessment.
Altruistic individual contributions to the enterprise	
Leadership and initiative.	Letters from Student Liaison, Provost, Dean, Center for Teaching, Dean of Students, Athletic Association, Student Association. Self-assessment.
Works in the context of the Mission and Vision.	
Willingness and reliability.	

Note: This demonstrates skills in administration, planning and leadership (based on Block, 1990; Kouzes and Posner, 1989, Woods, 1994)

6.3.1   Forms of evidence — Criteria for decisions

One major weakness of committees occurs when decisions are made without published criteria.

> *For example, on one campus, groups were asked to submit proposals for funding. After such proposals were received, the criteria for screening the proposals were created. Then the "best" proposals were accepted. The decision-selection was made based on criteria. However, those submitting proposals were not told the criteria.*

This approach of creating the criteria after-the-fact caused major frustration on this campus.

Since all decisions should be made based on published criteria, peer assessment of such criteria provides valuable evidence about the quality of the decision and about the skill and performance of the people making the decision.

6.3.2   Forms of evidence — Annual reports of committees

The annual report provides a rich form of evidence. The report should be assessed in the context of the University Mission and Vision statement (or equivalent), the terms of reference of the committee, the specific goals of the committee for this past year, and the efforts to benchmark performance and create recommendations for improvement in practice. The assessment would be done by the person commissioning the committee: the Chair, the Dean or the Provost.

6.3.3   Forms of evidence —
"Thank you" letters from the chair of each committee

People should be graciously thanked for their service. This polite thank you letter (with cc copies to the appropriate persons) should positively address the criteria given in Table 6.4. For example,

> *Dear Tom,*
>
> *Thank you very much for serving on the Graduate Curriculum Committee this year. I was pleased that you attended 13 of the 14 meetings. We had a very busy schedule this year. I appreciate that you were always well prepared and that you presented the opinions of your faculty objectively and clearly.*
>
> *Special thanks for your initiative in forming the special subgroup on "part-time students from industry." Your report, and our subsequent endorsement of your recommendations, addressed the issues and offered a really clear set of options to help us through this "minefield."*
>
> *Best wishes.*
>
> *Sincerely,*
>
> *Chair*
>
> *cc Dean*

When that letter is compared with the following, the relative contributions are clear.

> *Dear Jessica,*
>
> *Thanks for being on the Graduate Curriculum Committee this year. I was disappointed that you were only able to make 1 out of the 14 meetings.*
>
> *Sincerely*
>
> *Chair*
>
> *cc Dean*

6.3.4 Forms of evidence for chairs — Introduction to new members, agendas and minutes

Chairs play a crucial role in the decision-making process. Three important issues where evidence is available are:

Introduction of new members. The chair should meet ahead of time with each new member appointed to a committee. The chair can provide background reading (for example, legislation about health and safety for that committee), outline the general policies and practices and identify the stakeholders that the member represents. For example, are they appointed to represent all "graduate students' or are they appointed to "be themselves"? The form of evidence is letters from new members to the person who struck the committee.

Agenda. The following information make a good agenda:

- Name of the committee, chair, secretary and way of communicating "regrets."

- Date when the agenda was circulated. This should be at least three working days before the meeting.

- Mission and vision statement of the University. This forms the context in which the committee will make its deliberations.

- Mandate of the committee. This identifies the expected outcomes.

- Mechanics for this particular meeting — number of the meeting, date, start time, place, map (if it's a new location) and rain/shine options.

- Overall purpose of this particular meeting. Identify the context for the decisions to be made at this meeting.

- What to bring — data, reports that may be needed.

- How to prepare — Identify the issues that affect the decision and what research is expected of each member before the meeting.

- Actual list of agenda items or list of decisions with the approximate time allowed to reach consensus for each. The maximum time per decision is 20 minutes. This should not be a list of topics where no one has any idea what the issue is. For example, 2.3 "Report from the Student Executive." If this item is only for information, then e-mail it or include it in the "Information Section." If there is a decision that the student executive want made, identify it so that the members can think about it ahead of time, gather data and come prepared.

- Possible motion or decision. By framing a motion ahead of time, all can see the data needed. Members can think about it and bring revised motions.

- Time when the meeting will be over.

- "Information" section where news and information that do not require decisions are communicated.

Minutes should:

- Be a short and accurate representation of the decisions made.

- Give a clear indication of the decision and the amount of support it received.

- Identify the person or persons who are to implement the decision.

6.3.5   Forms of evidence — Leadership inventory (LPI).

The Leadership Practices Inventory (LPI) is a questionnaire developed by Kouzes and Posner to probe the dimensions of leadership.

6.4   Forms of evidence — Performance Summary

Just as in Sections 5.5 we described a *Performance Summary* to provide a personal interpretation of how the evidence satisfies the criteria for quality performance in Teaching and in Research, so a similar *Performance Summary* should be created for service. Examples and details are given in Chapter 13.

If you try only one thing from this Chapter

Effective service is more than a list of committees responsibilities. We can measure and reward excellence in service.

Reflection and self-rating of ideas

Create a summary of this Chapter. Reflect on the ideas in this Chapter and self-rate some of the ideas as listed in Table 6.5.

Table 6.5
Reflection and self-rating about service and administration

Reflection:

_____

_____

Rate the ideas

	already do this	would work	might work	not my style
General criteria				
High quality results	O	O	O	O
Goals met	O	O	O	O
Pertinence	O	O	O	O
Credit to the University	O	O	O	O
Other _____	O	O	O	O
Evidence for service				
Peer or client assessment of quality	O	O	O	O
Goals are met: time and budget	O	O	O	O
No discredit to University: articles, lawsuits	O	O	O	O
Letters from clients	O	O	O	O
Repeat requests from clients	O	O	O	O
Peer assessment of pertinence	O	O	O	O
Self assessment	O	O	O	O
Other _____	O	O	O	O
Evidence for administration				
Published criteria for decisions: peer assessment	O	O	O	O
Dean assessment of Annual Reports of committee: goals met	O	O	O	O
Minutes of meetings: peer assess	O	O	O	O
Peer assessment of agendas	O	O	O	O
Letter from chair	O	O	O	O
Use of LPI as measure of leadership	O	O	O	O
Peer assessment of chair's efforts to introduce new members	O	O	O	O
Letters about altruistic contributions	O	O	O	O
Other _____	O	O	O	O
Performance Summary for Service	O	O	O	O
Other _____	O	O	O	O

What conclusions can you draw from your response?

_____

_____

Make it happen

Intrinsic incentives
to improve teaching

The key idea is that to make any change — such as to improve teaching — the most powerful motivation is intrinsic motivation. The seven generic steps in intrinsic motivation are:

1. Understand the context — your personal goals and the context in which you are an academic.

2. Perceive a discrepancy between the current situation and a perceived desired state.

3. Acknowledge the ambivalence — *I would like to achieve the desired state but on the other hand, the* status quo *looks OK. Why change?*

4. Analyze the pros and cons related to the ambivalence and accept that the pros exceed the cons and embrace a desire to change, *I want to.*

5. Develop the confidence that you can make the change, *I can make the change.*

6. Develop a plan for the change process and;

7. Implement the plan.

What keeps you going when your emphasis on teaching is downgraded? You publish in refereed educational journals — and these count against you for salary advancement and promotion! You attend educational conferences, you try to bring principles of effective learning into your classroom and to your supervision of graduate students. You have explicit activities for your new graduate students to develop their critical evaluation of publications; with experienced graduate students you guide them in the process of refereeing papers. "Don't spend your time on that stuff. Spend your time getting research grants and publishing refereed papers," suggests a well-meaning colleague. Yes, what keeps you going in a cold climate for student learning? As outlined in Section 1.5, academics have an enthusiasm about their profession. They have a sparkle in their eye for what they do. That internal excitement, that internal or intrinsic motivation is the most powerful force you can let loose. It is far more effective than such external motivation as promotion and rewards (Sloan, 1989).

In this Chapter we focus on the seven-step process of internally intrinsic motivation. We say "internally" because this is personal. Only *you* can intrinsically motivate yourself. In the following chapter, Chapter 8, we consider specific actions to take.

7.1 Keep the sparkle in your eye — A general description of the process of intrinsic motivation

Intrinsic motivation usually follows the following seven-step process:

1. Be clear about the context. Enunciate your personal goals. Realistically address the environment in which you work as an academic.

2. You perceive a discrepancy between the current state and perceived desired state. The desired state can be considered as a goal. *I wish I could improve my teaching.*

3. Because of the discrepancy, there is ambivalence; the greater the discrepancy, the greater the ambivalence. Ambivalence is "I want to change but I don't want to change." For example, *I would improve my teaching but that takes a lot of work for no apparent reward.* Ambivalence is a common experience during change; resolving ambivalence is often a key to change and to resolve ambivalence requires an identification of what motivates you to maintain the *status quo*, to resist change.

4. Explore the ambivalence (perhaps by listing pros and cons or by a force field diagram; by self-rating the importance of this change and exploring what it

would take to shift the rating higher; list and address the concerns, exploring the goals and values as to what is really important in your life). Gradually increase the perceived important of change so that you are *willing* to change. You now see that change is important, intrinsically valuable and cherished.

5. Explore your confidence that you will be able to make the change. (Perhaps by brainstorming how you might do the task, reviewing past successes, drawing on a support network to facilitate your making the change.)

6. Develop a plan. The plan should include a goal statement (expressed as results instead of actions), a list measurable criteria related to the goals, and milestones and celebrations.

7. Implement the plan, pass milestones and celebrate.

Consider a general description of these steps in turn.

7.2 Understand the context

The context has at least three dimensions — your personal goals, the environment in which you work as an academic and your personal "life."

7.2.1 The context of "your goals"

Take time to write out your goals. They might be "to be the best teacher five years from now;" "to receive tenure," "to be promoted to Full Professor in six years," "to be awarded a Fellow of the American Society of Engineering Education," "acknowledge that *a little bit of me* goes out with every graduate of our program and I want that little bit to be....." or "to receive research grants of more than $500,000 per year."

7.2.2 The context of the "culture/system"

Familiarize yourself with the written policies concerning the measurable criteria, the forms of evidence and the process for promotion, tenure and annual performance. Beyond the written policies is the actual culture — what really happens. Consider carefully what is within your power and what is not. What can you control; what can't you control? Perhaps reconsider your responses in Table 2.3.

7.2.3   The context of your personal life

All of us have a personal life that balances our roles as friend, spouse, child, parent, colleague and that balances our personal dimensions of intellectual, physical, emotional, spiritual and social. Our goals for our career and the demands of the "system" in which we work must fit into the context of our commitments to others and to ourselves. We need to acknowledge our expectations from our personal life.

7.3   Be realistic in identifying a change to improve learning

We may recognize a discrepancy between our current teaching and our goal for being a facilitator of learning. Within the context (of your overall goals, the system and your personal life) identify a change to improve your teaching. Be cautious. I have had too many friends who devoted time improving their teaching and were denied tenure, and delayed in promotion. Effective teaching was unrecognized and not rewarded in their environment. Be realistic. Start small with simple things you can do that will make a dramatic improvement in student learning. Apply Pareto's principle: look for the 20% change that will have 80% impact.

Write out your goal.

7.4   Acknowledge ambivalence —
Some reasons given to keep the *status quo* for student learning

When it comes to being motivated to improve student learning, many reasons often come to mind as to why the *status quo* is preferred:

> *I've tried that, and it doesn't work;*
>
> *the real focus in this university is research, I won't be rewarded;*
>
> *I don't have the time; there is no merit in it for me;*
>
> *my student evaluations plummet whenever I try any thing new;*
>
> *I learned by the lecture, why can't they?*
>
> *I've already invested a phenomenal amount of time getting my lectures onto power point;*
>
> *I love to lecture; students like my lectures too. Why change?*

Let's briefly meet colleagues.

> *We met Nicole briefly in Myth #3, Section 2.3. Nicole struggles to get her research program established and has little time to improve her teaching.*

Comment: Nicole is also caught up in that old chestnut "good researchers = good teachers." She knows that in her institution it is the research that counts. The "institutional attitude" is that research is superior to teaching, model 4 in Section 1.3.

> *We met Jacques briefly in Section 4.4. He is tenured and has gradually moved away from research in his subject. Last semester he tried cooperative learning in the classroom. It sounded as though it should work well! His student evaluations plummeted. Students sent a petition to the chair suggesting that Jacques was an incompetent teacher. "Look, student ratings really just measure my "performance" at lecturing; I was trying to improve their learning. But the students don't see that. They think I'm not doing what I'm paid for. They think I should be lecturing and telling them what is important and what will be on the exam. OK. If that's the game they want to play, that's what I'll do. No more new stuff for me."*

Comment: Jacques probably missed out on the clues of how to implement a change. Students are very comfortable where they are: sitting in lecture, astutely identifying the professor's favorite testable ideas and succeeding very well with the established system. Rock the boat and their A+'s might drop to D's while they are figuring the new system. Don't rock the teaching boat (Benvenuto, 1999) or "If the conventional lecture is dead, why is it alive and thriving?" (Woods, 2006). Jacques might have used ombudspersons, and rationalized the choice of learning environment during his first meeting with his class and in his course syllabus. He also could use the Course Perceptions Questionnaire to obtain feedback about the learning environment.

> *Meet another colleague, Maria. "Why should I bust a gut to make this course into something special. I'll only be teaching this for another couple of years. Then, I'll rotate to another course. Someone new is going to take over and do something different. All my effort will be in vain. I won't make a difference."*

Comment: Maria, like many of her colleagues, is hoping that *all* the Department will take teaching as seriously as she does. If only the whole Department tried all these things, then I could do it too. Me do it alone? She has forgotten that we do it for the students we interact with right now. She has forgotten that students who are fired up about her approach will become a strong force for change. Yes, do it alone; don't wait for everyone to get on board, Maria.

> *"I love to lecture. I get a thrill from performing in front of the students. They love my lectures. Why should I change?" exudes Michelle.*

Comment: The students enjoy your presentations; you certainly entertain them. But what are they learning?

> *"I don't understand it. The students have suggested that I cancel lectures and pose a problem first and let them learn through problem-based learning. How can they learn if they haven't had my lectures first?" asks Henri.*

Comment: Henri states a commonly-held misconception about this learning environment called problem-based learning. In general, before we discard any option to improve student learning we should invest time learning details of how it might work and searching for evidence of its effectiveness.

> *Nausheen elaborates "I have just spent the last three months converting my lectures onto powerpoint. There even are jazzy cartoons and zippy music that really will appeal to the now generation." I don't have time to do more.*

Comment: using new technology is appealing. However, whatever we do should be based on research on student learning. Has Nausheen taken her lectures and converted them to another format? Or has she interspersed active or perhaps cooperative group activities? Will the new approach Nausheen has taken improve student learning or is it just a jazzed up version of the old format?

In summary, we may prefer the *status quo* because we have already tried to improve, there is no extrinsic reward, it takes too much time, my student evaluations will decrease, change is not needed, and I really enjoy doing what I am doing.

7.5 Overcome ambivalence —
Some important reasons for making a change

To overcome the ambivalence, one of the most effective reasons to "improving student learning" is that this is consistent with your overall personal goals listed in 7.2.1.

Other reasons to explore include self-pride, the pleasure of seeing students (and other teachers who adopt your approach) learn and succeed, the excitement of integrating teaching and research, the enthusiasm for discovery, curiosity, inventiveness, your positive attitude that drives you to set goals, your high self expectations, your pride in contributing to the university and to the profession, your increased portability, and your challenge to make something that has worked for others work for you. Overcome the ambivalence, downplay the attitudes that protect the *status quo*, focus on the positive advantages and say "I want to!"

7.6   Build confidence that "I can make it happen"

Now let us focus on saying "I can make this happen!" We prepare by drawing on your confidence and by interacting with our support system.

7.6.1   Drawing on your confidence; and anticipate and respond to possible obstacles

Confidence that one can make the change is nurtured by three general factors: 1) a feeling of competence, 2) by having autonomy and having the control over enough that allows you to achieve the change and 3) relatedness (with your personal goals connected with and consistent with those in the environment, people are affirmed by others). At the same time, it is astute to anticipate possible obstacles that might prevent you from achieving your goal and develop tactics for overcoming these.

A.   *Competence*

Visualize examples from the past when you have succeeded. Recall times you have won rewards, when others have commended you on your competence. You can visualize yourself achieving the goals. You might consider gaining additional expertise before starting the change.

B.   *Autonomy*

Assure yourself that you have enough self determination, freedom and resources to be able to achieve your goal.

C.   *Relatedness*

Connectedness. Confidence is high when you view your goals as being worthwhile; when others say "Hey that's a great idea;" when your working environment is supportive and when your goals are consistent with the institution's goals.

D.   *Anticipating and overcoming possible obstacles*

As you visualize the journey to achieve your goal you should identify any obstacle that might occur and develop strategies overcoming these proactively. Some possible issues include managing time and yourself well, gaining the required expertise first, and having a support system.

A useful approach is to use the Kepner Tregoe Potential Problem Analysis. In this approach possible obstacles (and causes) are listed, rated according to the probability of occurring and the seriousness if it does occur, the preventative actions for each obstacle and contingency action to monitor or cope if it does occur. (Kepner and Tregoe, 1981)

7.6.2   Receive informal support and encouragement

We continue to be intrinsically motivated if we have support and encouragement from family, friends, from colleagues from other institutions, from mentors and role models, from students and eventually from our home institution.

- **Support system from family.**
- **Support from people at outside institutions.**
  - Peers from other universities visit to observe you in your classroom. Introduce them to your colleagues and to the chair. Use the opportunity to illustrate that others find what you are doing is noteworthy. Highlight their visit without flaunting it.
  - Keep in touch with colleagues whom you met during an effective teaching workshop. They too may be experiencing the same doubts and difficulties you are experiencing; be a support to them and gain personal inner strength from helping them.
- **Support from mentors and role models.** Draw on the experience of mentors and role models who have succeeded.
- **Support from colleagues in Center for Teaching and Learning.** One of the strongest support from within the institution can usually come from colleagues in the Center for Teaching and Learning. They not only will encourage you but they also will have expertise to guide you along the journey.
- **Support from your students.** Be willing to spend time at the beginning of the semester explaining and rationalizing the new learning environment you will be using. Tell them what is in it for them. Use ombudspersons to provide you with continual monitoring of the effectiveness of the intervention. For example, when the learning environment in a course was changed from a traditional lecture to small group, self-directed, self-assessed problem based learning, the dramatic difference in the effectiveness of the new environment

occurred when a six-hour introduction was used instead of a two-hour introduction (Woods, 2007a).

- **Peers and peer acceptance within the institution.** Often peer acceptance within your home institution is slow in coming. For example, award-winning teachers usually have given workshops on effective teaching *elsewhere* for 10 to 12 years before their home university deigns to ask them to do workshops on home turf. Do not wait for others. Try new ideas about teaching as a pilot project for yourself. However, it is wise to let colleagues, especially with in the Department or Unit and the Dean know of the interventions that you are implementing.

7.7   Build a plan

Here is a summary checklist for a plan (based on Miller and Rollnick, 2002)

The main goals for myself in making this change are: _____
The most important reasons why I want to make this change are: _____
The pertinent measurable criteria I would use to tell me I have achieved my goal are:
The forms of evidence/measures/instruments that are pertinent include:
I plan to do the following things to accomplish my goals: milestones along the way specific actions   when
Other people could help me with change in these ways: person   possible ways   when I would contact them
These are some of the obstacles to change and how I could handle them: possible obstacle   probability x seriousness   how I will respond
I will know my plan is working when I see the following results:

7.8   Implement the plan

With the help of your support system, implement the plan. Monitor your progress; celebrate milestones of achievement.

If you try only one thing from this Chapter

Be intrinsically motivated to improve student learning; follow a seven-step model and, in particular, acknowledge and overcome ambivalence.

Reflection and self-rate the ideas

When we think of motivating faculty to improve teaching, too often we think of P&T, promotions and tenure. However, the real heart to motivation is not such external motivators but rather the internal sparkle in your eye about teaching. You should want to do it. Oh, you can get by if you *have to do it*. But, the really effective teaching is when you want to do it. Table 7.1 gives you a chance to reflect on and rate the ideas about internal motivation. Suggested actions to take to intrinsically motivate yourself are given in Chapter 8.

Table 7.1

Reflection and self-rating about intrinsic motivation to improve teaching

Reflection:

The most interesting idea in this Chapter was:

_____

_____

_____ I wish more was said about

_____

_____

_____

Rate the ideas

	already do this	would work	might work	not my style
Use a seven-step model of the intrinsic motivation process	O	O	O	O
Context:				
Have written long term goals	O	O	O	O
Understand the "system"	O	O	O	O
Include my personal life commitments	O	O	O	O
My goal to improve student learning				
Am realistic about goals to improve student learning	O	O	O	O
Explicitly address ambivalence	O	O	O	O
Have a variety of techniques to overcome ambivalence	O	O	O	O
Am confident because of my competence	O	O	O	O
Have autonomy to achieve my goal	O	O	O	O
See my goals as related to my academic environment	O	O	O	O
Anticipate potential obstacles and have plans to overcome	O	O	O	O
Have a strong and extensive support network	O	O	O	O
Can build a plan to improve achieve my goal	O	O	O	O
Other: _____	O	O	O	O
_____	O	O	O	O
_____	O	O	O	O

What conclusions can you draw from your responses? _____

_____

Actions for individuals

Using intrinsic motivation to improve teaching

The key idea is to systematically follow the process described in Chapter 7. Here we give actions to take as you follow the seven-step process for intrinsic motivation.

Step 1, understand the context.

Step 2, to create a goal, you can use evidence from students, from instructional development specialists, from research ideas to improve learning that you've read or heard about and use the MRIQ inventory to give feedback about your attitude and about your role as teachers. The goals should be written in observable terms with measurable criteria and agreed-upon forms of evidence.

For Step 3, one way to acknowledge ambivalence — as to why the *status quo* looks good — is to revisit the myths and assumptions given in Chapter 2.

For Step 4, select your choice of positive reasons for change.

In Step 5, build confidence, ideas include emphasize your competence, use your self management skills and gather your support network.

Step 6, create the plan. Include activities to bring in your support system.

Step 7, implement the plan and monitor and celebrate progress.

Some options to help you include the use of self-assessment or a *Private Teaching Dossier*. (A *Private Teaching Dossier* is compared with the *Teaching Dossier* described in Chapter 4). *I want to and I can!*

" I can improve my teaching!" exclaims Rochelle.

Improve your teaching as part of personal growth and development. Use intrinsic motivation! Easy to say, but how?

In this Chapter we provide practical suggestions as you work through the seven-step process of intrinsic motivation. We start with a clear understanding of your personal goals, of the university "system" and a realistic understanding of the demands on your time. To set a personal goal to improve teaching, a wide range of evidence and ideas can be used to create a goal to improve student learning in your classes. This includes student evaluations, being TV taped; using the triple student course evaluation technique, completing inventories and extracting neat ideas from the literature. Ambivalence might arise because of attitudes related to the Myths described in Chapter 2. Confidence that you can achieve the goal is increased through being skillful in the classroom; being a skilled research supervisor, by managing yourself well including integrating teaching research and service and by not spending an excessive amount of time preparing for class. Build support from your students; create a plan and implement the plan. In implementing a plan use self-assessment to improve performance. This includes creating a personal motto; creating goals for teaching; being scholarly in your educational activities; writing an annual, reflective Private Teaching Dossier; and sharing experiences. Consider each in turn.

8.1   Take time to understand the context

The context includes your long term goals, "the culture or system" in which you work and your personal life.

8.1.1   Write out your long term goals

Too often we float along with some general idea about what we want to achieve. As emphasized in Chapter 3, Table 3.9, performance improves when we have goals (Locke *et al.*, 1981). Goals should be written in observable terms, expressed as results (and not actions), with measurable criteria and some identified form of evidence.

For example, when I first joined McMaster my written goal was to be the best instructor possible by the age of 30. Good. I had a written goal, and it was expressed in terms of results. However, the goal was not written in observable terms; it lacked criteria and there was no explicit form of evidence identified. An inherent goal was my hope that "a little bit of me would go out with all my students." However, this was more a wish than a clearly defined goal.

Write out your long term goals.

8.1.2 Understand "the culture/system"

First we define "culture" and then offer suggestions about how an individual can identify the culture.

A. A definition of "culture"

A faculty handbook summarizes the policies of the university. But what we need to know is what really happens in this university "culture." The *culture* or the "system" might be defined as the environment determined by the collected actions, attitudes, standards, beliefs and practices about what is *really* important about the institution. The culture is the sum of many decisions.

For example, a provost might decide that the Center for Teaching should be relocated from a central to a remote location on campus. Furthermore, instead of reporting to the provost, the center would report to the librarian. I would interpret this decision as contradicting the Mission statement of that university "the improvement of teaching is important."

Another example, Bernard is an outstanding researcher and an average teacher; Bernie was promoted one year early. Regan is an outstanding teacher and an average researcher. Regan's promotion was delayed a year.

B. How one might determine the culture

Here are some suggestions about what you can do.

Familiarize yourself with the published policies, especially as they relate to promotion, tenure and annual performance. These should, but not always are, written in observable terms with measurable criteria, and stated forms of evidence. Take time to talk with the chair, a mentor, and a colleague about these published statements.

Talk with a member of the Promotions and Tenure Committee, a colleague, a mentor, or chair to determine how the policies are actually implemented.

For example, the published policy at one institution was that "the anecdotal comments on student evaluations" would never be presented as evidence to the promotions and tenure committee. Yet, in several instances, anecdotal comments were circulated to the committee.

Comment: there is not much that you can do to change this; it merely emphasizes that the published policies are not always followed to the letter.

At another institution, the policy was that the promotions and tenure committee shall consider the *Teaching Dossier* as evidence. Many faculty spent excessive time creating such a document. In talking with members of the P&T committee, we learn that no *Teaching Dossiers* were ever considered as evidence. P&T committee members did not consider them to be useful evidence.

If the culture says, "Don't be an idiot and take a course from the *Center for Teaching*. You'll become branded as a "teacher" and in this institution that's the kiss of death," then be cautious in devoting excessive time to improve learning. Some informal measures of "the culture" include:

- the career paths of the current President and Provost of the University;

- the credentials of academics who are promoted;

- the flavor of the "shop talk" in the faculty lounge;

- the flavor of the PR for high school students. Does it support Myth #1?

- the response of colleagues, and especially administrators, to the Myths outlined in Chapter 2;

- the response of colleagues, and especially administrators, to the Models of the relationship between teaching and research as outlined in Section 1.3;

- actions taken by colleagues, and more importantly, by administrators; the question is "do their actions provide evidence that both research and teaching are valued?"

- the response of colleagues to the annual student evaluations;

- the balance between "teaching" and "research" in the PR and articles in the University Newspaper and on the web;

- whether graduate education is considered "research" or "teaching;"

- the published criteria that are part of the University Mission and Vision Statements. Unfortunately, the Mission and Vision statements of many institutions are window dressing and grandiose hot air. They speak a good line. But does the university "walk the talk"? Ask for a copy of the criteria and forms of evidence that the administration uses to implement the Mission and Vision;

- talk to students.

Take time to obtain a realistic impression of the culture. A word of caution is that the culture and policies can change. For example, a University was known as "Teaching University;" effective teaching was expected and rewarded; discipline research was accepted but not emphasized. There was a change in administration that completely reversed the emphasis. The goal was to bring in research support money; excellent teaching was okay but not rewarded. The new hiring and emphasis was on research.

Take time to understand the system. You do not have to agree with the culture/system. But, you need to understand this context. Indeed, you may decide to improve your teaching *despite the system*.

8.1.3   Put your goal in the context of your life

Covey (1989) gives an excellent overview of how to manage time in the context of all the things going on in our life. This accounts for the different roles you play (spouse, friend, parent, child, colleague, community volunteer and so on) and the different dimensions of your life (intellectual, social-emotional, spiritual and physical).

8.2   Create a goal to improve student learning

To change from the *status quo* in teaching, we need to become aware of a possible desired state. For some people this occurs naturally. From the list describing peak performers, given at the beginning of Chapter 3, these people:

- are unsatisfied with past performance and believe they are capable of achieving much more,
- are curious and intellectually engaged,
- seek to grow personally and professionally throughout their career,
- want to expand their interests,
- want to acquire new knowledge and skills.

Regardless of whether this is a natural urge to improve or an explicit decision to "improve teaching," the next step is to identify an achievable goal.

The sources you might use to identify a discrepancy between current performance and an improved learning experience for the students include:

- input from student evaluations, feedback from specialists observing your class learning environment, and the discrepancies from the triple ratings;

- inspirational articles and conference presentations. See others do it and say "I could do that!"

Another option is doing an attitude check. Consider each in turn.

8.2.1 Evidence from students or instructional development specialists

Evidence can be obtained from course evaluations, from an analysis of a videotaped class or from triple student evaluations.

A. *Gather evidence from course evaluations (student ratings)*

In Section 4.3 we discussed student ratings as a form of evidence for performance review. For evidence of performance so that peers can make decisions, the important questions to use are about the overall effectiveness of the course and the instructor.

Here we focus on using the student rating as evidence to improve learning (and not for tenure, promotion and merit decisions which was discussed in Chapter 4). Look at questions that probe specific dimensions about your teaching, and especially ones that you can change. These include:

- course organization and planning,
- clarity and communication skills,
- teacher-student rapport and interaction (quality and extent),
- course expectations, grading and assessment policies,
- course difficulty and workload,
- student self-rated learning,
- your attitude toward the students,

plus a place for student comments. You might ask the students to list your five strengths and the two areas to improve.

As described before in Chapter 4, the ratings should be:

- done anonymously;
- gathered with the instructor absent from the class;
- collected by students and given to a third party to summarize for the instructor.

Knapper and Rogers (1994) emphasize the need to communicate to the students the value placed on the student ratings.

Interpreting the ratings. Summarize the results for yourself of student ratings in the context of ratings for the same course over the past six years. Treat the results with a grain of salt, especially if students include comments. Remember that about 10% will hate what you do no matter how hard you try ("Professor Nicole is so incompetent; how did she become a teacher?"); 10% will love you ("Professor Nicole is terrific. Why aren't there more like her in this Department?") Focus on the remaining comments and learn from them. Summarize for yourself the five strengths and the two areas you would like to work on.

B.   Be videotaped in class

Before class, record your answers to six questions:

1. What you hope the students will learn in this class?

2. How you plan to conduct the class to achieve these goals?

3. What is your criterion for success?

4. How students were asked to prepare for this class?

5. What you expect them to do during class?

6. How have you prepared the students for this class?

Videotape that class and then, as you watch a replay of the tape, analyze the tape in the context of the six questions. Identify five strengths and two areas to work on.

C.   Triple student evaluations

Using the traditional student evaluation form (described in Section 4.3), after one class or a series of classes, complete the form yourself based first on how you thought it went. Then complete the form based on how you think the students rated the teaching/learning in the class. Finally, ask the students to complete the form. Summarize the student's responses. Now you have three responses for each element on the form: your assessment, your prediction of the student's assessment and the actual student's assessment. Compare the responses and analyze the results. Identify five strengths and two areas to work on.

8.2.2   Be motivated by others

Network, attend conferences, talk to others, read books and articles about teaching and learning. For example, Chickering and Gamson (1987) note that learning improves for environments with prompt feedback, where there is cooperation (not competition), that are active (not passive), that expect student success, where there is extensive, quality teacher-student interaction, and that accounts for student's unique learning preference. Gibbs (undated) says "whoever owns the assessment owns the learning."

Other ideas include 1) limit teacher talk to 20 minute bursts (to overcome boredom) and 2) use ombudspersons to help monitor the quality of the teaching-learning. See Felder *et al.*, 2000 for other ideas.

8.2.3   Use an attitude check

Teacher attitude is relatively easy to change and, according to a student survey, is most influential in affecting student learning (Woods, 1999a). Your responses to the questionnaire My Role Is Questionnaire, MRIQ, in Appendix E, might help you identify goals.

8.2.4   Set your goals

Goals should be written, expressed in results to be obtained (and not actions to be taken) and coupled with measurable criteria.

My advice is to start simply. Don't be tempted to change to the educational "flavor of the month." Here is my structured list. These are relatively easy to implement; they have a mega impact. Hopefully you are doing some of these already.

- Know the names of your students; show them that you care about each as an individual.
- Provide an atmosphere where you expect them to succeed; you are not there to "weed them out."
- Limit teacher-talk to 20 minutes and then have activities to engage the students in the learning process.

Felder *et al.*, (2000) give other suggestions.

If you do not have tenure, I would discourage you from implementing more ambitious interventions such as cooperative learning groups; or small group self-directed, self assessed problem-based learning.

8.3   Acknowledge ambivalence

It is astute to acknowledge ambivalence right at the beginning. Yes, the goals generated in Section 8.2 sound great, but... after the initial enthusiasm wanes and obstacles occur, perhaps the reasons for maintaining the *status quo* and not trying to achieve these goals begin to undermine your performance.

One approach to acknowledge ambivalent attitudes is to address the myths presented in Chapter 2 and your attitude about teaching versus research from Chapter 1. To what extent might these affect your performance? Consider your response to myths from your ratings in Table 2.3.

- From Myth #7, Section 2.7 and the discussion in Chapter 1, first consider your personal model of the relationship between teaching and research. Confirm that you agree with Model 1 that there is a *synergistic interaction between teaching and research*. However, as Candy (1996), Brew and Boud (1996) and Kreber (1999b) suggest, the *practice* of synergistically integrating research and teaching builds gradually over one's career. In the early years, faculty may be better advised to focus on specific roles and to build the research infrastructure first.

  Comment: in most university climates the emphasis is on discipline specific research and that a line is drawn between graduate teaching and undergraduate teaching. Indeed, regrettably, teaching is often considered to be only your work with undergraduates. If you do not see teaching and research as a synergistic interaction, then an obstacle might be "why bother to improve my teaching? That is not valued at this institution."

- From Myth #2, Section 2.2 confirm that traditional lecturing is not the only way to teach. Remind yourself of the research that emphasizes the importance of such elements as active, cooperative and prompt feedback to improve learning. Also realize that teacher's attitude is probably the easiest and most effective to change. Embrace an attitude that you are there to develop the talent of each student, expect all the students to succeed, nurture the whole person development, focus on preparing them for their future careers and not restricted to the mastery of the specific subject in your course.

  Comment: If you persist in believing that the traditional lecture is the only way, then why change?

- From Myth #3, Section 2.3, acquire the attitude that you can be terrific at both "discovery" research and teaching.

  Comment: If we keep the attitude that discovery only occurs in "research" then our efforts to assess our progress and use measurable criteria in our journey to improve teaching will be flawed. We might give up because we cannot see progress and achievement. Another incorrect option we might take is that for any new learning environment we create, we will only test whether "they like it" and "we like it," we will diddle around and lose the opportunity to bring rigor to our efforts. This argument also applies to Myth #6, Section 2.6, related to being scholarly in our teaching and to Myth # 8, Section 2.8, requiring use the five principles of assessment.

- From Myths #4 and 5, Sections 2.4 and 2.5, confirm that your role as a teacher is to affect "the whole person" and that quantity and quality of teacher-student interaction is important to student learning.

  Comment: If we think that teaching is only the transmission of our discipline knowledge then we will avoid using powerful methods to improve learning.

- From Myth #9, Section 2.9, identify those forms of evidence about "excellence in teaching" with which you are most comfortable. Recall about 20 plus forms of evidence were listed in Chapter 4. From Table 4.1 reflect on all of the venues where your skill in teaching is used. Do not be limited by the traditional view that "teaching" is what you do for undergraduate students. Gather evidence from all of the places where you use your skill in teaching.

  Comment: if we fail to identify and gather forms of evidence as we make changes, then we may give up too soon. This isn't working! We might mistakenly rely only on the traditional student evaluations (that may have nose-dived) and leave the educational journey disheartened. This also applies to Myth #10, Section 2.10, related to the importance of gathering and presenting evidence to ourselves about our teaching.

In summary, the wrong attitudes about the university, your role, about teaching, research and assessment may prompt you to give up and return to the *status quo* because "this isn't working; there is no merit to doing this, I can't see progress, the student evaluations are killing me and the tried and true lecture still looks good to me, if it ain't broke, don't change it." Check your attitudes related to the myths.

8.4 Overcome ambivalence and identify advantages to achieving your goal

Some of these advantages include:

- **Consistent with personal goals.** This is probably the most powerful reason for change.
- **Self-pride.** Improve your teaching because you feel it is important. Do it despite the system.

- **The pleasure of seeing students learn and succeed**. A little bit of you goes along with all the students you touch. You might receive e-mails or cards from graduates saying "I succeeded because of you."

- **The pleasure of seeing other teachers and colleagues learn and succeed**. Others use your methods. They send e-mails seeking advice about your approach. They seek you out at conferences. They visit you.

- **The excitement of integrating teaching *and* research**. Nicole has convinced herself that it is teaching *versus* research. It is not! Teaching is a seamless activity that stretches from the entering freshman (with large classes, predominance of lectures and heavy on comprehending theories) through to the postdoctorate fellow (with its one-on-one intimacy, its problem-based learning and its discovery of theories). No chasm separates undergraduate from graduate education — except in the minds of those who really don't understand what universities are all about. Research shows that students see teachers with strong research programs as being enthusiastic, at the cutting edge of their discipline and able to bring the subject alive (Jenkins *et al.*, 1998; Lindsay, 1999). For Nicole, it's all a matter of seeing research and teaching as linked, and of sharing her research interests in class. Discover new ideas and effectively teach them to others.

- **Enthusiasm for discovery; the personal joy of synthesizing new ways of making knowledge understandable and integrating the new knowledge with your (and your student's) past experience.** Whitehead (1929) suggests that teachers are intrinsically motivated when they continually integrate new information. Initially, you may use texts, a syllabus and "teaching approach" similar to the one you experienced. As the subject knowledge changes and as you uncover sections of the course that students find difficult, you will create your own enrichment notes. Gradually the course evolves to become *yours*. I recommend that you start every course with the idea that you will create your own text for the course. As the course evolves, think big. Create an outline for *your* future text. The first year you might create section 25.2.1 for your text. Write it that way. Clear up the permissions and copyright releases. Experience the joy of synthesizing the material and have a sense of accomplishment. Here are seven other factors that might help you overcome ambivalence.

  1. **Curiosity and inventiveness**. You want to try to change your effectiveness. Set goals, create criteria, gather evidence and see positive proof of accomplishment.

  2. **Positive attitude that goals can be set and accomplished**. You are unsatisfied with past performance and convinced that you can accomplish much more.

  3. **High self expectation and strong orientation toward the subject**. You have set high personal standards; you want to grow personally and

professionally throughout your career. You are characterized by the 13 descriptors given at the beginning of Chapter 3

4. **Make your efforts contribute to the institution's value system.** The mission and vision statement of the institution might say "student success is paramount" or "our goal is to maximize the talent of each student." You might feel that you are not doing as much as you could in your course to make this happen.

5. **Contribute to the teaching profession.** You have a network of colleagues who value teaching. You want to evaluate a new intervention to improve student learning and so contribute to the teaching profession.

6. **Strengthen your personal portability.** You have a strong research record in your subject discipline, but you want to strengthen your effectiveness as a teacher fostering student learning so that, should you decide to apply for a position elsewhere, you will have a more attractive profile.

7. **Inspired by a role model.** A visit with Austin Doherty, Alverno College, inspired me to develop student's abilities. It worked for her. I tried to make it work in my environment. Be inspired by others.

These are example intrinsic motivators for change so that you have reached the stage of saying "I want to change."

8.5   Build confidence that you can achieve your goals

Many of these suggestions related to building confidence (discussed in this Section 8.5) also apply to implementing the plan (discussed in Section 8.7). Elements to build confidence include being skillful in the classroom, building support from your students, being skillful in supervising graduate students, managing your time and yourself well and gathering a support network. Consider each in turn.

8.5.1   Be skillful in the classroom —
Remind yourself of your competence
(or acquire the competence as needed to achieve your goals)

Learn to be a skilled teacher. Systematically map out a long range plan of study for yourself. Find a mentor. Visit the Center for Teaching. Learn the top seven ways to improve student learning (discussed in Section 2.2). Learn some key ideas about the fundamentals of teaching and learning (see, for example, Felder *et al.*, 2000 or Woods,

1999a). Attend at least one workshop a year. Keep up-to-date and form a network with skilled teachers.

8.5.2 Take time to build support from your students

In the classroom, go for success, not failure. Give your teaching interventions the best chance to be effective. Whenever you try something new, most students tend to resist.

Students prefer the familiar to something new. They know the "lecture system" and how to make it work for them to get the highest marks. If we change the familiar "system," most resist the change (Benvenuto, 1999). When they experience change, students often follow the eight-step grieving process of shock, denial, strong emotion, resistance, acceptance, struggle, better understanding and integration (Woods, 1994). Help them through the grieving process by running a workshop (MPS 49, 1999, Woods, 1999a).

- *Explain why* you are making the change.

- *Help students see their personal benefits* of the new approach in the short term and in the long term.

- *Explain your role.* Students may believe that they are paying for teachers to "lecture" (Benvenuto, 1999). Use Perry's inventory (described in Section 4.5 and Appendix C) to help students understand their perceptions; explain your role in terms of the Perry model.

- *Monitor the program frequently.* Use ombudspersons, one minute papers (described in Section 2.7) or CATS suggested by Angelo and Cross (1993) and adjust in response to their feedback.

- *Be flexible.* If this particular class is vehemently opposed to the new approach, explore options to achieve your goals and theirs. Perhaps scale down the intervention. Gather data on how to make the intervention more effective the next time you try it.

- *Bring in success stories.* Invite recruiters or students (from other programs where the intervention has been effective) to give testimonials at the start of your course.

- *Help students cope with the upheaval when old habits are identified and changed.* This is particularly true when developing student's skill in problem solving. For example, part way through a program to develop problem solving (Woods et al., 1997), students complained that "*focusing on the process of problem solving has meant that they could no longer solve problems.*" We used the following analogy to help them through this frustration.

Consider that you are a reasonably good tennis player. You go to an expert to improve your game. The expert takes your game apart. As you relearn how to do each part, your game is not what it used to be. Be patient. Gradually you improve and surpass your past skills.

For example, when the learning environment in a course was changed from a traditional lecture to small group, self-directed, self-assessed problem based learning, the dramatic difference in the effectiveness of the new environment occurred when a six-hour introduction was used instead of a two-hour introduction (Woods, 2007a).

8.5.3 Be skillful as a research supervisor of students

Research supervisors of graduate students use a research project as the vehicle for the successful development of their student's self confidence and skill in research. Research we defined earlier as "the curiosity, perseverance, initiative, originality, critical appraisal and integrity one uses to create new understanding and practices." The process is intensely interpersonal. The student enters that relationship with the understanding that the supervisor has the student's best interests at heart. The supervisor enters that relationship counting on the student to be interested, diligent and willing to learn and to complete the project effectively and efficiently. Before accepting a student it is wise for both student and supervisor to spend time outlining goals, aspirations and general expectations. One of the worst scenarios is when students wish to transfer supervisors or drop out of the program without completing the thesis because of "personality clashes" or "disillusionment." Rarely do Departments have effective ways of resolving such awkward "transfers." Part of this disillusionment can come if supervisors enter the student-supervisor interaction with unachievable expectations. Table 8.1 is a reminder of attitude expectations for supervisors. Here are some actions:

- Apply the principles of effective learning outlined in Chapter 4: encourage active learning, work cooperatively (not competitively), create an environment that expects success, account for different learning styles, be interested in developing the "whole person," provide prompt feedback, empower students with skill in self-assessment and nurture empowerment coupled with accountability.

- Develop your student's higher order thinking skills of critical appraisal and research. We can assess this development by using the eight criteria for research outlined in Chapter 5. For example, provide explicit training activities (such as enrichment reading and activities for the critical appraisal of past, published articles). Model your approach that you use to critique research proposals and grant applications.

Table 8.1

A checklist for the role and expectations from a graduate student supervisor

Supervisors I have met but hope students never encounter.	Supervisors I hope students encounter.
My students do what I tell them. That way we can get papers out promptly and on time. Get one student out the door and then it's on with the next. They get credit because my name is on the paper.	Students are colleagues with whom we will have a lifetime association.
The goal is for me to publish papers so that I can sustain my research empire.	The goal is to develop the research skill of each student in the context of nurturing the "whole person."
I pick risky blue-sky research projects that probably will fail or have negative results. But, if they succeed, wow! The credit results that will be fantastic!	Let hired research associates do the risky stuff. Give students positive reinforcement and select projects that have a high possibility to develop thinking skills effectively and discover new ways of doing things. Projects with negative results can be great learning experiences but are very difficult to sell and rarely result in publications.
I like good news. Come to me when you have positive results. Otherwise, leave me alone.	I'm here to help. Whenever things are not going as we planned, let me know quickly so we can solve the problem expeditiously.
I expect you in the lab all the time. For the next four years, you are mine and you are accountable to me for all your time.	This is a learning experience for the "whole person." Enjoy the intellectual stimulation from our research group and enjoy the options for enrichment from all that the campus offers.

- Be interested in the student as a person, in the research topic and the student's progress.

- Get to know your students well. These are colleagues with whom you will have a lifetime association.

- Know when to let the students make their own mistakes (knowing that such mistakes will not compromise the ultimate quality of the results nor unnecessarily delay the completion of the work).

- Motivate and help students create and stick to a realistic time schedule. Finishing on-time is a team effort. A graduate student who spends only 30 hours per week (when 60 to 80 hours per week are required) will not finish on time. Create a written time line which forms an informal contract between you and the student and which can be updated as time progresses.

- Empower and hold your students (and yourself) accountable through such activities as weekly meetings when progress is discussed and goals are set.

- Maintain good communication with all your students.

- Encourage students to draw on the full resources of the university (and not just depend on you and your research group).

- Create situations where student success builds upon success.

- Facilitate your student's production of research work through publications, the thesis and proposal reviews.

- Provide prompt and appropriate guidance, especially through the major hurdles, by elaborating on criteria and expectations.

- In selecting research projects, pick ones 1) that interest you, 2) that have potential to make a contribution, have positive results and be a good learning vehicle, 3) that have room for the student to have ownership and select issues of interest, 4) that tend to be narrowly defined at first (because they usually expand as the research progresses) rather than pick grandiose projects (where you and the students will extend a lot of effort trying to focus on major issues).

- Encourage your students to continually write up the work, rather than saving it all to the end.

- As a Department, create humane mechanisms to try to resolve potential conflicts between students and supervisors.

More suggestions are given by Kingman (1982) and in Chapter 7 of Davidson and Ambrose (1994).

8.5.4   Use your skill in managing yourself well

To achieve most goals requires us to manage ourselves well. Establish the emotional conditions so that, to achieve these goals, you will 1) manage your time well, 2) see all that you do as an integrated whole and 3) don't plan to spend an excessive amount of time preparing for class.

Academics already are putting in a 50 to 60 hours week. One of the keys to intrinsic motivation is to use that time wisely and see productive purpose for all that you do.

1. *Manage your time well.* Few of us can be the superhuman professors (Felder, 1994) expected of us. Set aside time for reflection and for being an excellent teacher, researcher, administrator and consultant. Create reasonable schedules for your time, plan ahead, shift urgent situations to non-urgent and learn to say "No!" to requests and activities that unnecessarily disrupt your

plans. Focus on important and non-urgent tasks. There are times when you need to say "No!" to invitations and opportunities in "teaching," "research" and "service." Some ideas about time management are given in the context of "service."

Committee work, that consumes about 15 to 28% of your time, is one area for proactive action.

- Seek advice about administrative and committee options that will provide the best learning experience. Committee work should not be shunned. Committee work provides a key experience in your development. Indeed, Kreber (1997) in factor #2 on teaching clusters committee work along with activities traditionally associated with teaching.

- Ask your chair if he/she will serve as an intermediary for all requests for committee work. It often is difficult to say "No!" to the wide range of administrative responsibilities and service requests one receives. Someone has to get the administration done, but the same willing soul shouldn't have to do it all. When asked to serve, respond by saying "I need to clear that through my Chair." Having said this, take the time to discuss with your Chair the merits of serving on this particular committee. If your Chair is the one making the request, then ask him/her to prioritize and indicate the time commitment for the different service functions you have.

- Once you are on a committee, perform the job 100%+. However, make it clear to the Chair that in order to be prepared for meetings, you need to have detailed agendas well in advance of each meeting. Gently let him/her know that if you do not receive an agenda, then you won't attend (Woods, 1994). Without advance warning and individual preparation, any meeting is a waste of time. Expect that meetings will have a fixed duration, instead of "we will meet until we have all the business done!"

- Learn the basics of effective meetings and how to chair meetings (Woods, 1994). Since many people do not know how to chair meetings and since committee work will be part of your responsibility, I have found the best option is to willingly accept being chair.

2. *See all that you do as an integrated whole; integrate teaching, research and service.* Have short and long term plans that address all roles. Don't feel guilty about spending your planned time on any of these activities. Share your findings, especially your research findings, with your undergraduate students. Here are some ideas:

- Assign projects that bring undergraduate students in contact with your research. In a communication skills course students can be teamed up with your graduate students to do appropriate literature critiques; ask them to do a literature search using the Science Citation data base to generate a list of people citing your work and to critique their extension of the work. Use experimental research equipment for the undergraduate laboratory course. Ask students to interview faculty members about their research. Create homework assignments based on your research.

- Bring to class concrete demos, based on your research, to illustrate the fundamentals. Use your research work to supply the context to balance concrete with the abstract as recommended, for example, by Felder *et al.*, 2000.

- Post articles and poster presentations outside your office, in the lab. or in the student lounge.

- Create a web page.

- As a Department post in the student home rooms or lounge a list of the Departmental Breakthroughs.

- Explain absences from campus and bring students into the action.

  Next week, I'll be at an international Conference presenting a paper on how to de-ink recycled paper. Fascinating stuff. When we recycle newsprint and want to reuse it. Briefly explain the problem.. Here's what we have found....Briefly explain your findings. Others who will be presenting their approaches include... Briefly outline from the abstracts what others have found. I'll report back to you after the conference. In the meantime, what's happening for you next week? Here are the arrangements I have made.

- Offer introductory graduate level courses as senior level electives. This means that both graduate students and undergraduates will be taking the same course. (Assign additional expectations for the graduate students but have a common examination and content.) This opens up the research expertise to undergraduate students.

Educational research (Jenkins *et al.*, 1998; Lindsay, 1999; Jenkins *et al.*, 2007) also suggests that undergraduate students fear that active researchers will not be available to them to answer their questions and that the researcher's attitude will be one of valuing the research activity more than the undergraduate teaching activity. Address this by protecting the faculty time devoted to each, and by openly communicating the vital importance of both. Other suggestions are available (Anon, 1999).

3. *Don't spend an excessive amount of time preparing for class.* Usually we want our classroom activities to be superb. As a guideline (Woods, 1983) the preparation time required for first-time offerings of courses are:

- undergraduate courses takes about three hours of preparation per hour of "class contact time,"

- graduate courses takes about five hours of preparation per hour of "class contact time."

These numbers decrease to about 1.7 hours and 3 hours respectively if only minor revisions are made to courses that have been given often before. This illustrates how much work it is to get that first graduate course going. You might consider sharing the graduate course with a colleague when you are developing the course for the first time.

For teaching, a reasonable annual allowance is 550 hours. This accounts for time to prepare for class, in-class activities, marking and about 60 hours per annum to improve, upgrade one of your courses per year. This allotment has been confirmed to be reasonable by Woods (1983), Howard (1985) and Simpson (1996). A template to determine the allowance for a course is given in Appendix H.

For suggestions about the preparation and delivery of the course see Section 8.2.

8.5.5   Gather your support network

Many are in your support network.

- **Support system from family.** Talk to your family about your goals and activities.

- **Support from people at outside institutions.**
  - Peers from other universities visit to observe you in your classroom. Introduce them to your colleagues and to the chair. Use the opportunity to illustrate that others find what you are doing is noteworthy. Highlight their visit without flaunting it.
  - Keep in touch with colleagues whom you met during an effective teaching workshop. They too may be experiencing the same doubts and difficulties you are experiencing; be a support to them and gain personal inner strength from helping them.

- **Support from mentors and role models.** Draw on the experience of mentors and role models who have succeeded.

- **Support from colleagues in Center for Teaching.** One of the strongest support from within the institution can usually come from colleagues in the Center for Teaching. They not only will encourage you but they also will have expertise to guide you along the journey.

- **Support from your students.** Be willing to spend time at the beginning of the semester explaining and rationalizing the new learning environment you will be using. Tell them what is in it for them. Use ombudspersons to provide you with continual monitoring of the effectiveness of the intervention. Details are given in Section 8.5.2.

- **Peers and peer acceptance within the institution.** Often peer acceptance within your home institution is slow in coming. For example, award-winning teachers usually have given workshops on effective teaching *elsewhere* for 10 to 12 years before their home university deigns to ask them to do a workshops on home turf. Don't wait for others. Try new ideas about teaching as a pilot project yourself. However, it is wise to let colleagues, especially with in the Department or Unit and the Dean know of the interventions that you are implementing.

Check with the chair that you have sufficient autonomy to implement your proposed changes to achieve your goal. Check with colleagues, within your institution and outside, that the goal is worthwhile and that they support you. Draw on support from students, alumni, mentors, family, colleagues and administrators.

8.5.6   Manage stress and maintain your high self esteem

Too easily we slip into the habit of negative self-talk that destroys self esteem and promotes distress. For more on building self esteem see McKay and Fanning (1987); for more on stress management see Woods (2007c) MPS 5.

Based on competence, skill at self management, a support network and high self esteem, you can now say "I want to and I can!"

8.6   Develop a plan

Take the principles of managing yourself well, from Section 8.5.4, and create a timeline, consult your chair, gather your support system, and create written ways to measure success and to see milestones achieved and celebrate. In creating a plan *bring research to your teaching*. Don't "diddle around" as discussed in Myth #6 Section 2.6 and in Chapter 5. When you decide to try something in the classroom, pause first and write out your hypothesis.

> *"I think that student's learning will improve if the students and I become more aware of the student's learning preferences."*

OK, now what? we might ask how might we measure the "improvement in learning"? Here are some options:

> *Get feedback from your students about the impact their new awareness of their learning style has had on their learning. Design a questionnaire and administer it several times in the semester.*
>
> *Ask students to keep a one-page, weekly log or journal in which they reflect about their learning style and the implications of why they attend class? What do they learn from the problem assignments? How do they study and prepare for tests? With whom do they study? How do they find "texts" that "talk to them." The log could be handed in and marked. This activity provides background information to help students respond to the questionnaire given above.*
>
> *Compare the marks for the class receiving input about the learning style with marks from previous classes who did not receive such information. The marks could be adjusted based on the overall average of the classes in the previous year. If you have a large class, one might do a control group study with one section receiving the treatment and the other receiving no treatment. Suggestions about how to set this up are given by Abraham and Cracolice (1994).*

Identify evidence to help you see accomplishment. We can only grow if we gain feedback about the positive and negative aspects of our teaching. A wide range of evidence is helpful. Here we use the five assessment fundamentals to evaluate the effectiveness of our teaching.

Gather pre and post-test data. Explore the possibility of using a professional inventory/questionnaire as a pre- and post- test for your students' performance. For example, for this experiment in learning described above perhaps the LASSI inventory might be useful (Weinstein *et al.*, 1987). With this inventory, you would need to apply for funds to support your project because most professionally-prepared inventories cost money. Information about inventories is given by Buros (annually), Murphy (1994) and Woods (1999b). Alternatively, others may have done similar research. Contact them and find out what instruments they developed or used.

Use a research approach based on the principles of assessment; don't diddle around. I encourage you to follow the general plan given in Chapter 7.

The main goals for me in making this change are: from Section 8.2.4.

The most important reasons why I want to make this change are: select the most pertinent ones from Section 8.4 or add your own.

The pertinent measurable criteria I would use to tell me I have achieved my goals are:

The forms of evidence/measures/ instruments that are pertinent include:

List the possible evidence; create or arrange for funding to purchase

I plan to do the following things to accomplish my goals: milestones along the way:

specific actions	when
Build support from students	First couple of days of class (8.5-2)
Class ombudspersons	First day
name cards	First day
write syllabus	

Other people could help me with change in these ways:		
person	possible ways	when I would contact them
family	support longer hours and discouragements	continually
colleagues		
chair	supports my approach to doubters	

These are some of the obstacles to change and how I could handle them:		
possible obstacle	probability x seriousness	how I will respond

I will know my plan is working when I see the following results:

write self-assessment

ombudspersons reports are working: feedback is objective; I take time to address each in class; ombudspersons see me spontaneously when there is a problem

>80% class attendance and participation

people walking by classroom ask "you seem to be having so much fun in your class. How do you do it?"

Create a plan.

8.7 Implement a plan

In implementing a plan, we follow the guidelines given in Section 8.5 — be skillful in the classroom and as a research supervisor, and manage yourself well. Focus especially on building support from your students. Apply the fundamental principles of assessment, are scholarly in your approach, and gather evidence based on the goals and criteria. From the evidence you gather you see progress, milestones achieved and you celebrate. Here are details of using self-assessment and a *Private Teaching Dossier* as forms of evidence.

8.7.1 Use self-assessment to motivate, to monitor and to improve your performance

One of the greatest self motivators is self-assessment. Self-assessment follows the five fundamental principles introduced in Myth # 8, Chapter 2. The key elements are set goals, identify criteria, gather evidence and rejoice in your accomplishments.

- *Create a personal motto or vision and set personal goals.* Improve your teaching by having a personal motto. "To be the best instructor by the age of 30." Very ambitious and I didn't make it. Nevertheless, that goal helped crystallize activities in the early years. What's your personal motto or goal? Enrich your motto by identifying goals, criteria and the type of evidence you plan to collect.

- *Gather evidence for research-in-teaching and to help you see accomplishment.* You can only grow if you gain feedback about the positive and negative aspects of your teaching. A wide range of evidence is helpful.
  - **Gather continual data about the teaching-learning task.** Use the one-minute paper, ombudspersons and the variety of options for getting feedback throughout the course that were described in Section 2.7.
  - **Gather student ratings of your courses.** Use research evidence to design the form and interpret the results (Cashin, 1995; University of Victoria, 1999). More is given in Section 4.3.
  - **Gather feedback from your students about the learning environment.** The Course Perceptions Questionnaire, CPQ, is recommended. This was described in Section 4.4 and Appendix A .

- *Document your achievements.* Keep a weekly reflective log of activities. Write articles about what you have done to nurture your sense of accomplishment. Submit these to peer-reviewed journals. Apply for grants and funds to support your activity. Create the framework for your future textbook.

- *Reflect about your teaching and summarize achievement* — Take time to reflect about your teaching. Put your reflections on paper. Create a *Private Teaching Dossier* and use this as a basis for setting goals for personal growth. A *Private Teaching Dossier* is described in Section 8.7.2.

- *Share your experience.* Share your goals and ideas with like-minded colleagues. Draw on them for suggestions about implementing and coping with the apparent downsides of making a change to the student's learning. Join professional associations; attend conferences. Create a community of learners on your campus (Boyer, 1990; Brent *et al.*, 1999). Give seminars and workshops to outside agencies. The Boy Scouts, Girl Guides, Service Groups, Gifted and Talented Programs — many are looking for speakers. Do any of the interventions apply in other contexts? Generously share your experience.

8.7.2   Create an annual *Private Teaching Dossier* to improve teaching

Take time to set goals and reflect about your teaching (Schon, 1987; Brookfield, 1990). Use critical appraisal to constantly inquire into what you are doing in the classroom — the merit, worthiness and sustained enthusiasm for your teaching and your student's learning.

> *"Hey, I have so much stuff to do, and now you are asking me to reflect about my teaching! You've got to be kidding," reacts Nicole (whom we met in Section 2.3). "I enjoy teaching but I've still got those n+1 grant proposals to get out the door."*

Here are some vital reasons why you should take the time to reflect, Nicole.

Reflecting now will save time in the future when you prepare for the next time you give this course. The course is finally over; you mark the last set of exams. You tried a few things differently. Some of them worked; some of them fizzled. Maybe next time. You are just glad that the semester is over and you can get back to research. But, in about four weeks you will get your student ratings for the course... and then in the fall, you'll pull out your notes and say..."Now what happened last time? What worked and what didn't work? What was it that I was going to try differently? Oh, I forget. I guess I'll just do it the same as I think I did it last time. If only I had spent some time writing down what I did when the course was over last fall. If only...." Take the time at the end of the course to write down your reflections about the course, what your goals were, what seemed to work and what didn't. Then, as you are preparing to do the course again, three to six months from now, you can refresh your memory from the reflections.

Writing down your reflections helps you have a sense of accomplishment. Summarize the courses you taught, write down what you tried to accomplish in each course. Consider the examination performance and see what parts of the course the students seemed to have trouble with and the parts the students really understood. Pat yourself on the back.

Reflecting will help you identify where you are and to set goals for what you want to achieve.

> *"OK, I'm convinced I should reflect, but what do I reflect about?" asks Nicole.*

The *Private Teaching Dossier* can provide a basis for reflection. A *Private Teaching Dossier* is:

1. Personal. This is for your growth and motivations.

2. Shared. Because it contains some evidence for your *Teaching Dossier* described in Section 4.16.

3. Inclusive. Because it includes all the areas where skill in teaching is used. Scan the column of Table 4.1. Identify, for you, the clients and activities where the teaching skill is applied. This can be undergraduate courses and counseling, graduate courses and supervision, community "service" courses, industrial, business short-courses, updating courses, workshops, Kreber factor # 1 (keeping up to date and learning, networking, mentoring), and Kreber factor # 4 (preparing to teach).

4. Not easy to prepare.

5. Rich with evidence that should not be used for any other purpose especially for performance review. For example, responses on students ratings to questions about "organization," "ability to inspire interest," and "attitude of the instructor toward the students" are extremely useful to foster improvement but should never be considered by peers doing performance assessment.

6. Integrative. This juxtaposes evidence from many different sources and perspectives about a single issue. For example, evidence about your attitude can be gleaned from the syllabus, from self-reflections, certain questions on the student rating and the "social climate" from the CPQ (described in Section 4.4 and given in Appendix A). As another example, your efforts to develop critical and creative thinking and research skills can be probed by gathering evidence from undergraduate research projects, from the supervision of graduate students but also from student ratings, from ASQ (described in Section 4.5 and given in Appendix B), from an analysis of examinations and assignments based on Bloom *et al.*'s taxonomy (described in Section 4.9) and from the exit survey.

The *Private Teaching Dossier* differs from the *Teaching Dossier* described in Chapter 4 because this is written to help you improve. A comparison between these two forms of Dossier is given in Table 8.2. To the ten components that form the major core of what has come to be called a *Teaching Dossier* you will add components to help **you** see a sense of accomplishment, to monitor progress and to set goals for development. Keep those goals in mind as you prepare the dossier. More ideas about preparing a *Teaching Dossier* are given by York University (1993), University Committee of Teaching and Learning (1992), McMaster Educational Services (1994), Brown et al. (1996), Shore *et al.* (1980), University of Alberta (1999), the University of Victoria (1999), Felder and Brent (1996) and Seldin (1991).

8.8   The importance of individual initiative

Gibbs *et al.* (2009) found, especially in the faculties of humanities and social sciences, that individual initiative and leadership were the prime mechanisms for departmental change. In the professional faculties, if the chair was not an outstanding teacher, the chair would often ask individuals to lead the way.

If you try only one thing from this Chapter

Get a sense of the culture/system in which you work. Say "I want to and I can improve my teaching."

Reflection and self-rating of ideas

When we think of motivating faculty to improve teaching, too often we think of P&T, promotions and tenure. However, the real heart to motivation is not such external motivators but rather the internal sparkle in your eye about teaching. You should *want to do it*. Oh, you can get by if you *have* to do it. But, the really effective teaching is when you want to do it. Table 8.3 gives you an opportunity to reflect on the ideas in this chapter and to rate those you are doing already and identify those that have potential usefulness for you.

Table 8.2
Comparison between a *Private Teaching Dossier* and a *Teaching Dossier*

	Private Teaching Dossier	Teaching Dossier
Purpose:	Intrinsic motivation. Private and personal. Used by you to reflect and improve.	Extrinsic motivation. Submitted as evidence to peers to assess performance in teaching.
People who see it.	You	Peers.
Perspective.	Reflect on the past but focus on setting future goals, measurable criteria and forms of evidence.	Focus on what has been done.
Student ratings: questions about attitude, organization, style, ability to inspire interest.	Yes, these provide insight to interpret what's going on and to suggest how to change.	No.
Student ratings: student comments.	Yes.	Never unless you give all of them and that's too much.
Student ratings: about the overall effectiveness of the course.	May be.	Yes.
Analysis from TV taping of you in action in class.	Yes. This can be a real goldmine of information to help you.	Not the analysis. Indicate that it was done.
Awards.	Not usually.	Ycs, and give the criteria, the pool of applicants and granting agency. Help the peers understand.
Long term goals.	Yes.	No.
Assessment of major contributions made in teaching.	No.	Yes.
Efforts to improve.	Analysis and implications.	Description of efforts made.
Syllabi.	Attached plus your written critique.	Peer assessment, based on criteria.
Examinations.	Personal interpretation of how students handled the questions, which questions tended to discriminate and style of questions. Bloom's taxonomy analysis.	Peer assessment based on the criteria in the context of the syllabi and mission and vision statements.
Student anecdotal comments from course evaluations.	Yes, especially those that give insight about what to do.	Definitely not.
Enrichment initiatives.	List of enrichment activities, rationale, self-analysis and put these in the context of your ultimate textbook.	List of enrichment done plus peer assessment of these based on criteria.

Table 8.3
Reflection and self-rating about intrinsic motivation

Reflection:

The most interesting idea in this Chapter was _____

I wish more had been written about _____

_____

Rate the ideas

	already do this	would work	might work	not my style
The context				
Have written personal, long-term goals	O	O	O	O
Have used a wide variety of sources to understand university culture	O	O	O	O
career paths of administrators	O	O	O	O
credentials of those promoted	O	O	O	O
responses to various Myths of Chapter 2	O	O	O	O
familiar with the policies	O	O	O	O
familiar with the practices and opportunities	O	O	O	O
Have academic goals in the context of my other commitments beyond academia	O	O	O	O
Understand your priorities				
be realistic about what you expect of yourself for teaching	O	O	O	O
Goal setting				
Use a variety of input to help identify personal goals to improve learning:				
Use course evaluations,	O	O	O	O
Be TV taped	O	O	O	O
Use the triple student course evaluation technique	O	O	O	O
Am motivated by others	O	O	O	O
Use MRIQ to gain feedback about my role	O	O	O	O

... continue

Rate the ideas

	already do this	would work	might work	not my style
Attitude check:				
Teaching and research interact synergistically	○	○	○	○
I can excel at both teaching and research	○	○	○	○
My role is to affect the "whole person"	○	○	○	○
I want to bring "research" to what I do in the classroom	○	○	○	○
I am aware of the five principles of assessment	○	○	○	○
"Teaching" is all activities where I use my teaching skills (and not just undergraduate activities)	○	○	○	○
Have written observable goal to improve student learning	○	○	○	○
I want to **Improve teaching because:**				
Consistent with long term goals	○	○	○	○
Self pride	○	○	○	○
See students succeed	○	○	○	○
See colleagues succeed by using my methods	○	○	○	○
See teaching integrated with research	○	○	○	○
Enjoy synthesizing information	○	○	○	○
Curiosity & inventiveness	○	○	○	○
Positive attitude that goals can be set and accomplished	○	○	○	○
High expectations	○	○	○	○
My goals contribute to the Mission and Vision of Institution	○	○	○	○
Strengthen personal portability	○	○	○	○
I'm inspired by others	○	○	○	○
Contribute to the profession	○	○	○	○

... continue

Rate the ideas

	already do this	would work	might work	not my style
***I can* Improve teaching because:**				
Competence in the teaching intervention	O	O	O	O
Have student support				
– explain purpose of your approach	O	O	O	O
– explain personal benefit to them	O	O	O	O
– explain our role	O	O	O	O
– monitor the student-teacher team	O	O	O	O
– show flexibility	O	O	O	O
– use success stories	O	O	O	O
– help students through the change process	O	O	O	O
Have research student support				
– use fundamentals of learning	O	O	O	O
– focus on developing eight research skills	O	O	O	O
– show personal interest in their success	O	O	O	O
– allow astute autonomy	O	O	O	O
– monitor the time schedule and help them finish on time	O	O	O	O
– good communication	O	O	O	O
– provide prompt feedback	O	O	O	O
– select research project that develops confidence in research skills	O	O	O	O
Manage time well				
Learn to say No!	O	O	O	O
Use committee work effectively	O	O	O	O
– expect agendas				
– learn the basics of effective meetings				
Integrate teaching and discipline subject research	O	O	O	O
Explain your research to students	O	O	O	O
Illustrate teaching with cases from research	O	O	O	O

... continue

Rate the ideas

	already do this	would work	might work	not my style
Use projects to bring students in contact with research	○	○	○	○
Post your articles	○	○	○	○
Post Departmental research breakthroughs	○	○	○	○
Explain absences from campus	○	○	○	○
Offer senior elective course in your research specialty	○	○	○	○
Protect time for teaching and research activities	○	○	○	○
See Masters and PhD research as teaching	○	○	○	○
Don't spend excessive amounts of time preparing for class	○	○	○	○
– use the 550 h/year template	○	○	○	○
Additional support I receive to motivate me to improve my teaching:				
From family and friends	○	○	○	○
From peers outside my university who visit	○	○	○	○
From your network of peers outside my university	○	○	○	○
Have a mentor	○	○	○	○
Have a role model	○	○	○	○
Support from colleagues in the Center for Teaching	○	○	○	○
Support from your students	○	○	○	○
Don't wait for strong peer support within your home university	○	○	○	○
Manage stress well, especially negative self-talk	○	○	○	○
Be scholarly in your educational activities	○	○	○	○

... continue

Rate the ideas

	already do this	would work	might work	not my style
Gather evidence about learning effectiveness	O	O	O	O
Pre and post tests	O	O	O	O
Monitoring evidence	O	O	O	O
Course ratings ("course evaluations")	O	O	O	O
Use CPQ about learning environment	O	O	O	O
Document achievements	O	O	O	O
Keep a daily/weekly reflective log book	O	O	O	O
Write articles	O	O	O	O
Table of Contents for your future texts	O	O	O	O
Write out your plan and include criteria	O	O	O	O
and obtain instruments/tests/measures	O	O	O	O
Monitor your implementation of the plan				
– use self-assessment	O	O	O	O
– use a research approach	O	O	O	O
– gather evidence of learning effectiveness	O	O	O	O
– document achievements	O	O	O	O
– write an annual, reflective *Private Teaching Dossier*	O	O	O	O
Include critical appraisal of teaching	O	O	O	O
Setup filing system to store data for annual Dossier	O	O	O	O
Share experiences	O	O	O	O
With colleagues	O	O	O	O
Form a "community of learners"	O	O	O	O
Give seminars and workshops	O	O	O	O
Other _____	O	O	O	O

My conclusion from these responses is _____
_____

9

Actions for administrators
Creating an atmosphere for intrinsic motivation

The key idea is that the environment in which we operate plays a crucial role in intrinsic motivation. Even though intrinsic motivation is personal — you decide — administrators should create environments that promote intrinsic motivation, especially intrinsic motivation to improve student learning.

Crucial elements in that environment that affect the intrinsic motivation process include creating and supporting a culture that promotes student learning, providing individuals with a feeling of competence, with a sense of autonomy and with a relatedness between the institution and the individual.

> *"Let me tell everyone about the terrific job Sarah is doing in the classroom!"*
> *exclaims the proud chair.*

Intrinsic motivation is personal. So what can administrators do? Lots! Consider the first in the intrinsic motivational process (described in Chapter 7): the extent to which the culture encourages student learning. As mentioned in Section 8.1.2 the culture of the university is a key component in what happens in a university. The administrators play key roles in determining that culture. How do administrators create a culture to nurture student learning? There are three answers depending on whether you are a chair, dean, provost or president. Three major elements that affect the culture are:

1. The written overall university culture, and policies. These include the mission and vision statements, the P&T and performance review policies, financial incentives, the cultural climate and the myths. These are determined primarily by the president, provost, and the senate. This is explored in chapter 12.

2. The actual practices of how the policies are interpreted and applied. These are determined by most administrators and decision-making committees.

3. Within this culture, the decisions and actions of administrators to support and encourage individuals and help them exploit the culture.

In this Chapter the focus is on the third element — how the administrator can help the individual understand and use the culture to achieve personal goals. Hence, in this Chapter an administrator's first activity is to find out the personal goals of the colleague. Then, in Section 9.2, the administrator can provide guidance as to how the culture can help achieve the goals.

Then, in this Chapter we shift the emphasis to step 5 in the process of intrinsic motivation — have confidence that you can make the change. In Section 9.3 we consider how an administrator can help provide a feeling of competence, a sense of autonomy and relatedness between the institution and the individual. Above all the administrator can provide emotional support and encouragement and be fair and trustworthy. Consider each in turn.

9.1   Learn their goals

As astute chair is one who interviews each departmental colleague to discover their personal short and long term goals; and reflects on how the chair and the Department can do the best to help the individual achieve those goals.

As a follow up, the chair can give gentle guidance on the goal setting and on the assessment process.

In addition during the interview the chair might seek input as to the perceived strengths and areas to improve within the Department (Woods, 1983).

9.2   Help them see how the culture supports their personal goals

Help them see how the Mission, Vision, and culture can help them achieve their personal goals.

For intrinsic motivation, the first step, as seen in Section 8.1.2, is to understand the culture of the institution. If the culture expects a focus on student learning, then it is relatively easy for each of us to try to improve student learning. It is expected that you improve student learning. Depending on your administrative position, you may or may not be able to influence what might be considered extrinsic motivators such as the Mission, Vision, P&T, performance review policies. However, you can clarify the culture and help individuals see how the culture can help them achieve their personal goals. Financial incentives and help from the professionals in the Center for Teaching are two components that can help anyone achieve goals to improve teaching.

9.3   Help develop an individual's confidence

Step 5 in intrinsic motivation is "Develop confidence that you can achieve your goal." Three elements toward building confidence include 1) competence, 2) autonomy and 3) relatedness. Consider, in turn, actions that administrators can take to help individuals develop their confidence.

9.3.1   Instill a feeling of competence

We feel confident when we work in an environment where we feel competent. Our colleagues provide supportive praise; the Department, faculty and university have celebrations honoring our achievements; the chair provides an annual interview based on the five principles of assessment outlined in Section 2.8. Example activities for administrators include:

- Provide support and praise; brag to others about an individual's competence. *Celebrate and publicize achievements.* Feature those who live the mission statement in frequent letters to journals, industries, recruiters, alumni, state or provincial legislators and high school counselors. Help those who support your institution and be aware of your accountability. Identify one person in each Department who is responsible for contributing the information monthly to your Public Relations Department. Have the names of award winners posted on a "Wall of Fame" near the President's Office.

- Interview each to identify personal goals and to learn what the chair can do to help individual achieve those goals (Woods 1983).

- Foster "teaching excellence" and give visibility to teaching improvement activities. Expect improvement of competence (Woods, 1983).

- Ask individuals to do things that are within their personal sense of competence.

- Encourage educational enrichment (whether it was encouragement to visit the Center for Teaching, invitations to the Center for Teaching to provide feedback about your program and serve as a resource; providing Departmental funds to attend workshops, inviting experts to visit department.)

High expectations of all; all are expected to be highly competent.

9.3.2   Provide autonomy

We feel confident when the goals we set are within our control. We have the power to work toward achieving the goals. Administrators can provide a wide range of opportunities through which individual faculty can achieve personal satisfaction and growth.

Again, this includes an annual personal interview. Resources are provided, in terms of specialized training, time, budget and space, to achieve the goals.

9.3.3   Provide relatedness

We feel that we are valued and a vital part of the system. There is a consistency between our goals and those of the institution. Communication and feedback are excellent. We know and feel related to the mission, vision, outcomes and expectations of the institution.

A warm, supportive, encouraging, team — all for one and one for all — everyone embracing the motto *innovation in learning, excellence in research and high quality of student life* — each of us having unstinting pride in the accomplishments of all colleagues — an environment where each is encouraged to develop his/her own style and skills. This describes an environment where each feels relatedness is high. What might be some elements that created such an enterprise?

Good communication and feedback. Everyone knows the Mission, Vision and expected Outcomes. Furthermore, performance indicators are in place to help us get feedback and monitor progress.

Here are some other dimensions. As an example, Dean Jack Hodgins, McMaster University, clearly enunciated a goal for the Faculty — his goal was that Mac would be the MIT of the north. The graduate program started when the undergraduate program started; strong support was given to any idea that would help the faculty move toward that goal. Jack's enthusiasm for Mac and for his goal was contagious; he attracted students, faculty and corporations. Jack also lived the philosophy that everyone was important. For example, the birthday celebration of the janitor John was as important as the celebration of a major research publication. He always took the time to find out what your latest news was; what you were doing and where you were going. He bragged to all about the achievements of his faculty.

Adair is Dean. He and colleague Husain were walking across campus after a very eventful meeting with the Industrial Advisory Committee. At the IAC meeting Husain had elaborated on the team building activities he had introduced into his course. Bill from Arch Industries was extremely impressed and praised Husain for his leadership. As they walked Dean Adair said, "Husain, your activities to develop team skills are OK, but you should realize that everyone in the faculty is doing that already. Bill was impressed but you are not doing anything special."

Are you Dean Adair or Dean Jack Hodgins?

For *esprit de corps* the faculty coffee lounge was connected to the Dean Jack's office. Since, in the 1960s, the time slot from 10 to 10:30 am was chapel break. All of us went to the lounge for coffee, to chat with our colleagues from all departments and to get support and ideas. Dean Jack would inevitably be there too.

Faculty social events also contributed to the sense of family and worth. The annual Christmas party in the lounge of the Engineering building for faculty, administrators, staff and spouses. This included square dancing; faculty skits or the inevitable treasure hunt throughout all the engineering building.

High expectations of all — all would be great teachers, all would bring in large amounts of research funding, all would annually present papers at international conferences, all would support each other. All faculty were dedicated to teaching research and professional service. No one focused only on one to the detriment of the others. All submitted papers to conferences and all attended at least one national conference each year. Initially, we all went to national and international discipline conferences and to specialty conferences in our research discipline.

All went to various student events during the year. Yes, we had faculty parties and social events, but we all supported and attended student events. Some of the more athletically inclined also played hockey, golf and went skiing.

We all knew details about our colleagues research, shared equipment and supported each other.

The spouses provided exceptional support. To develop *esprit de corps* we needed the continual support of our spouses who opened their houses to host our numerous departmental parties.

An approach might be to revisit the vitality checklist given in Table 3.12, in Chapter 3, and note what an administrator might do to encourage individuals to do the 11 items listed.

9.4   Provide emotional support and encouragement

Many options are available to provide support and encouragement. These include praise and celebrate, talking up what is happening and setting up informal support networks.

9.4.1   Praise and celebrate

When you learn about outstanding performance, promptly write a personal letter of congratulations. Arrange for celebration events.

9.4.2   Talk it up

Start your biweekly Departmental meetings with individuals briefly talking about the "latest" in research and teaching. This helps build *esprit des corps*, helps you keep up with events in the Department and continues to emphasize what is important.

9.4.3   Consider informal support networks

Bag lunches that focus on teaching, informal discussions with students, circulating announcements of events sponsored by Center for Learning and from Universities that are close, encouraging all to participate in educational listservs, such as Forum for Teaching & Learning in Higher Education.

9.5   Be fair and trustworthy

Develop trust, expect and assess all aspects of academic responsibilities, equitably distribute teaching responsibilities and lab space, know your limits and give feedback empathetically.

9.5.1   Develop trust

Table 3.1 lists the key elements of building trust — do what you say you will do, be willing to self disclose, be a good listener, understand what really matters to others, ask for feedback, tell the truth, keep confidences, honor and claim the seven fundamental rights and don't embarrass others. Apply the principles of assessment.

9.5.2   Encourage and assess all components of academic responsibility

One might be tempted to focus primarily on the research contribution, perhaps with some attention to the teaching contribution but rarely are service, "good citizenship" and contributions to the vitality of the Department explicitly and acknowledged fairly and encouraged.

9.5.3   Fair and equitable teaching loads, research space

Openly discuss with colleagues who will teach what undergraduate and graduate courses each year. The mechanics of how this might be done, using the course loading document in Appendix H. By discussing this openly, using the loading system, all the teaching commitments were covered and all faculty were pleased with their assignment. Where possible use a consultative approach for decisions that affect others.

9.5.4   Know your limits

Do not promise something that is out of your control. "I'll do my best to have your case presented" as opposed to "The committee will give you tenure."

9.5.5   Give feedback empathetically

Chairs usually have many opportunities to give feedback to colleagues. Indeed, often that is expected. Here are some guidelines about how to give feedback empathetically.

1. Look for the good in others; expect the best.

2. People don't care about how much you know; just how much you care about them.

3. Show empathy; indicate that you have listened and understand. Focus the response on being flexible so that you show willingness to listen and try to understand another's point of view.

4. Identify five strengths for every two areas to work on.

5. Provide positive feedback often, honestly and as soon as possible after the noteworthy event.

6. For feedback to improve performance, focus on the value of the feedback to the recipient rather than on the power or release it gives the person giving the feedback.

7. For feedback to improve performance, focus on the behavior and performance and not on personality or personal worth.

8. For feedback to improve performance, give the amount of information that the person can productively use (rather than the amount you want to unload at that time. For example, don't say, *"Here are your five strengths and here are 25 things you should change."*)

9. Focus on descriptions of behavior and not on advice or judgments about the behavior (unless you are asked explicitly for advice. However, it is usually better to help them explore options rather than for you to give your answer to their problem).

10. Focus on what is said and not why it is said.

11. Focus on being equality-oriented rather than superiority-oriented.

9.6   Be a role model

Talk openly about your own approach to teaching; about the mistakes you made. Ask colleagues for ideas about how to improve your own teaching. Ask for guidance from the Center for Teaching and share ideas you received with others. Apply for grants in research-in-teaching.

9.7   Learn details about research-in-teaching

Since some colleagues may wish to apply their research skills to teaching, administrators should become familiar with the rigorous extension of research to teaching, learn the standards and qualities of the refereed journals and be able to give support, advice and encouragement. Help colleagues distinguish between excellence in teaching and excellence in research-in-teaching. Remind colleagues of the nine-step research process that applies equally to research in a subject discipline and to research-in-teaching.

Details were given in Section 5.1. Learn about the quality of the refereeing in journals that publish articles about research-in-teaching. Table 5.3 might be a useful start. Peruse reviews that colleagues have received. Ask advice from those who have served as reviewers for the journals and draw on the experience of the professionals in the Center for Teaching. Check with Research Services about the availability and standards for grants that support research-in-teaching.

9.8   Common threads

Be intensely proud of your colleagues and brag about their accomplishments to others.

Listen well and know what everyone is doing, in the faculty, in the Department.

Be trustworthy.

If you try only two things from this Chapter

Learn their goals. Build trust.

Reflection and self-rate the ideas

When we think of motivating faculty to improve teaching, too often we think of P&T, promotions and tenure. However, the real heart to motivation is not such external motivators but rather the internal sparkle in your colleague's eye about teaching. They should *want to do it*.

In this Chapter we suggested ideas for you, an administrator, to nurture intrinsic motivation to improve learning. Table 9.1 gives you a chance to reflect on and rate the ideas about nurturing internal motivation.

Table 9.1

Reflection and self-rating about nurturing intrinsic motivation to improve teaching

Reflection:

_____

_____

Rate the ideas

	already do this	would work	might work	not my style
Interview each to learn goals	O	O	O	O
Help each see how the culture supports their goals	O	O	O	O
Help develop teacher's confidence by:				
Strengthening their competence by				
praise	O	O	O	O
celebrations	O	O	O	O
positive environment expecting "teaching excellence"	O	O	O	O
providing resources to strengthen competence	O	O	O	O
providing individual autonomy so that individuals have the power to improve student learning.	O	O	O	O
showing the relatedness between individual's goals and those of Department, Faculty, University via:				
– good communication about M&V and program outcomes	O	O	O	O
– supportive environment via pride in individual's achievements	O	O	O	O
social events	O	O	O	O
Provide emotional support and praise	O	O	O	O
Be fair and be seen to be fair	O	O	O	O
Be trustworthy	O	O	O	O
Know your limits	O	O	O	O
Give feedback empathetically	O	O	O	O
Be a role model	O	O	O	O
Learn details about "research-in-teaching"	O	O	O	O
Other: _____	O	O	O	O
_____	O	O	O	O
_____	O	O	O	O

My conclusion from these responses is _____

_____

Overview of extrinsic incentives and rewards

The key idea is that extrinsic incentives must not be neglected. The overall culture is the sum of the extrinsic incentives. An effective and well-crafted Mission and Vision statement is a good start. Policies and practice related to tenure, promotion and performance have a major impact on one's willingness to improve teaching. Other external incentives are listed.

This is an overview for the next three Chapters.

"I'm so close to getting the Nobel Prize that I really want to concentrate on my most recent research breakthroughs. I really don't have time to try to improve my teaching. Besides, on the University webpage they cite the number of Nobel winners so it must be important in this culture," responds Jared.

The best motivation is *intrinsic* motivation described in Chapters 7 to 9. However, the sparkle in our eye gradually diminishes if our efforts are not externally acknowledged, appreciated and rewarded. Sometimes our efforts may even be denigrated.

Sloan (1989) suggests that *extrinsic* motivators should be used to create environments which increase *intrinsic* motivation. We want the extrinsic motivators to create an environment that nurtures teachers to *want* to improve teaching rather than forcing them to *have* to do it. For example, the clients that personnel in the Center for Teaching dread having to work with are those instructors who are sent by the Dean because their teaching ratings are unacceptably low. Chapter 9 explored approaches administrators could take to nurture *intrinsic* motivation.

Extrinsic motivation to improve teaching includes external items that either through prestige or money prompt performance. In general these might include:

- celebrations and awards from within the institution or from outside. Internally, these include citations, celebrations and awards. Externally, these include fellowships in professional organizations, fellowships, best paper awards, national and international recognition, entry in *Who's Who*.

- financial include salary, awards and financial support to improve teaching.

Internally, the culture — whether it uses celebrations and prestige awards or direct salary remuneration — should be open in its equitable recognition of each individual's contributions. In other words, the performance expectations and goals should be published and the extrinsic rewards presented based on published measurable criteria. The process should have sufficient transparency that all believe the decisions are fair, yet not so transparent as to publish confidential personal details.

Many perceive the most influential extrinsic motivators to be the promotion and tenure and annual performance reviews. Wright's survey (1996) of 51 Canadian Universities and his analysis of the 950 responses from Directors of *Centers for Teaching* and Deans and Chairs of Departments showed that University policies and practices for tenure and promotion were the single most important motivator to improve teaching. Gmelch *et al.*, (1986) identify inadequate faculty reward and recognition as the major factor contributing to faculty stress and burnout. However, I believe it is important to consider more than just P&T and performance reviews. I would like to focus on the importance of the culture as being seen by all to be equitable and generous in its recognition and rewarding of good teaching.

In this overview Chapter, we consider first the ideas related to creating extrinsic motivation within the University Culture that are equitable. Then we consider the extrinsic motivators beyond the University that impact on the culture and thus directly on the individual performance.

10.1 Creating the extrinsic motivators within the university — Culture of accountability and equity

Good performance should be acknowledged and rewarded. The culture/system should be seen by everyone as being fair and equitable. One approach to achieve both these goals is to ensure that personal performance assessment is based on the five principles of assessment

From Chapter 2, Myth #8, the five principles of assessment are:

Principle 1 — Assessment is about performance: not personalities.

Principle 2 — Assessment is based on evidence: not feelings.

Principle 3 — Assessment should be done for a purpose with clearly defined performance conditions.

Principle 4 — Assessment should be done in the context of published goals, measurable criteria and pertinent agreed-upon forms of evidence.

Principle 5 — Assessment should be based on a wide range of evidence.

Three examples where these principles are not applied well include:

- Mission and vision statements (typically the criteria are not published)

- P&T policies and practices (typically the criteria are not published and inadequate evidence is accepted for effective teaching and service; Tables 4.2, 5.2, 6.2 and 6.4 may be useful starting examples)

- Design of evidence — sometimes the forms of evidence are not consistent with the criteria.

> *For example, the chair decides to use peer observation of classroom effectiveness. The observation/rating form selected should not be selected arbitrarily. It should not be similar to the traditional student course evaluation. It should include the criteria used for effective teaching (as given, for example, in Table 4.2.)*

The questions on the student course evaluation should not be worded so as to imply that the lecture is the expected form of in-class learning.

When we apply the principles we realize:

1. The University should publish Mission and Vision statements that work. They should describe goals and culture within the institution. The key word is *publish*. From the principles of assessment, measurable criteria must be published to provide a measure of how well the goals are being achieved. These should be created with a 20 year perspective and not "fine-tuned" every couple of years. This is explored in more detail in Section 12.2.

2. Performance indicators related to the goals and criteria and student learning should be gathered and published for faculties, schools and departments. See Section 12.3 for more.

3. The Promotion and Tenure and annual performance review published policies and practice — as well as having published goals, measurable criteria and lists of forms of evidence — should be consistent with the overall M&V of the university. As an aside, this means that we cannot continually be "improving" our M&V statements. The M&V statements should be created with, for example, a 20-year perspective. This is because every policy and procedure internally will be affected by the M&V statements. Candidates for tenure, for example, need to know the expected performance goals over the next six years having confidence that they are not going to change in the interim. For example, if in year four the M&V statements were changed to include "extensive faculty-student interaction" with measurable criteria that faculty are expected to attend more than half of the undergraduate student events per year and to attend convocation and more than half the alumni events per annum, and subsequently these are expected in the T&P decision, then many candidates will feel that they are not being treated fairly. Section 12.4 gives more suggestions.

4. Monitor the culture and help individuals understand the culture. Sections 12.5 and 12.9 explore these ideas.

5. Provide resources. Financial support for Centers of Teaching, course and materials development, individual release time should be set up consistent with the M&V. Section 12.6 describes some options.

6. Celebrations and internal awards to motivate improvement in teaching should be created consistent with M&V. Section 12.8 offers suggestions.

7. Practices in implementing the above-mentioned policies should be transparent, should follow the principles of assessment and the culture created in the M&V statements.

10.2 Be sensitive to external extrinsic motivators

Three external *extrinsic* motivators are the criteria used by the accreditation agencies, those used by external "ratings of universities" and those used for external awards. For these, universities have little direct control although members of the University community may serve on boards or be consultants. Nevertheless, it is astute for us to be aware of and respond to these criteria. When the external criteria are consistent with the internal culture, then it is astute to use these criteria internally. Consider each in turn.

10.2.1 External accreditation agencies

For schools of engineering, the national engineering accreditation boards (the Consejo de Acreditacion de al Ense anza de al Ingenieria, CASEI (Rugarcia, 1996; Rocha, 1998) in Mexico, the Accreditation Board for Engineering and Technology, ABET (Peterson, 1995; ABET, 1997; Felder, 1998) in the United States and the Canadian Engineering Accreditation Board, CEAB (CEAB, 1999) in Canada) have a major impact on programs. The accreditation requirements provide extrinsic motivation for Departments to revamp their programs to meet the standards. Their influence has been illustrated by the spate of papers, pronouncements, workshops and resulting innovative curricular changes that have occurred in the United States because of the new ABET Engineering Criteria 2000 expectations. The ABET 2000 criteria shifted the emphasis from:

- what we teach to how much students have learned,

- course-based to outcome-based, and

- from courses taught to the process used for continual improvement, benchmarking and accountability of the educational process.

Thus, external agencies put pressure on programs, and hence upon faculty, to change the curriculum, to improve the quality of the student learning and to monitor and assess that learning process.

Higher Learning Commission (2003) lists five major categories for accreditation — mission and integrity, preparing for the future, student learning and effective teaching, acquisition, discovery and application of knowledge; and engagement and service.

10.2.2 External surveys and ratings of universities

Other forces, external to the university, that provide extrinsic motivation include published national surveys and rankings of universities and programs (NSSE, Macleans, 2010; Gourman, 1996; Angus *et al.*, 1999; *US News and World Report*). The pressure these ratings have to improve teaching depend on the degree to which effective teaching is accounted for in the ratings.

National Survey of Student Experience (NSSE), for example, has had a major impact because it publishes the criteria, the criteria include elements to improve learning (especially active and cooperative elements) and this provides benchmark data annually for programs in North America.

10.2.3 External awards, citations and fellowships

The Nobel Prize, the Canadian Killan Awards, fellowships in The Royal Society and in professional organizations — these are examples of external awards that may motivate faculty as each adjusts priorities along their career.

10.3 So what do I actually do?

The policies and practices of the University *extrinsic* motivators should be public and equitable. An overriding concern is that policies and practices should be consistent with the overall mission and vision of the university. Although details of how to put various elements of *extrinsic* motivation into practice are given in Chapters 11 to 13, much depends on each person in the University being aware of the culture and being trustworthy and fair in implementing the policies.

If you try only one thing from this Chapter

The culture should promote equity in rewarding performance. Base policies and practices on the principles of assessment.

Reflection and self-rating of ideas

Reflect on the ideas presented and rate some of the ideas in this Chapter in Table 10.1.

Table 10.1

Reflection and self-rating of extrinsic motivators that promote excellence in teaching

Reflection:

_____

_____

_____

I wish more was said about _____

Rate the ideas

	already done well	a little more needed	much more	completely missing needed
In my context, the extrinsic motivators include:				
Recognition of teaching in tenure and promotion policies	O	O	O	O
Recognition of teaching in tenure and promotion practices	O	O	O	O
Clarity in criteria and forms of evidence to be used for P&T	O	O	O	O
Recognition of teaching in annual performance review policies	O	O	O	O
Recognition of teaching in annual performance review practices	O	O	O	O
Clarity in criteria and forms of evidence to be used for performance	O	O	O	O
Clear definitions of what constitutes "service," "research" & "teaching"	O	O	O	O
Acceptance of "seven key skills" of an academic outlined in Section 1.5	O	O	O	O
Cultural attitude about research and teaching (Section 1.3) synergy; rejects research is superior to teaching	O	O	O	O
Culture that supports good teaching	O	O	O	O
Hiring practices that require demonstration of teaching ability	O	O	O	O
Strong *Center for Teaching* with colleagues to help	O	O	O	O
Deans/chairs fostering the importance of teaching	O	O	O	O
Numerous excellent workshops on teaching methods	O	O	O	O

... continue

	already done well	a little more needed	much more	completely missing needed
Mentor program	○	○	○	○
Grants for instructional development	○	○	○	○
Internal awards available for teaching	○	○	○	○
Celebrations for effective teaching	○	○	○	○

Other

_____

_____

_____

_____

My conclusion from these responses is _____

Some models for teaching and research in the context of promotion, tenure and performance review

Since Promotion and Tenure tends to be perceived as a major extrinsic motivator, how best might that concept of research-in-teaching be integrated into the P&T policy and practice?

Answering this requires a) a clear distinction between in-class teaching (described in Chapter 4) and research-in-teaching (described in Chapter 5) and b) selecting a best way for your institution to juxtapose research-in-teaching with in-class teaching and with subject discipline research. For the purposes of tenure, promotion and performance review, options for handling teaching, research and research-in-teaching are discussed.

> *Michael knew it was bad news as soon as he opened the door. "Sit down," chair Christine curtly said. "Your request for tenure has been denied. June 30th will be your last day." "But the students love me. I am the top-rated teacher in this Department, and I have five papers in refereed journals describing my courses." "I know," conceded Christine and added, "June 30th."*

In denying tenure, the P&T committee members, in this research-intensive University, had the following attitudes and beliefs:

1. Being an outstanding teacher is not enough.

2. When asked for Michael's specialty in teaching, the response was "teaching."

3. Writing papers, refereed or not, about your teaching is "teaching."

4. Scholarship about teaching, yes, we've heard those words. We've heard about the scholarship of discovery, the scholarship of teaching, the scholarship of integration, the scholarship of application. Next we'll hear about the scholarship of scholarship. We don't consider scholarship to be research.

5. This candidate does not do research.

Michael's mentor might have guided him to:

- clarify the difference between "teaching" (activities to promote student learning) and "research about the effectiveness of the student learning" that includes identifying an area of interest, creating a goal or hypothesis, developing measures related to that goal, using the measures to decide whether the goal has been reached or the hypothesis confirmed. Describing what happens in the classroom is not research. Michael needed to read Chapter 5 that differentiates between excellence in teaching and research-in-teaching and that highlights why research-in-teaching is important.

Michael asks, "How do you get tenure and still be an outstanding teacher?" Faculty are expected to discover new knowledge as well as transmit and that knowledge to others. That's a given. Discovery of knowledge is usually called research and is characterized (as described in Chapter 5) as the curiosity, perseverance, initiative, originality, critical appraisal and integrity one uses to create new understanding and practices.

Some faculty prefer to use their research skill to discover how best to help students learn. They prefer research-in-teaching or a combination of this with research in their subject discipline.

The current challenge, as I see it, is that "research-in-teaching" lacks credibility in most research-intensive institutions. The reasons might be those discussed in Section 5.7. The question then is, how might we best handle research-in-teaching in the policies for P&T and performance review.

In Chapter 10, we learned that the most effective way to encourage excellence in teaching is through the policies and practice of promotion, tenure and annual performance review. In Chapters 4, 5 and 6 we demonstrated how to measure excellence in teaching, research and service. In this Chapter we offer several models to include such measures in policies for promotion, tenure and annual performance review. But first, we see from Michael's case that definitions are needed for "teaching" and for "research-in-teaching." Then we explore various models that might be used to include "research-in-teaching" in the P&T policies. In Model 1 research-in-teaching is combined with in-class teaching. In Model 2, research-in-teaching is considered alongside research in a subject discipline. Model 3 offers alternatives. Then a critique is given about these options. Consider each in turn.

11.1   Distinguish between "teaching" and "research-in-teaching"

A key element in Michael's case is the need to clearly distinguish "teaching" from "research."

Michael *described* what he did in the classroom but did not apply the research process to evaluate how effective was his teaching. The committee also rejected the very concept of scholarship and refused to equate it to research.

Some of the challenges mentioned in Chapter 5 include:

- the culture.

- I have given my definitions of "teaching" and "research-in-teaching." Definitions may differ in other institutions. The distinguishing definitions should be publicized for your university.

- individuals need to ensure that when they are claiming scholarship/research-in-teaching that it is not "teaching,"

- all documentation related to performance should clearly distinguish between "teaching" and "research-in-teaching."

- deans, chairs and members of the T&P committees should accept "research-in-teaching" as "research" and invest time learning which are the quality refereed journals for educational research. Members know such journals in their subject discipline, but may not be aware of them in the educational arena. Table 5.3 may provide a start.

Now consider four models for "teaching" and "research" in P&T policies.

11.2   Model 1 — Include research-in-teaching in what we call "teaching"

In this model we identify two areas, research in a subject discipline (such as, oil-water separations in chemical engineering) and "teaching." Here, the research-in-teaching is linked to the in-class effectiveness as a single entity called the "teaching stream." This is probably the easiest model for subject researchers and administrators to accept. Indeed for years, whatever research (and "diddlin' around") that has occurred has been linked with "teaching." For example, consider the Chair's comments in Section 2.6. *"Oh, Ahmed doesn't do research; he's the strong teacher in our Department!"*

Table 11.1 illustrates what this model might look like for promotion and tenure. We acknowledge that the service component is important; we have not included it because it would be the same requirement regardless of the stream elected. For tenure or promotion Nicole (a colleague introduced in Myth #3, Section 2.3, and in Section 7.4) would elect either a combination of columns 1 and 2 (Research in the subject discipline plus in-class teaching) or column 3 (the teaching stream). The quantitative numbers in this table will vary; they are included here as an illustration. Column 1 summarizes the traditional expectation for "research in a subject discipline." Indeed, publications, research grants and external recognition are commonly expected.

 The elements listed in Table 11.1 called seminars, external recognition and a clearly-defined area of specialization are usually inferred. Some candidates make these very explicit. Column 3 includes the same items for the "research" in teaching component. The only difference is that a variety of methods can be used to illustrate *impact*. Some might argue that the number of publications may be less simply because we have few recognized, refereed journals where we can publish. The numerical values of how many seminars, how many refereed publications will be decided in each institution.

In-class teaching component is the same regardless of which stream is elected. Traditionally, student ratings seem to have been the prime source of evidence used. Here we suggest other dimensions that reflect effectiveness as an in-class teacher as outlined in the 15 plus forms of evidence suggested in Chapter 4.

Table 11.2 illustrates how this model might be used for annual performance review and merit increase. This is consistent with the expectations for tenure and promotion but described on an annual basis. More explicit activities are reported: refereeing activities, awards, seminars and impact.

A model of teaching as research is given by Martin, 1999a, complete with a template matrix that can be used to prompt your description of the context within your discipline, your reflection upon, inquiry into, responsiveness to and communication about your teaching and the students learning (Martin, 1999b).

Table 11.1

Model 1 for promotion and tenure (Assistant to Associate Level)

Research Stream		Teaching stream with in-class teaching combined with research-in-teaching
1. Research in subject discipline	2. In-class teaching	3. Teaching Stream
	In-class impact: ratings above the norm on the "Faculty-wide" student evaluations over the past three years	
	Course development: revise 1/3 of a course per year	
	Efforts to improve: 20 pages of enrichment notes per year for a course you teach or develop a new laboratory experiment or a new design project	
	Efforts to improve learning: attend annually one seminar or workshop on improving teaching/learning over the past three years	
Publications about subject research: 10 to 17 refereed	Publications about teaching: 1 every several years in a lightly refereed journal or paper presented at a conference	Publications about teaching research: 10 to 17 refereed
Research grants:		Research grants:
Contribution independent of PhD supervisor:		Contribution independent of PhD supervisor:
Impact: through citations		Impact: through citations or adoption of educational approaches or adoption of textbooks in other schools
Seminars: approximately 1 per year over the past three years		Seminars: approximately 1 per year over the past three years
External recognition: letters of support from three independent national and international authorities		External recognition: letters of support from three independent national and international authorities
Area of interest: specific areas of expertise such as hydrocyclones, process design, reaction injection molding		Area of interest: specific areas of expertise such as assessment, active learning, problem solving development, knowledge structure

Other variations that I consider to be similar are the models from Oxford Polytechnic and from Western Australia Institute of Technology (WAIT). Gibbs and Openshaw (1983) describe other options that have been used at Oxford Polytechnic and at Western Australia Institute of Technology (WAIT). The Oxford Polytechnic model asks for "teaching excellence and general academic excellence, as demonstrated by course development, research, consultancy, publications, practice or other achievements that might lead to a member of staff being recognized as exceptional." They suggest the use of a 33-item *Teaching Profile* where the candidate documents

Table 11.2

Model 1 for annual merit increase

1. Research in subject discipline	2. In-class teaching	3. Proposed Teaching Stream
Publications: two per year in refereed journals	Publications: 1 every several years in a lightly refereed journal or paper presented at a conference	Publications: two per year in refereed journals
Referee: four papers and proposals per year		Referee: four papers or proposals per year
Grants: receive		Grants: receive
Impact: through citations		Impact: through citations or adoption of educational approaches or adoption of textbooks in other schools; visitors
Seminars: approximately 1 per year		Seminars: approximately 1 per year
Awards: receive awards for publications or for research one in five years		Awards: receive awards for publications or for research one in five years
Area of interest: specific areas of expertise such as hydrocyclones, process design, reaction injection molding		Area of interest: specific areas of expertise such as assessment, active learning, problem solving development, knowledge structure
	In-class impact: ratings above the norm on the "Faculty-wide" student ratings	
	Course development: revise 1/3 of a course	
	Efforts to improve: 20 pages of enrichment notes for a course you teach or develop a new laboratory experiment or a new design project	
	Efforts to improve learning: attend one seminar or workshop on improving teaching/learning	

general aims and specific objectives, how the aims and objectives are translated into practice, efforts to monitor and assess the outcomes of the learning and activities that demonstrate continued study of teaching and learning.

The WAIT model gathers the following data — student and peer rating of teaching, peer appraisal of leadership and peer appraisal of research.

11.3   Model 2 — Include research-in-teaching in what we call "research"

In this model, research-in-teaching is grouped with scholarship/research in a subject discipline.

Table 11.3 suggests what this model looks like for promotion and tenure. The same general criteria, as presented in Table 11.1 are included here; they are just in a different category. Table 11.4 gives some options for the purpose of annual merit review.

Table 11.3

Model 2 for promotion and tenure (Assistant to Associate Level)

1. Research in subject discipline	2. Research-in-teaching	3. In-class teaching
Publications: 10 to 17 refereed		Publications: 1 every several years in lightly refereed journal or a paper presented at a conference
Research grants:		
Contribution that is independent of PhD supervisor:		
Impact of research: through citations and alumni		Impact: student ratings above the norm on the "Faculty-wide" student ratings for the past three years
Invited seminars: approximately 1 per year over the past three years		
External recognition: letters of support from three independent, national and international authorities		
Area of interest: defined; for example, distributed control, polymerization of PVC, data reconciliation	Area of interest: defined; for example, use of Perry model, writing across the curriculum, developing interpersonal skills	
		Course development: revise 1/3 of a course per year
		Efforts to improve: 20 pages of enrichment notes/year for a course you teach or develop a new laboratory experiment or develop a new design project
		Efforts to improve learning: annually attend one seminar or workshop on improving teaching/learning

Table 11.4

Model 2 for annual merit review

Research in subject discipline	Research-in-teaching	In-class teaching
Areas of interest: general with specific topics of expertise: stability of oil-water emulsions and applications to polymer production and environment	general with specific topics of expertise: cooperative learning in large classes; learning styles and their impact	
Publications: 2 per year in journals with rigorous, 3 independent reviewers		
Supervision: 2 M Eng and 1 PhD candidates	no supervision, but individual researcher does collaborative and independent research	
Visitors and post docs: have one every three years		
Referee: serve as a referee for journals and for grants		
Seminars: invited to give one seminar		
Awards: receive awards for publications or for research: one in five years		
Grants: receive grants from funding agencies		

11.4   Model 3 — Teaching without the explicit documentation of research

Not all subscribe to the need for research. Some feel that being a great teacher is not only sufficient but that it should be acknowledged and rewarded just the same as research in a subject discipline is acknowledged and rewarded. This model (Instructional Development Centre, 1983) offers an interesting blend of in-class teaching and inferred research. Table 11.5 summarizes the elements.

In this model, the teacher shows an on-going interest in teaching and in improving the student's learning. Little emphasis is placed on communicating that expertise beyond the local university. Some of the expectation is on service — through presenting seminars, workshops and serving on committees. The intent for research is present in the model; the demand for evidence related to the research is implicit.

Table 11.5

Model 3 for promotion and tenure (Assistant to Associate Level)

1. Research in subject discipline	3. Teaching stream
Publications: 10 to 17 refereed	Publications: 4 or more on topics in higher education
Research grants:	Grants: recipient of 3 or more internal grants for educational development work
Contribution independent of PhD supervisor:	
Impact: through citations	
Seminars: approximately 1 per year over the past three years	Seminars: presentation of four or more seminars or workshops on topics in higher education, one of which to be at another institution of higher education
External recognition: letters of support from three independent national and international authorities	
Area of interest: specific areas of expertise such as hydrocyclones, process design, reaction injection molding	
	Presentation of 1 or more workshops on a specific teaching skill
	In-class impact: ratings above the norm on the "faculty-wide" student ratings over the past three years
	Above average skill in lecturing, tutoring, supervising, facilitating group discussion or in the candidates identified area of expertise for the delivery of courses.
	Production of significant course materials that are likely to result in improved student learning
	Responsible for one of the following: − major course revision to enhance student learning − creation of new course to enhance student learning − major curriculum development to enhance student learning
	University service to promote teaching and learning
	Specific developmental work on student study skills (with application beyond a particular course)

11.5 Other models

The University of Texas at Austin has challenged Departments to develop alternative reward systems that would better recognize the importance of teaching, university and community service and applied research. Financial incentives were provided to Departments willing to overhaul their existing procedures. This is reported to have resulted in substantial changes in faculty roles and attitudes, as well as provoking lively debate throughout the institution (Knapper and Rogers, 1994).

11.6 Summary and personal critique of the models

One of the models likely has elements that might be acceptable is your environment. The overall goal is to put into practice the statement "teaching is valued **and** rewarded in this institution."

All models require effective in-class teaching **and** require that data be gathered from a variety of different viewpoints — student ratings, peer assessment, self-assessment and, where possible, from alumni and trained observers. All include some form of evidence demonstrating **research**. In Model 3, the allowable evidence is more inferential. In Model 1, the required evidence is to be explicit and lumped with the in-class teaching; in Model 2, lumped with research in the subject knowledge.

From my experience, here is my critique and recommendations.

For **Model 1**, the advantages of this model are that the educational research is a natural outcome of the teaching practice. The disadvantages of this approach are that this leads to the idea of dual pathways — the teaching stream versus the research stream. This does not strengthen the synthesis of teaching and research as promoted in Model 1 of Section 1.3. Instead this tends to polarize the two areas and support either Models 3 or 4 from Section 1.3 (research versus teaching or research is superior to teaching). Unfortunately, if the research is not formally recognized as being part of the teaching stream (in the criteria and in attitude) then teachers may continue to "diddle around," be dedicated in-class instructors with high student evaluation ratings and be confused when they are rated five out of ten by their peers on their "teaching" because for ratings higher than five we would expect evidence of research. Furthermore, there will be a tendency to give higher teaching loads to faculty in the "teacher" stream. This defeats and undermines the whole effort for research-in-teaching.

Model 1 does not support the principles outlined in Table 1.3, tends to polarize "teaching" as being undergraduate teaching and will cause confusion as to where to place "graduate education." Researchers will tend to view graduate education as "research" and "teaching" as undergraduate education. By linking the research-in-teaching with the in-class teaching it is easier for all to confuse the teaching element with the research element.

Model 2 is perhaps a harder model to sell to traditional researchers who may consider research in education as "second-class citizens." On the positive side, this allows one to demonstrate (and count) research in both a subject discipline and in teaching. Indeed, one can argue that research is research regardless of the context. A disadvantage of this model is the research-in-teaching is separated from the practice (in-class teaching). I recommend the use of this model because it focuses on the skill application which has been the main theme presented in Table 1.3 and throughout this book.

In **Model 3** the research skills described in Chapter 5 are not required explicitly. The evidence, for the most part, sounds like evidence you would use for excellence in teaching and not evidence for research-in-teaching.

In summary, in my culture, I would recommend the use of Model 2.

11.7 Criteria for teaching, research and service

In Chapters 4, 5 and 6 we focused on the highest expectations of *excellence* in teaching, research and service. In this Chapter we considered the *norm* expectation or break point between acceptable and unacceptable behavior. What criteria might be used for a range of ratings from very poor to excellent? Table 11.6 offers some guidelines.

If you try only two things from this Chapter

Distinguish between and define "teaching" and "research-in-teaching."
Use a reward system where *research-in-teaching* is considered research.

Reflection and self-rating of ideas

Table 11.7 gives you a chance to reflect on and rate the applicability of the ideas given in this Chapter.

Table 11.6
Example ratings for teaching, research and service

"Average expectations for annual performance ratings

for "teaching"

- a response from student course evaluations to the question "overall effectiveness of instructor" is > 5 out of 10.

- published >15 observable goals for each course.

- a value for Peer Evaluation of Educational Programs of <4.

- a value for the Course Perceptions Questionnaire of >20.

- 200 pages of enrichment notes per annum; the quality to be judged by the Chair and by two peers as being "good" based on criteria of purpose, quality and quantity of citations, consistency with required text, coherence and communication skills.

- one visitor from outside the university to learn about your educational methods in a two year period.

- three refereed research papers per PhD graduate.

- PhD candidates graduate within four years from entering with a Bachelor's degree.

- external evaluator of the thesis rates it "good" in contribution to knowledge.

- Peer assessment of the *Teaching Portfolio* is that the candidate addressed all ten parts, that the reflections, documentation and synthesis were consistent and related to the 11 criteria.

for "scholarship/research-in-teaching or subject discipline"

- two publications per annum in refereed journals.

- reviewer of four papers or grants per annum.

- invited to give one seminar per annum.

- receive an award for research, for publications, or for presentations once in seven years.

- papers receive three positive citations in the first five years after publication.

for "service"

- serves on two committees per year with >80% attendance at functions.

- letter from chair of the committee indicates reliable, prepared, completes tasks willingly and on time.

- positive letters from clients of consulting work.

Table 11.7

Reflection and self-rating of models and policies to promote excellence in teaching

Reflection:

_____

_____

_____

_____

_____

_____

_____

_____

Rate the ideas

	already do this	would work	might work	not my choice
Model 1 — Link research-in-teaching with in-class teaching				
Your preference	○	○	○	○
University response	○	○	○	○
How you would adjust the expectations in				
Table 11.1 for promotion _____				
Table 11.2 for annual performance				
Model 2 — Link research-in-teaching with research in subject discipline				
Your preference	○	○	○	○
University response	○	○	○	○
How you would adjust the expectations in				
Table 11.3 for promotion _____				
Table 11.4 for annual performance				

... continue

Rate the ideas

	already do this	would work	might work	not my choice
Model 3 — Without explicit documentation for research				
Your preference	○	○	○	○
University response	○	○	○	○
How you would adjust the expectations in				
Table 11.5 for promotion _____ _____ _____				
Other Model				
Your preference	○	○	○	○
University response	○	○	○	○
Expectations for promotion _____ _____				
Expectations for annual performance _____				

Actions for administrators

Extrinsic motivation to improve teaching

The key idea is that principles of assessment should be applied to Mission and Vision statements and policies about P&T and annual performance.

Nausheen was pleasantly shocked. No one had ever told her she was doing a good job. Yet, her chair Carolyn had just completed an annual performance interview and she said "Nausheen, you're a terrific teacher. Thanks being part of our Department." Carolyn is using just one of a dozen highly-effective ways that an administrator can use to motivate colleagues. And motivate and reward faculty to improve teaching is vitally needed.

Usually less than 50% of the graduates are ultimately satisfied with their university experience (White, 1990) although more recent data of Cote and Allahar (2007) suggest the number is 70 to 80%. Students rated the "attitude of the faculty toward students and toward student learning" as the dominant cause of student dissatisfaction (Woods, 1991). "Inflate grades for undergraduate students" is the way to make more students happy and for more students to graduate (Cote and Allahar, 2007). "We used to use an exit survey, but our results were so far below the benchmark data that we stopped using the exit survey" admits Dean Jones. "What can I really do?"

Slow to seek input from customers, slow to respond, not providing the types of skills needed, student dissatisfaction with the university experience... how much more evidence is needed before Chairs, Deans, Provosts and Universities change... and implement policies and practices to extrinsically encourage effective teaching while nurturing and expanding the research in technical research and professional service?

The good news is that there are notable examples of institutions that succeed in focusing on student learning. Kuh *et al.* (2005) analyzed the unique characteristics of schools that rated highest on the National Survey of Student Engagement, NSSE, questionnaire related to the quality of undergraduate education. The NSSE results report the level of challenge, the amount of active and collaborative learning, the quality of the student-faculty interaction, the extent of enriching education experiences, and the extent of the supportive campus environment. The institutions with the highest NSSE ratings were characterized as having:

1. A "living" mission and "lived" educational philosophy.

2. An unshakable focus on student learning.

3. Environments adapted for educational enrichment.

4. Clearly marked pathways to student success.

5. An improvement-oriented ethos.

6. Shared responsibility for educational quality and student success.

Based on their analysis, they recommended the following actions that administrators could take:

1. Make student's success everybody's business.

2. Feature student success in the institution's enacted educational mission and purpose. This relates to item 1 above.

3. Make talent development a central tenet in the institution's operating philosophy. This relates to items 1 and 5 above.

4. Cultivate an ethic of positive restlessness.

5. Put money where it may make a difference in student engagement.

6. Feature diversity inside and outside the classroom.

7. Attract, socialize and reward competent people.

8. Encourage collaboration across functional lines and between campus and the community.

9. Lay out the path to student success. This relates to item 4 above.

10. Reculture the institution for student success. This relates to items 2 and 4 above.

Gibbs *et al.* (2009) found, for leadership in teaching in research-intensive universities, that there was clearly no one way but there were common behaviors. These were that leaders:

1. had credibility that teaching is important,

2. were willing to involve students in the process to improve learning,

3. were strong advocates for teaching (both internally and externally),

4. promoted an environment of collaboration and exemplary practice,

5. provided clear goals and rewards,

6. gave autonomy to teachers.

In this Chapter we offer some details or practical actions administrators can take to implement these ideas.

12.1 Action to improve the assessment process

As emphasized in Chapter 10, policies and practices should be seen as being accountable, equitable and fair. Basing policies and practices on the fundamental principles of assessment is a wise foundation. Here are some examples.

- Motto, mission and vision and policies should include criteria.

- Mission and vision statements usually neglect publishing criteria and identifying acceptable forms of evidence.

- Policies for promotion, tenure and annual performance review should include criteria. Tables 4.2, 5.2, 6.2 and 6.4 may be useful starting examples.

- Create forms of evidence that are consistent with the criteria.

In this Chapter we outline how to embed the principles of assessment into policies and practices. Consider first the university's motto, mission and vision statements and published program outcomes. Then, suggestions are given about selecting and using appropriate performance indicators. Policies for promotion and tenure and annual performance reviews are considered next. Then a range of ideas are given to extrinsically support and motivate faculty to improve teaching. The word assessment refers to an individual's performance; evaluation, to the effectiveness of a program or an institution.

12.2 Create a motto, mission and vision statements and program outcomes that work

As we have seen for intrinsic motivation, the administration can create an environment that nurtures intrinsic motivation to improve teaching. Furthermore, one key factor in creating such an environment is for the University to publish a motto, mission and vision statements and program outcomes.

12.2.1 A motto

The climate of a university is usually captured in its motto. Our search of the Internet found few universities with mottos related to mission and vision statements. One positive motto is "Innovation in education, excellence in research and quality of student life." So what? Within the institution, the climate should shift to make the motto a reality. For example, individuals, departments and faculties can identify with and try to increase their contribution to "innovation in education." What is your University's motto? and what is its impact on your culture and environment? If you do not have one, you might decide on a motto for your Department, then encourage the faculty to accept the same motto and so use a grass roots movement to implement change.

12.2.2 Mission and vision statements

One of the most influential elements to affect the "culture" should be the mission and vision statements. Such statements should:

- embody the five principles of assessment

  Comment: as pointed out in Myth #8 most, if not all, institutions have M&V statements but these are worded generically in unobservable terms and lack measurable criteria. In short, most of the M&V statements I have seen are of little use.

- include performance indicators related to the M&V that are gathered at the Departmental and Faculty level to hold such units accountable for implementing the "culture" of the University

  Comment: regrettably the performance indicators are usually numerical statistics about class size, or the number of faculty with Nobel prizes that are not measures of student learning. If measures such as NSSE are used, then, unfortunately, they are not gathered at the Departmental or Faculty level.

- be the basis for resource allocation to a unit based on the degree to which the unit embodies the M&V of the institution.

Universities that have mission and vision statements inevitably include teaching and learning as a vital component. However, to make these part of the daily decision-making processes of the university, these must contain measurable criteria and example types of evidence as illustrated in Table 2.2. Without the criteria, every department comes to the University Budget Committee claiming "We're the department that is 'living' the mission and vision statement; give us more funds than the others!" The development of such statements and criteria is an investment of one to two years of negotiations and Town House meetings that is well-worth the effort.

Here are explicit actions administrators can take. Create a mission statement that emphasizes the importance of student success and learning. Once these are created then where does one start? Following the principles outlined in Table 3.9,

performance improves if we have goals (in this case, to improve the culture)

assessment must be related to the goals.

As chair you might acknowledge the University's mission and vision statement and make it more relevant to your department. Monitor the progress and celebrate the successes.

A. Set Goals

At the University level, the context might be that the University's Mission includes "expectations of student learning and success" and "we have an unshakable focus on student learning." Are such statements expressed in observable terms?

Comment: these statements might be altered to read as follows. *Faculty rate their prime role as being to facilitate student learning, as reflected, for example, in Section D of MRIQ, Appendix E. Expect a value of >30 on a scale from 0 to 40.* Other options might focus on known interventions to improve learning, for example, 30% of the classes are taught using non-lecture options that include active, cooperative or problem-based mode.

In creating the M&V statements it sometimes is useful to use the evidence and criteria as a starting guide.

B. *Create criteria and list forms of evidence*

At the university level, the criteria should be given, as suggested in Table 2.2, Section 2.8. Usually there are many criteria and forms of evidence. The most pertinent ones should be explicitly selected.

At the departmental level, although individuals can do many things in each course to try to improve student learning, a departmental approach might be to increase the ratings on the ACL and SFI dimensions of NSSE by 10%. They might use pre and post semester evidence using NSSE. Others might elect to focus on "a shared responsibility for student success" and change the wording on their syllabus to express this commitment. An example is given in Table 3.2.

C. *Monitor progress and celebrate success*

Progress and success should be monitored and celebrated at all levels. At the Departmental level, for example, the chair supports the individual efforts by monitoring progress, sending personal letters, talking about the progress and having departmental celebrations.

12.2.3 Publish program outcomes

At the institutional level, for example, Alverno College has published eight abilities that graduates must possess.

Deans could

> *Expect all programs to create a list of outcomes.*

It is noteworthy that many of the criteria and forms of evidence (criteria # 1 in Table 4.2 on teaching; Section 4.6 on the assessment of the syllabus; Part II in the

PEEP evaluation, Appendix D; Section 3 in the *Teaching Portfolio* described in Section 4.16) require a defined set of program outcomes. If the programs do not have such outcomes, then individual teachers cannot complete their expected mandate.

Example outcomes are given in Table 3.2 as part of a course syllabus.

12.3 Gather and use performance indicators (accountability measures) that are related to learning and to the criteria in the mission and vision statements

Gradually universities are posting performance indicators on their web page. Such indicators include basic data and occasionally data relative to M&V and to student learning.

12.3.1 Gather basic data

As a start, the provinces and states publish statistical information. For example, the Universities in Ontario provide Common University Data Ontario (CUDO) that lists the number of degrees awarded, student enrolment and entering averages, number of students living on campus and activities offered, student satisfaction, first-year tuition and ancillary fees by program, number of teaching faculty, undergraduate class size by year level, research awards granted and graduation rates and employment rates by program. Similar types of data are published for the state of Texas. Additional information could include the percentage of the total university budget that is spent for instructional development to include salaries for staff for the *Centers for Teaching*, internal grants, faculty release time for mentoring or taking courses for improve teaching, and internal faculty awards (0.4% of the overall operating budget is a reasonable criterion at this time).

12.3.2 Gather data more relative to student learning

Performance indicators linked to student learning should be used to monitor and improve performance. Options include:

- Exit polls/end of program reviews, as used, for example by Evergreen State College and Queen's University (Appendix F). A reasonable target satisfaction measure might be 50% in all programs.

- The Course Perceptions Questionnaire (Appendix A), as used, for example, by Universities in Australia to measure departmental effectiveness for the purpose of academic audits and resource allocation (Knapper and Rogers, 1994).

- My Role Is Questionnaire (Appendix E) that explores the faculty's attitude about his/her role.

- The National Survey of Student Engagement. Particularly relevant are the NSSE data that allow us to see the changes we make between first and final year.

- Alverno College is exemplary. They listed the outcomes — eight abilities. They selected 16 instruments to measure the student's acquisition of the abilities as they progress through the program (Mentkowski *et al.* 2000).

Select performance indicators that relate to student learning.

12.3.3 Use data to create an Institutional Plan for growth and for improving learning and to create an environment that will intrinsically motivate faculty to improve student learning

An example 10-year plan with goals and criteria has been published for North Carolina State University (Brent *et al.*, 1999). In the SUCCEED program (Brent *et al.*, 1999), a model of an action plan to encourage excellence in teaching was created. Queen's University has used the NSSE data which they benchmark with a comparable group of US schools and then create a plan. For details about Queen's see www. queensu.ca/irp/pdfiles/nsse/NSSE_2006_Presentation.pdf.

12.3.4 Use data as input for funding departments and programs

One might start with a motto and well-designed M&V statements that are linked to measurable performance indicators. These can be measured at the faculty and departmental level. Performance can be related to funding. For example, how well a department is meeting the M&V goal of "focus on student learning" could be determined by five performance indicators (NSSE ACL and SFI, CPQ, MRIQ and exit survey)." Table 12.1 provides some example data.

The results are relatively consistent and suggest avenues for change. For Department B, from the MRIQ, the attitude of the faculty tends not to focus on student learning. The low value of the CPQ suggests heavy dependence on formal lectures (which is somewhat consistent with the low values of NSSE, ACL).

Table 12.1

Example performance indicators for "focus on student learning"

Department	NSSE, ACL, sr. year, benchmark score	NSSE, SFI, sr. year, benchmark score	CPQ, ranges from -24 to 72	MRIQ, Focus on learning; ranges from 0 to 40	Exit survey, overall educational experience; excellent, % respondents
A	53.6	40.3	38	32	45
B	35.6	27.3	18	20	12
C	45.2	30.7	22	24	20

12.4 Use well-crafted policies for faculty performance that follow the principles of good assessment

Policies are written to guide decisions. As cited in Chapter 10, P&T and the reward system are claimed to be the single most important extrinsic factor we can use to improve teaching. Consider first written and public documents about P&T and then about performance review.

12.4.1 P&T

Here are some suggestions. As a start,

- *Ensure that excellence in teaching is valued* as much as excellence in research in all policies about promotion and tenure.

- *Acknowledge that research-in-teaching is research* and is valued regardless of whether the discovery research is applied to teaching or in a subject discipline.

- From Chapter 11, *select a model* for research and research-in-teaching that best fits your university.

Now consider more details. I have served as an external referee for many promotion and tenure cases. The documentation sent to me by those Universities inevitably say something like this,

> *"FOR PROMOTION FROM ASSISTANT PROFESSOR TO ASSOCIATE PROFESSOR. The appointee should be a very good teacher and have an acceptable teaching load. The appointee's research work should be independent and show high quality as judged by experts in the appointee's field of specialization. Service contributions to the department or university should be taken into account. Contributions to his/her profession may also be pertinent."*

Comment: Such statements do not satisfy the five principles of assessment. The statements are not expressed in observable terms, no criteria are given, and forms of evidence are not suggested. For example, in one case I received a 5 cm thick pile of individual student's course evaluations of the candidate. I guess I was expected to read all these individual reports and reach some conclusion about the candidate's teaching ability. In addition, the form used was faulty and did not ask the recommended questions (described in Section 4.3).

In another instance, the provost explained privately to me that for promotion to associate professor the criteria that the P&T committee used were:

- six refereed publications in major journals and the candidate's major professor should not co-author the papers.

- three positive letters from internationally-known experts in the candidate's area of expertise (selected from a list of seven provided by the candidate). The letters should say something like "the candidate is in the top 10% of professionals at this stage of their career."

- acceptable ratings in most of the student course evaluations.

- good citizenship.

Comment: This is an improvement for the research component. However, these details should be public. Secondly, for teaching only one form of evidence is used and the criteria are "wishy washy." For service and "citizenship" performance goals, criteria and forms of evidence are missing.

So what might Deans and Provosts do?

A. *Publish performance goals, criteria and forms of evidence* to be used for performance assessment in "in-class teaching," "scholarship/research," "service" and "good citizenship." Tables 4.2, 5.2 , 6.2, 6.4 and 3.12 might be a place to start. For research, the criteria might vary from faculty to faculty or from department to department. Okay, but those should be published and known information.

For example, in one case, the agreed-upon criterion (for internal use) was eight refereed publications. A candidate had one "major" chapter in a "research monograph." The Departmental Chair argued that "in this discipline, that was equivalent to eight refereed publications in other disciplines."

Comment: While there can be exceptions to the criteria, such major interpretations about individual Departmental expectations should have been agreed-upon and published before hand.

For teaching, more than just student ratings should be required. Chapter 4 lists options from which at least seven might be selected. The rating form itself should be well-designed.

For example, only one of about a dozen student ratings forms I was asked to review was well-designed.

If *Teaching Dossiers* are expected forms of evidence, then I recommend that examples of good and inferior *Dossiers* be published as examples of the standards expected.

Make service accountable; select at least four options for documenting and assessing excellence in service and committee work; ideas are given in Chapter 6. For example,

   i. require improved evidence of service.

   ii. require chairs to write "thank you" letters to all committee members documenting the contributions.

   iii. require annual reports from all committees.

   iv. include in the terms of reference of all committees:

> *"shall review the terms of reference for the committee and, in the context of the University's Mission and Vision Statement, shall make recommendations to improve the contribution to the University. This could include a recommendation to disband."*

> *"shall gather benchmark data about performance."*

   v. require the chairs to write letters to file about the operating procedures used and recommendations for improvement.

   B. *Explicitly address the issue of research-in-teaching*

For research, identify the model selected from Chapter 11 on how and where to include "research-in-teaching." Negotiate and acknowledge that research-in-teaching is valid as research.

Gain acceptance among faculty that research-in-teaching is "research" and subject to the same criteria and forms of evidence as subject-discipline research. After this has been written into the policies, help colleagues understand and apply the terms. The policies usually are not at fault; rather the fault is with a restricted view of "research" that excludes "research-in-teaching." This requires primarily an attitude shift. Training would start with the deans, then the chairs and then in-turn, they can communicate this to faculty through personal interviews. Invest time to learn the details of research-in-teaching. Suggestions are given in Section 9.7. These include such ideas as:

Distinguish between excellence in teaching and excellence in research-in-teaching.

Learn details about research-in-teaching to apply policies equitably.

Learn the quality refereed journals that publish articles in research-in-teaching.

C. *Consider acknowledging the importance of the five skills*

In Chapter 3 we elaborated on the research that identified the five skills beyond teaching, research and service. Perhaps the easiest to implement is citizenship. Select at least four options for documenting and assessing excellence in "citizenship;" suggestions, criteria and forms of evidence are listed in Chapter 3.

12.4.2 Disconnect salary from rank

Some institutions provide a salary range for the rank of assistant professor, for associate professor and so on. They do not allow, for example, an assistant professor to receive a salary in the associate professor range. Furthermore, once a person is promoted to associate professor, his/her salary is adjusted to the floor of the associate professor level. Such a policy means that the annual merit decisions are secondary to the promotion decisions. On the other hand, if the salary is disconnected from the rank, then, it is possible for an assistant professor (who might be a superb teacher but does little subject research) to have a salary equivalent to a mid-rank associate professor (who might have a mediocre teaching record but who has a research record sufficient for promotion). Thus, in institutions where the promotion criteria focus on discipline research requirements, outstanding teachers can at least be encouraged and rewarded through the annual performance reviews.

12.4.3 Annual performance reviews

Consider the principles and suggestions for P&T given in Section 12.4.1 and apply these to the annual performance review as applicable. In addition, consider the following.

Deans can

A. *Expect chairs to have annual personal interviews with each member of the department for performance reviews.*

B. *Expect all programs to create a list of outcomes.* It is noteworthy that many of the criteria and forms of evidence (criteria #1 in Table 4.2 on teaching; Section 4.6 on the assessment of the syllabus; Part II in the PEEP evaluation, Appendix D; Section 3 in the *Teaching Dossier* described in Section 4.16) require a defined set of program outcomes. If the programs do not have such outcomes, then the individual teachers cannot complete their expected mandate.

Yes, there should be an annual review to determine each persons's salary increment for the coming year. The increment should be based on performance.

C. *The performance expectations should be published, with descriptions of expected performance, criteria and typical forms of evidence used.* For example, I had been a faculty member for 18 years before I was learned the general basis the chairs and dean used to determine my annual salary change. It was not until I became chair that I learned that the relative ratings were 9 points of teaching, 9 for research and 7 points for service. In addition it was required that if I assessed one person as a +2 then I must rate another colleague -2.

Comment: There are three elements here. First the relative rating should have been published so that all knew the relative importance. Next, no criteria or forms of evidence were given. All I knew was that the chair had to justify my ratings so that the Dean agreed with the ratings. The third element was that the Dean was requiring norm-based assessment instead of the correct criteria-based.

So what might a Chair do?

A. *Publish the relative ratings of the three elements of performance — teaching, research and service.*

B. *As a Department agree on the performance goals, the measurable criteria and forms of evidence.* As an example, (Woods, 1983).

An average expectation (given a value of 5) in this Department is:

Teaching: 1) an overall teaching evaluation of 5 in the category "How does this course compare with others in the university?" and 2) doing major revisions on one course/annum or developing a new laboratory or developing a new design project for senior or freshman design course, and 3) developing a set of course notes (200 pages) over a ten year period and 4) publishing one education paper every three years and 5) having a normal load of about 550 hours a year of teaching.

Research: 1) two refereed publications per year, with about 10 pages per publication and 2) asked to give two invited seminars per year and 3) asked to review three papers or grant proposals per year. In lieu of some of these, additional support for research from one agency besides NSF/NSERC. For young staff members with less than two to three years, these criteria cannot be applied because of the time it takes to establish oneself. Hence, evidence, as perceived by the chairperson, to indicate an "expected commitment to research" (in terms of application for funds, supervision of students, papers being written or submitted) will be used to yield an "average" or as-expected rating.

Departmental responsibilities: 1) completes all willingly, meets all deadlines, treats staff thoughtfully and participates fully, and 2) with the college has a responsible role in one major faculty committee (such as curriculum or graduate committee) or 3) is editor of an international journal or 4) is chairperson of a session at a national or international conference, or 5) provides service courses to local engineers on updating courses.

    C. *Ensure that criterion-based assessment and not norm-based assessment methods are used.*

12.4.4 Hiring practices

Although universities usually expect quality research and in-class teaching, the degree to which these are valued varies from university to university. Universities are recruiting based on both discipline research **and** in-class teaching effectiveness. Candidates should be asked to present a research seminar and to present a sample "lecture" to students.

12.5 Monitor the practice of the policies

Policies can be published. But the real action is the practice of implementing the policy. For example, at one University the policy said "Each candidate for promotion shall submit a *Teaching Dossier* that shall be considered as part of the evidence to effective teaching." In practice, the promotion and tenure committee ignored the *Teaching Dossiers*.

Monitor the application of the performance criteria. Once agreement has been reached as to the criteria and forms of evidence for hiring, promotion and performance, monitoring is needed to ensure that the criteria are applied consistently.

The provost and senate committees need to ensure that the committee applies the criteria consistently. For example, a candidate might be a research superstar. But the criteria say acceptable teacher. The evidence is that his student ratings are 3 out of 10; peers, alumni and students all note that he cares little about teaching and uses the same notes he used 12 years ago. He walks into class; says his thing and then disappears into his lab where, as he says "the real action is!" He rarely even knows who is in his class. He refused to prepare a *Teaching Dossier*. No other evidence is submitted. The evidence is inconsistent with the criteria for an "acceptable teacher."

12.6 Provide resources to empower faculty to be excellent teachers and researchers

Resources are needed to help faculty improve in-class teaching and to do research-in-teaching.

12.6.1 Resources to improve teaching

A variety of resources can be made available to help faculty improve student learning. These range from direct financial support to professional assistance.

- *Allocate at least 0.4% of the annual operating budget for faculty development.* The monies can be used to support Centers for Teaching, provide mentors, runs workshops, send faculty to workshops, provide faculty relief salary and internal grants and awards (Brent *et al.*, 1999).

- *Fund Centers for Teaching to help faculty.* Most universities already support such centers. These provide a cadre of trained professionals with expertise in a variety of areas. Centers usually provide links to other campuses, run courses and seminars and provide workshops for Teaching Assistants, young and experienced faculty. They show leadership to improve teaching (Brent *et al.*, 1999). In the SUCCEED program (Brent *et al.*, 1999), Faculty Development coordinators are also hired within the Faculty of Engineering to provide local support and leadership. Such Centers should be located centrally on campus where it is easy and attractive for faculty to visit. Don't locate Centers in an isolated part of campus. The Director of the Center should report directly to the Provost. They should not be part of audiovisual, or the Library or the Student Learning Center or the Computer and Internet Services. For most Centers the mandate is to help faculty. If you want a separate center to improve student learning, that's okay but don't combine the two functions.

- *Provide internal grants.* Usually a pool of money is set aside to fund the direct, out-of-pocket expenses for projects. For a school of 13,000 students, the budget was about $500,000 over a 10-year period to support about 250 projects to promote effective learning. With inflation, this is around $80,000/ annum in the year 2011.

- *Run workshops for outsiders and use the revenue and resources to help internal projects.* Once faculty at your home university has identified an educational niche, they can then invite others to attend workshops given in that specialty. This has been done, for example, in "assessment" by Alverno College and in "problem-based learning" by University of Southern Illinois and McMaster University. The profits and personnel from such ventures can then be used internally to promote excellence in teaching.

- *Create the position of teaching fellows who become mentors* (Brent *et al.*, 1999). Interested faculty are given a stipend to serve as mentors to help others improve teaching. However, the teaching loads of teaching fellows should not be different from other appointees. Teaching fellows need the same amount of time to do research-in-teaching as non teaching fellows need for research in the subject discipline. Teaching fellows should be expected to do discovery research.

- *Provide relief time.* Departmental chairs can implement this idea. For example, provide relief time to allow one to develop a course, to convert a traditional lecture course into a cooperative learning course. Here's how it might be done. Each year when the chair is assigning equitable teaching loads, allowance can be given to each faculty member to "revise 1/3 of a course." (The example course loading form used in our Department is given in Appendix H.) Each is held accountable in next year's performance review (Woods, 1983). This approach has been validated at other universities (Howard, 1985) and in faculties other than engineering (Simpson, 1996). Sometimes more time is allowed, especially for a teacher who received low student ratings and who wants to change. As a department we recognize that some will have more class contact hours because others need time to improve their courses by revising more than 1/3 in any particular year.

- *Create a "book" account.* To help faculty write textbooks, create an account that provides money for the creation of course notes. These course notes will eventually evolve to become a textbook but during this journey a range of costs will be incurred. Make it easy by creating a departmental book account to support this work.

12.6.2 Research services for those who wish to do research-in-teaching

Research services are available on most campuses. They alert faculty about grants and funding for research; they guide in the preparation of grant applications and usually provide accounting services for the grant.

Such services should be provided for those who wish to apply their research to teaching. Regrettably few professionals in research services may be familiar with granting agencies, sources of funding, and they may not be experienced in providing assistance in writing and obtaining research grants for research-in-teaching.

12.7 Ask departments to summarize departmental performance

Just as individuals might be encouraged to create *Teaching Dossiers and Performance Dossiers*, ask Departments to prepare similar documentation. Universities in Australia are exploring the use of Departmental Performance Dossiers for the purpose of academic audits and resource allocation (Knapper and Rogers, 1994).

12.8 Action to celebrate achievements

Praise and celebration of achievement are very strong motivators. Administrators can nominate colleagues for external awards and they can create internal awards.

- *Nominate colleagues for external awards*. Reklaitis (1992) of Purdue University and Wood (1992) at McMaster University aggressively promote nominating colleagues for teaching awards. Usually one colleague within the Department is asked to assume this responsibility. This is not a trivial task. We have found that one must first become aware of the external awards, then contact the agencies to obtain the criteria (and talk to the personnel at the agency to obtain a reliable description of successful nominations). Table 12.2 lists some example awards for which faculty in Chemical Engineering are eligible. Next, one circulates the list to colleagues and gathers feedback about eligibility. Working with the colleague and creating the nomination usually takes about three months of work per nomination. With this approach, we received about three awards annually. Indeed, colleagues were very appreciative that the effort was extended to nominate them, even if they did not receive an award.

- *Create internal awards*. Awards can be created by the students, Department, Faculty School or University. So what might you do? If you do not have any awards available, you might start small. Suggest that the students develop a "golden apple" award to be given to the most effective teachers/supervisor. Encourage student organizations to create student awards to outstanding teachers. At McMaster University, three notable awards are the President's

Table 12.2

Some awards for educators

Award	Details
Ben Dasher Award	Best paper at the Frontiers in Education Conference. Selected from among papers presented at the conference. No application required.
Canadian Society for the Study of Higher Education Research Award	Distinguished contributions to research in Canadian Postsecondary Education. Canadian Society for Study of Higher Education 1001- 151 Slater St., Ottawa ON K1P 5N1
CCPE Faculty Teaching Award (Canadian Council of Professional Engineers)	Exemplary contribution to teaching and learning of the engineering profession in Canada. National Awards Program CCPE 401-116 Albert St., Ottawa, ON K1P 5G3
CASE Award (Council for the Advancement and Support of Education)	Any discipline, extraordinary commitment to undergraduate teaching. CASE Professor of the Year Award, Suite 400 11 Dupont Circle Washington DC 20036-1261
Catalyst Award (CMA)	Excellence in teaching: Chemical Manufacturers Association 2501 M Street NW Washington DC 20037
Chester F. Carlson Award (ASEE)	Innovation in engineering education. ASEE 11 Dupont Circle, Suite 200 Washington DC 20036
Corcoran Award (CEE)	Best paper in the journal *Chemical Engineering Education*. No application required.
Ray Fahien Award (ASEE)	Terms of reference given in Chemical Engineering Education.
Fellow SRHE	Sustained and significant contribution to knowledge and understanding of higher education. The Secretariat, SRHE University of Guildford, Guildford, Surrey, England GU2 5XH

... continue

Award	Details
Fellow ASEE	ASEE Fellow Member Committee 11 Dupont Circle, Suite 200 Washington DC 20036
Grawemeyer Award in Education	University of Louisville, School of Education Louisville, KY 40292
3M Fellow Award (Canada)	Sustained excellence in teaching and leadership. Society for Teaching and Learning in Higher Education c/o Instructional Development Centre, McMaster University, Hamilton ON
Gustav Ohaus-NSTA Award	Essay on how science teaching can be made more effective. NSTA, 1840 Wilson Blvd, Arlington VA 22201-3000
Union Carbide Award for Chemical Education (CSChE)	CIC National Office, 130 Slater St., Suite 550 Ottawa ON K1P 6E2 Canada
George Westinghouse Award (ASEE)	Young educators, excellence and innovation in teaching. ASEE 11 Dupont Circle, Suite 200 Washington DC 20036
Warren K. Lewis Award (AIChE)	Important contribution to ChE Education: AIChE 345 East 47th St, New York, NY, USA 10017
William H. Walker Award (AIChE)	Outstanding contribution to the literature of ChE: AIChE 345 East 47th St, New York, NY, USA 10017
Wighton Award (Canada)	Undergraduate laboratory innovations. National Committee of Deans of Engineering Concordia University, Montreal. Quebec H3G 1M8

Award for outstanding teaching, educational leadership and course materials development. The winners receive cash, attend the President's dinner, and receive a certificate that is presented at convocation. Their names are placed on the President's Wall of Fame.

Have frequent celebrations of the achievements of your colleagues.

12.9 Help individuals use the culture and assist new faculty get started

Much can be done to help all faculty understand the culture and to assist new faculty get started in their career at your university.

12.9.1 Help individuals understand and use the culture

It is foolish to create M&V, use performance indicators, create astute P&T policies and practices and then keep these well-kept secrets from the individual faculty. Take time to help each faculty member understand the policies and culture. This affects that crucial sense of relatedness (discussed in Section 9.3.3). All administrators should attempt to build trust-in themselves, in the process, and in the culture. Some suggestions are given in Section 9.5.

12.9.2 Action to help new faculty get started

It is very difficult for new faculty to learn the system, write research proposals and get funding, attract graduate students and get their work published. I found it challenging to get papers out within four years. In addition each is expected to develop new course notes, and select a good learning environment and do the expected service.

- *Reduce the teaching load.* Give new, untenured faculty a chance to get their research in their subject discipline going. Cut the teaching load for undergraduate classes in half. Suggest that they read Section 8.2.4 about giving your teaching interventions the best chance of success. Address Myth #7, Section 2.7. Provide an overview of the Departmental outcomes; elaborate on how the course helps students reach those outcomes. Provide examples of a possible syllabus.

- *Suggest that they share the teaching of a graduate course.* Although young faculty want to "own" their own graduate course in their specialty, for the first time suggest that they share the course with an experienced faculty member. (As an example, we find in engineering that it takes about 5 to 12 hours of preparation time per hour of class time for first-time graduate courses.) For example, offer a graduate course that has two related, but different, parts.

- *Provide internal grant funds to startup the research program.*

- *Encourage team supervision of research projects.*

- *Strongly recommend that the new faculty select a mentor.*

- *Assign committee duties after discussion with the new faculty member.*

- *Have a performance interview.* Follow the principles outlined in Section 12.4.3.

- Provide written policies and answer any questions about them.

12.10 Leadership to improve teaching

Gibbs *et al.* (2009) indicate that a Departmental change to improve learning can be caused by 1) an external requirement, 2) a previous problem that was not addressed or 3) individuals who feel it's needed or "value-driven." Whatever the cause, the change usually required more than three to five years. For Faculties of humanities and social sciences departmental improvements evolved because of individual initiatives. For professional faculties, such as veterinary science, medicine, science and engineering, departmental improvements usually occurred through collaborative activity (whether the cause was value-driven or a past problem to be solved.)

If you try only one thing from this Chapter

Create an overall environment that focuses on student learning through well-crafted Mission and Vision statements designed on the five principles of assessment.

For deans, change the P&T and performance review documents to correctly promote effective teaching. For chairs, have an annual private performance interview with each departmental colleague.

Reflection and self-rating of ideas

Table 12.3 provides an opportunity to reflect and rate the ideas.

Table 12.3

Reflection and self-rating for Administrators—Promoting excellence in teaching

Reflection:

_____

_____

_____

Rate the ideas

	already do this	would work	might work	not my style
Publish a motto	○	○	○	○
Mission and Vision statement with criteria and evidence specified	○	○	○	○
Publish program outcomes	○	○	○	○
Post performance indicators related to M&V	○	○	○	○
– include basic data	○	○	○	○
– include data relevant to student learning	○	○	○	○
Use an Institutional plan based on performance indicators	○	○	○	○
Use performance data as criteria to fund Departments	○	○	○	○
Publish "excellence in teaching" in P&T documents	○	○	○	○
Include research-in-teaching in P&T	○	○	○	○
Publish criteria and forms of evidence for P&T	○	○	○	○
Policy re P&T follows principles of assessment	○	○	○	○
For P&T select at least 7 options for assessing excellence in teaching	○	○	○	○
For P&T make service accountable; select at least four options for documenting and assessing excellence in service	○	○	○	○
For P&T make citizenship accountable; select at least four options for documenting and assessing excellence in "citizenship"	○	○	○	○
For P&T explicitly address the issue of research-in-teaching by incorporating a model where research-in-teaching has credibility	○	○	○	○
Distinguish between excellence in teaching & excellence in research-in-teaching	○	○	○	○
Learn details about research-in-teaching to apply policies equitably	○	○	○	○

... continue

	already do this	would work	might work	not my style
Learn the quality refereed journals that publish articles in research-in-teaching	O	O	O	O
For P&T gradually include the five skills from Chapter 3	O	O	O	O
Disconnect salary and rank	O	O	O	O
Publish "excellence in teaching" in annual performance review	O	O	O	O
Include research-in-teaching in annual performance review	O	O	O	O
Publish criteria and forms of evidence for annual performance	O	O	O	O
Monitor practice of policies	O	O	O	O
Disconnect salary from rank	O	O	O	O
Empower faculty to be excellent teachers				
Allocate at least 0.4% of the budget for faculty development	O	O	O	O
Fund "Centers for Teaching"	O	O	O	O
Provide internal grants	O	O	O	O
Use local expertise to run workshop & generate $	O	O	O	O
Create the position of teaching fellows	O	O	O	O
Provide relief time to improve courses	O	O	O	O
Create an account to support textbook writing	O	O	O	O
Provide research services for research-in-teaching	O	O	O	O
Publish Departmental Performance reviews	O	O	O	O
Celebrate				
Nominate colleagues for awards	O	O	O	O
Create internal awards	O	O	O	O
Celebrate and publicize achievements	O	O	O	O
Have a "Wall of Fame"	O	O	O	O
Help young faculty get started	O	O	O	O
Help individuals understand and use the culture	O	O	O	O

Other

_____

_____

_____

What conclusions can you draw from your responses? _____

Actions for individuals
Extrinsic motivation

The key idea is get tenure first. Learn how to document and describe your performance accurately and well. Work to improve credibility for excellence in teaching and research-in-teaching.

"Yeah, I know we have a Mission and Vision and we've had Town Hall meetings till we are sick and tired. So how does the M&V affect me anyway? That's just the President and Provost talking so as to raise money," claimed Hebert.

"Promotion delayed; what more can I do?" exclaimed a frustrated Juliette.

So far, the suggestions for action have been primarily for administrators. But you, without the administrative power, have much that you can do. Do all the suggestions given in Chapter 8 with which you are comfortable. Then, work on the *extrinsic* factors that support your *intrinsic* drive. In this Chapter we consider understanding the system, understanding your priorities, building credibility for excellent scholarly teachers, being an agent for change, keeping good records, creating a performance summary, and learning how to present your case. Consider each in turn.

Your university has enacted a variety of extrinsic motivators — the Mission and Visions, the policies for P&T and performance review, resources and awards. Faculty should ensue that they understand the real culture and system.

In this Chapter we start with the process of getting tenure and then move on to other actions you can do to use effectively the extrinsic motivators.

13.1 Get tenure

1. Know the system, what is the basis for tenure in your institution?

2. In most universities, you must have evidence of research and, in 2011, research-in-teaching does not have the credibility to make the grade in many universities. (As outlined in Section 5.7).

3. Start with your role primarily as a researcher, as described in Myth # 7. Be realistic about the amount of effort needed to get your research program going. Write grant proposals, get funding, set up labs, attract graduate students, write and publish papers. In my experience it takes about five years to get those first papers out.

4. You love to teach. But if you don't have tenure, then you may not be able to continue teaching. For the teaching emphasis, then, my recommendation, as cautioned in Section 8.2.4, and Myth #7, is to start simply.

13.2 Keep up-to-date about "the culture or the system"

The overall guidelines about how to determine the "culture" or the system are given in Section 8.1.2. The culture may change over the years, especially if there are changes in the President, Provost and VP Academic; keep up-to-date.

Request an interview with your Chair to discuss your performance and understand how your performance fits into the culture. Our experience has been that many Chairs are not only uncomfortable with the task of doing performance reviews of all their colleagues but they also may be uncomfortable openly discussing their review with you. On the other hand, some Chairs interview colleagues annually already. If he/she does not, ask to have an informal meeting. Prepare documentation, like the *Teaching Dossier* or annual Performance Summary, and give this to him/her about two weeks before the meeting. At the meeting focus on performance and evidence, rather than on personalities. Follow the principles of assessment (outlined in Myth # 8, Section 2.8). Then get feedback about how your performance relates to the Departmental, Faculty and University culture.

Ask a mentor to lead you through the ropes. If you don't have a mentor, consider asking for one.

13.3 Build credibility for excellent teaching

We lose credibility for excellence in teaching whenever:

- academics get awards from peers as outstanding teachers when discussions with them reveal that they really do not understand the subject knowledge. It is great to be an effective teacher but you have got to teach the correct stuff. We all must be experts in the subjects we teach. We need to know our subjects cold! (I can understand dramatic teachers who don't know the subject discipline getting awards from students. But not from peers!)

- academics are touted as being outstanding teachers when discussions reveal they do not know the first thing about the fundamentals of effective teaching. I remember visiting a campus and being told "Wait till you meet Prof. Brian! He's our hotshot teacher." My later attempts to discuss the development of learning objectives, applying the principles of assessment and the application of Bloom *et al.*'s taxonomy caused nothing but confusion. Prof. Brian hadn't a clue what I was talking about. This was embarrassing all round.

- awards for "teaching" go to outstanding subject discipline researchers who are inadequate teachers. Let outstanding researchers get their awards from societies sponsoring research! Awards for teaching should go to excellent teachers; who know their subject cold, who understand and apply the fundamental principles about facilitating learning and who bring scholarship to what they do in the classroom. If there are no candidates, then give no awards.

- Solicit feedback. Check out the services provided by the *Center for Teaching*. Polish up your syllabus. Have peers review your syllabus using the form Peer Evaluation of Educational Programs. Gather personal benchmark data from CPQ, NSSE and MRIQ and ask your mentor or personnel from *Center for Teaching* to help you interpret the results of the inventories. For CPQ, some of the guidelines are given in Section 4.4. For MRIQ see Appendix H.

- benchmark and set goals as described in Section 8.2.

So what? Be clear on your claims. Do not overstate your cases. Apply criteria consistently and ensure that quality is there before claims are made, awards given and accolades handed out.

13.4 Build credibility for research-in-teaching

We hope that all strive to be excellence teachers. Some, not all, may wish to apply their research skills to teaching; others will prefer to focus their research in their subject. Others may wish to be researchers in both.

13.4.1 Learn details about research-in-teaching

In your university, help build the credibility that research-in-teaching is as valued as research in the subject discipline. Consider the issues raised in Section 5.7.4 and explore what you might do to improve the credibility. This includes having clear definitions for excellence in teaching and excellence in research-in-teaching. Perhaps use the distinctions listed in 5.7.3. Recognize that there are quality refereed journals for research-in-teaching. Ideas about how to rate and identify these are given in Section 9.7. Discuss with the *Center for Teaching* how to fairly assess research-in-teaching.

13.4.2 Be a researcher and not a diddler

If you have tenure and if you elect to focus on research-in-teaching, then be rigorous. Reread Myth #6. Follow the research guidelines suggested in Chapter 5.

13.5 Be an agent for change

Here are four ideas:

- *Proactively work on campus for the development of excellence in teaching.* Continually refer to the "research-in-teaching" at the same time anyone is talking about "research" in subject discipline only.

- *Actively seek membership on the promotion and tenure committee.* On the committee, be an advocate for the recognition of research-in-teaching; expect a range of quality evidence for "effective teaching."

- *Lobby for the publication of criteria and forms of evidence for decisions about employment.* Books have been written about the forms of evidence to seek for P&T decisions but they do not describe the criteria. Other books and articles have been written about the criteria but they do not list example forms of evidence. You need **both** measurable criteria and forms of evidence.

- *Gather evidence about the quality of refereeing from journals publishing in education.* In Table 5.3 are listing my ratings of the quality of the refereeing used by various journals in teaching and learning. A three star rating may mean very little to those who are unfamiliar with these journals. However, if you share the criteria and referee's comments from articles you or colleagues published in such journals as *Academic Medicine, Cognition and Instruction,* or others, then skeptics may begin to see the quality of the publications.

13.6 Use the resources to improve effectiveness

Visit the *Center for Teaching*; learn about their expertise and the services they offer. Apply for grants.

13.7 Keep the chair and dean informed

The chair and the dean have access to many within the University. Keep them informed about your goals, your progress and your successes.

13.8 Learn how to gather evidence

The first step in proactively addressing Myth #10, Section 2.10, about an academic's ability to present data, is that we need to learn what type of evidence to gather and how to do this efficiently.

You and you alone know certain information about your performance and its impact on others. Gather all the pertinent evidence that relates to the criteria. Written records are needed.

13.8.1 Keep good records of what you do

Do not spend days looking for letters or missing records. Here are five convenient ways to keep track of what you do:

1. A calendar or diary on which you record commitments. Include enough information that you can understand what you did. For example, do not note "Meeting with visitors, Aug 5, 10: to noon." Identify the group and names of people.

2. A guest book, where guests "sign in." Ask them to include the date, their name and their home institution.

3. A bound log book in which you record telephone calls, decisions made with students, discussions and the outcomes, and general notes. This is very helpful to identify activities throughout the year. In addition, for critical decisions and recommendations for students you can record the decision and then both of you date and sign the decision.

4. A separate chrono file for correspondence, Fax and e-mails. Although you may file copies of correspondence by topic (for example, correspondence with E. Ruckinstein; letters of recommendation and so on), I find it useful to have a separate file where the correspondence is added chronologically by date.

5. A file folder of miscellaneous information. This could include unsolicited letters from alumni, feedback from workshops and invitations.

13.8.2 Record what you were invited to do but you declined

Invitations that you could not accept because of previous commitments are also valid evidence. For example,

Turned down:

1. Invitation to review two chapters in the new textbook *Plant and Process Design* for McGraw-Hill Publishers.

2. Invitation to be plenary speaker to 350 engineers at XPORT Company, Tulsa, OK at the annual Engineering Excellence conference.

3. Invitation to be a Director of the United Church Extension Council.

These are easy to neglect and forget; create a file folder or folder in your annual activity file.

13.8.3 Anticipate and gather evidence for performance reviews

In Chapter 4 and in Chapter 8, Section 8.5, a variety of data were suggested as evidence for excellence in teaching. Gather such data and note any benchmark data. For example, for students ratings of courses, often the chair will record the departmental averages and standard deviations for the key questions. The Registrar's Office may have data from the exit surveys. Obtain the Mission and Vision statements, the criteria, the Program outcomes and the corresponding criteria. Some documentation will be available about the criteria for awards you receive and the size of the pool from which you were selected. Collect material in folders: anticipate, benchmark, gather data and record. The evidence should be consistent your institution's criteria and expectations (as illustrated in Tables 4.2, 5.2, 6.2 and 6.4).

13.9 Create a performance summary in teaching, research and service

The *Performance Summary* interprets, for the purpose of extrinsic reward and decision-making, such evidence as your Curriculum Vitae, publications, grants, presentations, awards, committee work, student ratings, courses taught, student supervised, consulting done, external service and the *Teaching Dossier*. Here we describe how to prepare a summary for an annual performance review. A case for tenure or for promotion can be created by a synthesis of five or six years of annual *Performance Summaries*.

Step 1 — Decide on the classification of each activity. List all of your activities in the past year, and using Table 1.3 and your institutional definitions as guides, decide the classification for each activity.

For example, if the activity, (for example, a workshop for college teachers on the use of cooperative learning) required:

1. primarily your skill in teaching

   then call it "teaching" and criteria in Table 4.2

2. primarily your subject expertise

   then call it "service" and criteria in Table 6.2

3. primarily your skill in research

   then call it "research" and criteria in Table 5.2

4. primarily your skill in administration

   then call it "service" and criteria in Table 6.4

Step 2 — Identify the criteria the evidence supports. For example, for a workshop for college teachers on the use of cooperative learning: What skill in teaching did you demonstrate? and How does this evidence match a criteria? A statement that you "gave a workshop" provides evidence for criterion #8 in Table 4.2, willingness to share. On the other hand, the letter of invitation demonstrates that a peer at another institution identifies you as having expertise in the area of cooperative learning. Scrutinize that letter of invitation, the thank-you letter you received after the workshop and any other feedback you received to identify how the workshop experience relates to a claim of excellence based on the criteria. For example,

> *The letter of invitation might be evidence for criterion #1 — expertise because it said "We have heard of your expertise in cooperative learning and want to invite you...."*

> *A thank you letter, or a summary of the evaluations of your workshop might give evidence for criterion #6, selecting an appropriate learning environment, because it said "This workshop 'walked the talk.' You didn't tell us about cooperative learning; you asked us to experience and evaluate it for ourselves. I hope you will return and give another follow-up workshop at Red Deer College next year."*

Start with the criteria and ask "What evidence do I have for each criterion?"

Don't forget the invitations you turned down.

Step 3 — Write a draft Summary based on the criteria.

List the criteria. For each, cluster the evidence that demonstrates the degree to which you have achieved each criterion. Some evidence may be appropriate for more than one criterion.

Step 4 — Consider the following Do's and Don't's.

Here are some suggestions:

Do...

- Address all of the criteria with separate sections for each part of your job: teaching, scholarship and service.

- Put the information into context. Summarize student ratings and compare them with previous years. If you try something new in the classroom, help others see why you tried this, where you learned of the idea and the rationale. The evaluation of that activity would be described under scholarship.

- Help the reader interpret the evidence. For example, convert "attached is a letter from the Chair commenting on my administrative work." into "The Chair commended me for the initiative and follow-through that I brought to the Departmental Curriculum Committee that met 15 times this year and shepherded five major curricular changes through the Senate. (letter attached in Appendix C)."

- Think of the point you are trying to make and amass the evidence to support that claim. Succinctly summarize how the evidence supports the claims. Include the original evidence in an appendix (if appropriate).

- Be frank and open. Do not stretch the credibility by claiming too much.

Don't...

- Think that more paper is better. Verbose and unfocused *Summaries* (Portfolios, Dossiers) make the reader leery of your claims.

- Include peripheral material that is not directly pertinent to the issue.

- Confuse in-class teaching (and the preparation for that activity) with scholarship or service. Take your contributions and classify them the way you want. If you do not put your scholarly papers on teaching under "scholarship," the assessor might incorrectly put it under "teaching." You decide where the evidence fits.

- Think this can be written up in 30 minutes. A good presentation requires careful and systematic collection of data and about 10 to 30 hours of deliberation and writing.

- Try to do the task alone. Your *Center for Teaching*, peers, mentors and others can help you present your case.

Table 13.1 gives an example description (without the detailed evidence) that was prepared by Ahmed for his annual performance review. In Ahmed's institution, he is rated for research, teaching and service. The criteria are published and an idea of these is given in the "Context" given at the top of Table 13.1. Ahmed is an untenured Assistant Professor in a "research university." For research, he makes his claim for scholarship in teaching and intermixes both; for "teaching" he focuses on only the activities critical to being effective in the classroom. We note already that he has included scholarship in education under his scholarship category. That's how he thinks it should be presented.

In the section on scholarship, Ahmed should have a section describing his most significant contributions, in both chemical engineering and in teaching, and how these contributions have influenced the field; excerpts from reviewer's comments (especially from his paper on teaching because he is trying to establish his scholarship in teaching), and the citations of his work by others. When he reflects on these missing elements Ahmed should realize that he has been "diddlin' around" in his scholarship in teaching. The evidence does not support a claim for scholarship in teaching.

13.10 Present your case effectively in an interview

Whichever model is used to encourage, nurture and reward good teaching and scholarship, we require documentation and evidence. Here is where John has the most difficulty. "I find it difficult to brag. It's easy to list my publications, my research grants, the courses taught, the students supervised but I find it awkward to brag about what I've done in teaching. Besides, when I give a workshop on cooperative learning at the University of Keeners, is that "scholarship", "teaching" or "administration and professional service"? How can I put this effectively in a *Performance Summary*?

You are not alone John. Most would have difficulty, especially because of the words and attitude. Your comments really have two parts, "bragging" and classifying your activities. Consider them one at a time.

Presenting your case is **not** bragging. You are documenting the evidence to substantiate claims or to satisfy criteria. Inevitably when chairs interview colleagues about their annual performance review, any disagreement is because of a lack of documentation. Let's eavesdrop (with permission) on the chair talking to John. The

Table 13.1

Ahmed's Performance Summary (for annual performance review for merit)

Context Annual performance review for merit

Criteria: 9 points in-class teaching (student ratings; revisions of presentations); 9 points research (publications, reviewing, grants, invited seminars and papers presented) and 7 points administration/service (type of committee, extent of work, services, visitors)

Scholarship Ahmed Singer

I have attempted to apply my creativity to three areas of activity: technical research, educational research and professional affairs. I see my scholarly contributions as a combination of research papers and textbooks. My publications are in all three areas: technical research, education and professional.

Total: 26

Technical Research in Reaction kinetics

refereed: 6+3= 9

non-refereed: 4+5 = 9

accepted: 1

submitted: 2

Education and Education Research:

refereed: 3+1 = 4

non-refereed: 2+0 = 2

accepted:

submitted:

Professional

refereed:

non-refereed: 1+0 = 1

accepted:

submitted:

In this past year, the breakdown of the 9 publications was

in the area of reaction kinetics: 3 refereed; 1 accepted, 2 submitted; 5 non-refereed;

in the area of cooperative learning: 1 refereed; 0 accepted; 0 submitted, 0 non-refereed.

I was pleased to see the major work from Tracey's thesis published this year.

Two students completed their theses this past year; four papers should result.

Presented three invited seminars on reaction kinetics. Reviewed papers for Chemical Engineering Science and the AIChE Journal. Reviewed two grant proposals for NSF.

Turned down an invitation to be on a panel to review "New Directions for Research" because this came at a time when I had too many other commitments.

... continue

Teaching

The main emphasis this year was the complete reworking of two courses: Reaction kinetics and Reactor Design and my graduate course Advanced Reaction Kinetics and Catalysis course into a cooperative learning format. This required me to create a one-page description (and questions) for each day of class and tutorial. This produced excellent improvement in the Reactor Design class and mixed reaction for the graduate class.

I was delighted that the graduate students worked with me to create a course for those interested in going into academia. My contribution was through organizing different sessions (complemented my comments about developing CVs and obtaining research funds through separate sessions by Pierre and Shaun) and by presenting about five workshops on course development. Harietta talked to them as well. I hope this type of course is made available to graduates from any department.

I attended a seminar by Karl Smith on Cooperative Learning.

Administration/service

This year has been a very challenging one: last spring the curriculum changes required an extensive amount of work: I had to create the calendar copy, the bridging and scheduling details for all programs and for the next four years as we phase in the new curriculum. Added to this was the ongoing debate about the Faculty Mission and Vision that I found to be particularly draining.

I turned down two invitations to present workshops on cooperative learning; I am just starting this approach and I feel it is premature for me to present these.

I had some visitors to my laboratory this year: J. Smith and K. Brown from Exxon and Professor J. Riopelle, U. de Paris.

In the community, I continue to chair the Village of Smithville's Recreation Committee and work once a month with the Red Cross at their blood donor clinic.

For the AIChE, I continue to serve on the Reaction Kinetics and Undergraduate Education. I was session co-chairman at the Chicago meeting and will be session chairman for two sessions at the Los Angeles meeting. The responsibility is not onerous.

---

performance criteria used by the Chair are those given on the top of Table 13.1 (and reported in more detail by Woods, 1983).

Chair: "I see you have had a reasonably successful year in teaching, John. I note that you just reported your ratings this year. I like to consider them over a longer period of time and have summarized your student ratings over the past years. The Departmental average is 7.1, so on the student ratings you are above the norm. Considering the Departmental criteria for the teaching component, I would see your rating as being between 4 and 5 out of 10."

John: (rather taken back by this news... To himself he asks "I thought I would be at least 6 out of 10 this year. Where's the chair coming from to give me only 4 out of 10? what do I say now? I guess it won't hurt to be assertive.") That's a disappointment for me. I thought this year's work would merit a 6 to 7.

Chair: "That's a disappointment to me too because you seem to have been devoting a lot of your time to your teaching this year. In your record of activity forms that you submitted to me several weeks ago, you did not include anything about courses you attended, additional enrichment notes you prepared. I thought I saw you spending a lot of time with one-on-one counseling with Beatriz. However, I don't see any record of that. Can you elaborate?"

John: "I felt that adding that detail would only be bragging. I attended the week-long workshop in June on improving teaching. I read a series of papers about "Teaching Methods that Work" (Felder *et al*, 2000). From that I tried ombudspersons for the classroom and had several sessions on "active learning" in each of my classes. That seemed to work well. For the Course 306 I prepared about 20 pages of notes on a topic the students seem to find difficult. Beatriz...she is a very talented student. Her marks in my course were not her usual high performance. After some private discussion, she revealed that she has been having personal and family problems that have distracted her from study. I offered to be a listener for a few minutes each week. That seems to have helped... not to solve her problems... but to have her realize that we care about her. So what should I put down about Beatriz in my record of activities?"

Chair: "Performance reviews are not negotiations. They are assessments based on evidence... evidence that is written out objectively and succinctly. To your record of activity form, add the dates, title and duration of the workshop. Cite the paper. List the two ideas that you gained from the workshop and that you tried with your class. Document the number of pages of enrichment notes, the reason for their preparation, the student response and the topic of the notes."

John: "What about Beatriz? I don't want to bring her personal problems into the discussion."

Chair: "Correct. There is no need to. But what you can record is 'spent about 2 hours per week **counseling** students.' That indicates time spent above and beyond the norm and the use of the word counseling separates this activity from the usual tutoring and answering questions about homework assignments."

John: "That makes more sense to me, now. Still it's a lot of work documenting it all."

Chair: "No doubt about it! But, if your contributions are not documented, then others, such as the dean and the provost who do not know you well, will not support higher ratings for your performance without documentation. Help us all to see your contributions as you see them. Incidentally, you might consider using a *Performance Summary* format. No doubt you have your own Private Teaching Dossier (described in Chapter 8) to help you improve. You can follow the format given in Chapter 4 and create a *Teaching Dossier* in which you summarize your thoughts and reflections about your teaching. In particular, highlight what you see as your major contributions. The *Teaching Dossier* becomes some of the evidence you summarize in your Performance Summary."

John: "Thank goodness I am in this Department where the chair interviews each of us. Without this interview, I would not have known how important it is to include and document all that I have done. Thanks."

The second question John raised is how to decide what is scholarship, what is teaching and what is administration/service. John gave an invited workshop on "Cooperative Learning" at the University of Keeners. The workshop was on an educational topic, but it could have been on statistical planning of experiments or on using fractals or any Chemical Engineering topic. Regardless of the topic, the choice is to classify the workshop as "teaching," "scholarship" or "service." For his workshop, John should ask:

- "did I learn any new ideas and new approaches from my interaction with the participants?" (if so, then call this scholarship) or

- "did I present material and ideas that I have given numerous times before and I didn't really learn anything new from having presented the workshop?" (if so, then call this teaching since I used my skill in teaching).

If you try only two things from this Chapter

Learn how to present your performance more effectively. As a young faculty member, be a researcher in your subject discipline and get tenure first.

Reflection and self-rating

Use Table 13.2, reflect on the ideas in this Chapter and rate their appropriateness to your situation.

Table 13.2
Reflection and self-rating for academics

Reflection:

_____

_____

_____

_____

Rate the ideas

	already do this	would work	might work	not my style
Get tenure:				
understand the culture/system	O	O	O	O
have interview with chair	O	O	O	O
start with research in your subject discipline as your goal	O	O	O	O
use simple-to-apply principles of effective learning	O	O	O	O
Keep up-to-date about the culture/system				
have interview with chair	O	O	O	O
Build credibility for excellence in teaching				
be clear on your own claims about teaching	O	O	O	O
don't overstate your case	O	O	O	O
apply criteria consistently	O	O	O	O
provide evidence	O	O	O	O
If interested in research-in-teaching then apply research skills	O	O	O	O
Be an agent for change				
proactively talk about research-in-teaching	O	O	O	O
seek membership on P&T committee	O	O	O	O
lobby for publication of criteria	O	O	O	O
distinguish between effective teaching & research-in-teach	O	O	O	O
share example reviews as data about refereeing quality	O	O	O	O

... continue

Rate the ideas

	already do this	would work	might work	not my style
Use resources and keep others informed				
frequently consult with your Center for Teaching	○	○	○	○
keep chair and dean informed	○	○	○	○
Gather evidence				
keep good records:	○	○	○	○
calendar	○	○	○	○
guest book	○	○	○	○
bound log book for calls and decisions	○	○	○	○
chrono file for correspondence and e-mail	○	○	○	○
file folder for evidence about performance	○	○	○	○
list invitations "turned down"	○	○	○	○
obtain benchmark data for campus courses	○	○	○	○
exit survey data	○	○	○	○
student course evaluation data	○	○	○	○
feedback on course syllabus	○	○	○	○
results of CPQ, NSSE	○	○	○	○
use MRIQ and Centers of Teaching for guidance	○	○	○	○
details about awards	○	○	○	○
Create Performance summaries in teaching, research and service				
addresses criteria	○	○	○	○
help reader interpret the evidence	○	○	○	○
Present case effectively in your interview				
base preparation for and responses on principles of assessment	○	○	○	○
Other _____	○	○	○	○

What did you learn from your answers? _____

_____

Ideas for administrators for coping with underperformance

The key idea is that too often chairs or deans encounter underperformance in all dimensions — teaching, research and service. Underperformance must be distinguished from unacceptable performance and difficult behaviors. Detecting underperformance early is vital. Symptoms to look for are cited.

The central theme of this Chapter is to reignite the sparkle via facilitating intrinsic motivation following the principles of Chapter 7 — but now viewed from the point of view of facilitating this process for others.

> *"What do I do with the deadwood in my department? They are ineffective in teaching, research and even administration!"*

This is a commonly-voiced concern in workshops I have given on motivation and is extremely frustrating to administrators, students and colleagues because this is a terrible waste of potentially vital human resources and giving them an opportunity to retire early usually leaves a lack of continuity in the program.

In this Chapter we focus first on renaming this behavior, then we consider symptoms that usually accompany underperformance. Some possible causes are given, and an action plan suggested. Consider each in turn.

14.1 Clarification of terms is essential

Three words need to be clarified — difficult behaviors, unsatisfactory performance and underperformance. Consider each in turn.

Focus on *performance* not personal worth. The term "deadwood" or underperformers — must be renamed underperformance. From the first fundamental principle of assessment we realize that we need to focus on performance and not on personal worth. The term "deadwood" (as does the term underperformers) attacks personal worth. The term "underperformance" more accurately defines the situation. In the context of this Chapter our focus is on underperformance in all academic responsibilities (and not just underperformance in teaching and learning).

Before going further discussing underperformance we need to also distinguish this from dealing with *difficult behaviors*, unsatisfactory performance and underperformance.

Each person is unique. They can display such behaviors as "my way or the highway," stubbornness, brusqueness, egotistical, extreme pessimism, obnoxiousness, individualist non-team player, foul language, know-it-alls, anger and aggressiveness, whining and complaining, the quiet ones. These might be called difficult behaviors. These behaviors might be exhibited in meetings, between colleagues, toward students or toward the Department and the culture you are trying to create.

Unsatisfactory performance refers to functioning at level below the employment contract. This could include such unacceptable behavior as sexual harassment or physical violence; not handing in grades. The immediate action is to get advice from HR and act together.

Underperformance is performance that is not up to expectations.

> *For example, Professor Noname's performance used to be good when he was hired and when he was given tenure. But now, in teaching, Professor Noname lectures from notes that have not been revised in the past ten years. The student evaluations are the lowest in the Department. The majority of the student comments are "Professor Noname does not care." "This is the worst Prof. I've ever had!" "Noname can't and won't explain anything." "Noname is incompetent and should be fired."*
>
> *As Chair of the Department you do not want to ask him to teach any course.*
>
> *In research, Noname has no grant money, does not apply for grants and has no graduate students. He reluctantly serves on supervisory committees where he is a presence with no input. Colleagues to not want him on their committees.*
>
> *In service, Noname complains to you that you are picking on him and have given him too many committee responsibilities but he rarely shows up at meetings. The chairs of two committees have asked that he be removed from their committees.*

The situation has gotten out of hand. Actions should have been taken long ago to prevent his performance from deteriorating to this extent.

We need to detect underperformance early and take action to re-ignite the spark.

(Hopefully, if we have followed some of the suggestions given in the previous Chapters, we will never encounter a Professor Noname.)

14.2 Dealing with difficult behaviors

Since *difficult behaviors* are so disruptive to the collegial and supportive environment you are trying to create, you should take action. Suggestions about how to cope are given by Cava, 1990; Solomon, 1990, Bell and Smith, 2004 and Brinkman and Kirschner, 1994. Many of the difficult behaviors are learned responses individuals have adapted to cope with conflict. For example, one response to conflict is to collaborate; the extreme behavior is to "know it all." The *chronic complainer* tends to be an extension of *withdrawal* as an approach to coping with conflict.

Although the actions taken depend, to a great extent, on the type of behavior, some common actions include:

1. Gather background information from colleagues and former chairs to obtain a sense of whether this behavior.

a) has always been this way. "That's just Roger."

b) something happened; the behavior changed to be a difficult behavior. Find out as much as you can about the triggering event(s).

2. Have a private interview. Describe the performance assertively. "When you.... I feel..."

3. Listen.

4. Work out an acceptable approach to behavior.

Next we turn our attention to underperformance. In Section 14.3 we consider how to detect underperformance early. Then in Section 14.4 some options are given for dealing with it.

14.3 Detect underperformance early

In this section we describe typical symptoms and then suggest possible causes.

14.3.1 Be sensitive to the symptoms

Early detection requires monitoring, showing continual concern for your colleagues, preventing underperformance in one area (say service) from undermining performance in teaching or research. (Kelly, 1990; Wood and McCarthy, 2002; Indiana University East, 2008; Wiked, 2008; Moonwomon, 2008)

Underperformance is usually accompanied by some of the following behaviors:

1. less enthusiastic about their work; lost interest in their discipline.

2. suffer an overwhelming sense of failure, loss of pride, no prospects of change.

3. work far below their potential.

4. tend to withdraw, not participate, distance themselves from colleagues and students.

5. are exhausted.

This often hits the *best* performance.

Be sensitive to these and take action promptly.

14.3.2 Possible causes

If you encounter underperformance as an administrator, then most of the causes are not items that are under your control. You have to cope with the here and now and help the person find the best options for the future. However, being aware of the causes may help prevent future cases of underperformance in your Department. The causes could be within the organization or outside. Consider each in turn.

A. *Within the organization*

Three major factors within the institution include hiring practices, lack of motivational incentives, and stress.

i) *Faulty hiring practices; hiring mistakes*

The person can't meet performance expectations because they are not capable. Maybe they were hired as a research Post Doc or research associate and then evolved into the Departmental appointee without going through the usual hiring procedures. Alternatively, a wrong decision was made in granting tenure and now you are stuck with them in the Department. Hopefully, this is rare.

ii) *Intrinsic and extrinsic motivational elements missing in the past; past policies, past chairs, past deans*

These might include ideas discussed in Chapters 7, 9 and 12 and in particular:

- continually assigned tasks without discussion or the resources;
- not being accountable for performance or perceived unfairness in the loading, in the reward system, in the expectations;
- drifting away from the vitality of the institution;
- apparent lack of recognition, support, encouragement leaving them feeling unappreciated;
- no Departmental or Faculty meetings leaving them feeling uninvolved, uncommitted, detached, unappreciated;
- performance activities deemed important by "the University" are not considered in performance assessment; for example, citizenship, attending student and alumni functions;

- rank and salary determined automatically based on years of service and not on achievement and performance.

iii) Stressful environment

Key issues related to stress and burnout include workload excessive and pressure to do too many tasks in too short a time, uncertainty about expectations or the future, poor performance by administrators, changes in administrators, rapid changes in policies and "difficult behavior" of colleagues.

B. Outside the organization

Three factors outside the University include stress, change in interests and health.

i) Stress in their personal life

The life changes inventory, given in Table 14.1, gives feedback about one's annual stress. Note that both positive and negative events affect stress. Values below 200 are usual. The items in the inventory remind us of the wide variety of factors that stress us.

ii) Changes in interests and "what is important in life"

A colleague may decide that he/she wants to devote more time to gardening, music, painting, writing, religion, traveling, volunteering, helping others, dancing or a complete change in career. "I really wanted to be a veterinary technician instead of an academic!" They find a new theme in life. They lose interest in their academic career but may feel they will keep their academic position to financially support their "other life."

iii) Medical or health issues

Some may develop health problems that allow them partially fulfill their academic obligations — and they desperately want to do this... and even more.

14.4 Possible actions — First find the cause

Possible actions you could take depend on the cause. Find the cause. This was a colleague, a friend. He or she could underperform for a wide range of reasons. The goal of a private discussion is to describe the performance as you see from the written

Table 14.1
Life-change units as a measure of psychological stress
(adaption from Holmes-Rahe)

Event or stressor	No. of times in past year	Life-change impact per event	Total for year:
Death of spouse	_____	100	_____
Divorce	_____	73	_____
Marital separation	_____	65	_____
Jail term	_____	63	_____
Death of a close family member	_____	63	_____
Personal injury/ illness	_____	53	_____
Marriage	_____	50	_____
Fired at work	_____	47	_____
Grants cut off	_____	47	_____
Marital reconciliation	_____	45	_____
Retirement	_____	45	_____
Change in health of family member	_____	44	_____
Pregnancy	_____	40	_____
Sex difficulties	_____	39	_____
Gain new family member	_____	39	_____
Business/ school readjustment	_____	39	_____
Change in financial state	_____	38	_____
Death of close friend	_____	37	_____
Paper rejected by refereed journal	_____	36	_____
Change at work/policies or practice	_____	36	_____
Change in the number of arguments with spouse	_____	35	_____
Mortgage > $50,000	_____	31	_____
Foreclosure of loan/ mortgage	_____	30	_____
Change in responsibilities at work	_____	29	_____
Son/daughter leaves home	_____	29	_____
In-law troubles	_____	29	_____
PhD student leaves your group for another	_____	28	_____
Outstanding personal achievement	_____	28	_____
Spouse begins/ stops work	_____	26	_____

... continue

Event or stressor	No. of times in past year	Life-change impact per event	Total for year:
Begin/ end of semester	_____	26	_____
Change in living conditions	_____	25	_____
Revise personal habits	_____	24	_____
Trouble with supervisor/ chair/dean	_____	23	_____
Change in work hours/ conditions	_____	20	_____
Change in residence	_____	20	_____
Change in schools	_____	20	_____
Your PhD student fails the qualifiers	_____	19	_____
Change in recreation	_____	19	_____
Change in church activities	_____	19	_____
Change in social activities	_____	18	_____
Mortgage or loan < $50,000	_____	17	_____
Change in sleeping habits	_____	16	_____
Change in family get-togethers	_____	15	_____
Change in eating habits	_____	15	_____
Vacation	_____	13	_____
Christmas	_____	12	_____
Minor violation of the law	_____	11	_____
Parking ticket/ speeding ticket	_____	11	_____
Total in a year			_____

evidence, be a good listener to discover what his/her interpretation of the performance is and then explore options.

Miller and Rollnick (2002) provide excellent guidelines about asking questions using what they call the OARS approach.

O — use open-ended questions but no more than three in a row before using Reflective listening statement.

A — be affirming via compliments and appreciation, "*Thanks for coming in today.*"

R — reflective listening. Reflection is responding with a concise restatement of the content and feelings expressed in the listener's own words as to meaning. The purpose is to show the talker that you have heard empathically. In general you might start by saying "As I understand it, you..." Try to include both the content and feelings of what was said, express it in the listener's own words, do not add any new ideas nor leave out any ideas. Never overstate the feelings; perhaps say annoyed versus angry. There might be two to three reflections for every question you asked.

S — Summarizing link together and reinforce ideas.

Using astute questioning and listening you will probably uncover the cause of the underperformance.

If the cause is faulty hiring practices, then see Section 14.5.

> For lack of intrinsic/extrinsic motivation see Section 14.6.
>
> For stressful work environment, see Section 14.7.
>
> For stress in live outside the university, see Section 14.8.
>
> For change in life interests, see Section 14.9.
>
> For change in health issues, see Section 14.10.

Consider each in turn.

14.5 Overcome faulty hiring practices

One approach to overcome faulty hiring practices in the past is to have continual assessment of tenured faculty that includes loss of tenure and dismissal. Much has been written about this option. Here is one example from the University of Alberta. www.ualberta.ca/AASUA/agreements/Agr/Art13.htm.

All faculty are required to undergo an annual performance review. The chair makes a recommendation about salary increment that is reviewed by the Faculty Evaluation Committee, FEC. If the resulting recommendation is for zero salary increment, then one of four comments must be included with the recommendation. These comments are:

a) that maximum for rank has been reached and standards for promotion have not been met but performance is acceptable notwithstanding;

b) that performance requirements for an increment have not been met but performance is acceptable notwithstanding;

c) that academic performance while on authorized leave could not be properly evaluated;

d) that academic performance is unsatisfactory and unacceptable.

A recommendation of *zero (d)* is seen as negative. A series of years with a *zero (d)* can result in loss of tenure and dismissal. It is used.

Either the Department Chair or the FEC could recommend that no increment be awarded to a staff member.

Congratulations if this type of approach is already in place in your University.

14.6 Reignite intrinsic/extrinsic motivation

In general, to reignite the sparkle in their eye we follow the seven-step process for intrinsic motivation given in Chapter 7. The difference is that in Chapter 7 the context was that individuals would apply the process. In this present context, the chair or designate facilitates the process. Chairs can also reconsider the ideas given in Chapter 9.

Some guidelines to help you facilitate an increase in intrinsic motivation are given by Miller and Rollnick (2002). In general, ask questions using the OARS guidelines described in Section 14.4.

Now consider the seven-step process outlined in Chapter 7.

Step 1 — **Identify the context.** From the personal interview process described in Section 14.4 you probably will have discovered the specific cause of the loss in motivation. One of the more-common causes is lack of appreciation. Use questions to help your colleague elaborate and put this in his/her overall context.

Step 2 — **Identify a goal.** The goal might be to improve teaching, to improve research or improve service. Select only one. Do not encourage him/her to improve all of them at once.

To try to get this "improve" talk the facilitator can:

1. Ask them to share stories about when they really enjoyed teaching, or research or service.

2. Explore goals and values. What things are most important in your life?

3. Ask evocative questions. An excellent list of open questions to evoke change talk are given in Table 6.3 in Miller and Rollnick's book on *Motivational Interviewing* (2002).

4. Ask your colleague to rate the **importance.**

How important would you say it is for you to *get your research going again*? 0 means not important; 10 means extremely important. Where would you say you are?

Why are you at a _____ and not zero?

What would it take for you to go from _____ to a higher number?

5. Explore the decisional balance pros vs cons or force field diagram.

6. Elaborate on the topic before moving on; clarification... In what ways? How much? When?

Could you give me an example?

Continue to use the OARS model plus listening as you support and encourage your colleague to complete the remaining five steps in the motivational process.

14.7 Stressful work environment

Remind individuals of the actions to manage stress (MPS 5) or encourage them to attend local workshops on stress management. Useful actions include the following ten — focus on things you can control; include physical activities like jogging, swimming; use destimulating techniques such as muscle relaxation, music, hot bath, take a break or a holiday; use positive- not negative- self talk; plan ahead and avoid surprises; rename the anxious event; draw on your support system; develop positive addictions such as hobbies, music, talks, nature, pets; be decisive; draw on your spiritual base; use role models, and put the situation into perspective. In Ontario, the Employee and Family Assistance Program, EFAP, provides services that are proactive to help deal, for example, with stress.

14.8 Stress in life outside the university

Use the life change inventory to suggest the course of your major stressors. Follow the actions for stress management given in Section 14.7.

14.9 Change in life interests

Help them to identify what is really important in their life. If the spark is outside the Department, help them find opportunities within the University context or outside. They may assume a position within the university in alumni relations, in the Art gallery, promoting concerts and plays or other activity that more closely matches their new interests and the interests of the University.

Another option is to explore retirement options so that they leave the university to find career options more aligned with their new life interests.

14.10   Change in health issues

Be empathic. Check with HR to understand the University policies and benefits concerning health and disability. Perhaps recommend that HR administer an independent audit of your colleague's abilities. With the colleague's permission this could include medical information from the treating physician. In addition a review could be made of the workplace accommodation needs, such as providing a quieter working space or wheelchair accessibility or darkened rooms for light sensitive eyes.

If the illness is not completely debilitating and your colleague wants to continue contributing to the Department, identify the degree of participation that could be mutually successful. Without revealing confidential information and with permission of your colleague, let all in the Department understand the degree of contribution/reduced load so that all can support your colleague.

14.11   Overall skills needed

As with any interpersonal interaction, communicate well. Since this relates to an assessment of performance, the expectations, criteria and forms of evidence should be written.

14.12   Actions for individuals

This Chapter is addressed to administrators. However, individuals can learn much from this chapter because things change and we, too, might become unmotivated and our performance is not as high as we expect.

Recognize the symptoms.

Make an appointment to talk to your chair.

Review the principles of intrinsic motivation in Chapters 7 and 8. Although these Chapters were written in the context of "to improve teaching" the general principles apply to all aspects of an academic life.

If you try only one thing from this Chapter

As an administrator, facilitate the process of intrinsic motivation. As an individual, be sensitive to the symptoms and, as appropriate, revisit Chapters 7 and 8.

 Reflection and self-rate

Table 14.2 provides an opportunity to reflect and rate the ideas.

Table 14.2
Reflection and self-rating for Administrators—Promoting excellence in teaching

Reflection:

_____

_____

_____

Rate the ideas

	already do this	would work	might work	not my style
Focus on performance — not personal worth	O	O	O	O
Bring in HR when unsatisfactory performance occurs	O	O	O	O
Can cope with difficult behaviors	O	O	O	O
Can recognize symptoms of underperformance	O	O	O	O
Can identify underperformance because of				
– faulty faculty hiring/tenure decisions	O	O	O	O
– loss of intrinsic motivation	O	O	O	O
– stress from work	O	O	O	O
– stress from personal life	O	O	O	O
– health problems	O	O	O	O
Can use the life-change chart to identify possible cause of stress	O	O	O	O
Skilled at using OARS and listening	O	O	O	O
Can use a private interview to identify cause of underperformance	O	O	O	O
Can use post tenure review with potential of dismissal	O	O	O	O
Can facilitate motivational interviewing to help colleagues be intrinsically motivated	O	O	O	O
Am skilled at stress management	O	O	O	O
Can assist colleagues find positions elsewhere that match their new goals or interests in life	O	O	O	O
Can empathetically explore options for those with health problems	O	O	O	O

Other

_____

What conclusions can you draw from your responses? _____

Appendix A
Course Perceptions Questionnaire (CPQ)

Purpose: to provide feedback from the students about the degree to which the learning environment promotes deep vs surface learning. May be used to describe "an individual course", or "the Department."

To be completed by: students in your class.

Description: 24 Likert-type. This was developed by Paul Ramsden and modified by Chris Knapper for North American use.

Results: Provide feedback on the eight dimensions found to affect student learning.

Can be reported as: individual values for each factor; a total of all factors and the ratio of factors suggesting whether learning environment is student controlled or teacher controlled.

Factors are:

The six elements that positively promote learning are:

1. **good teaching**—the perception of the preparation, confidence and skill of the faculty in facilitating learning.

2. **openness to students**—willingness of faculty to help, friendliness and flexibility of faculty.

3. **freedom in learning**—the degree to which the students feel they have a choice in what they learn and how they learn it.

4. **clarity in goals and standards**—a degree to which the students feel that the assessment is clearly defined and appropriate; for example, a low rating would be given if the students feel that "professors are more interested in testing what we have memorized than what we have learned."

5. **vocational relevance**—how pertinent the students perceive the course content to be for their future careers.

6. **social climate**—students report good academic and social relationships with each other.

The two elements that tend to negatively promote learning are:

7. **workload**—excessive demands from the curriculum and the assessment procedures. "The sheer volume of work to get through in this course means that you can't comprehend it all thoroughly."

8. **formal teaching methods**—the student's perception that timetabled lectures (versus self-directed, group or individual study) are the main source of learning.

For example, the elements that tend to promote surface learning include inappropriate assessment methods (especially the use of short answer and multiple choice questions for factual recall), heavy workload [#7 above], perceived inadequacies in teaching [#1 above], inadequate feedback on assignments, long delay before feedback, spoon-feeding through handouts and lack of relevance or choice [#3 & #5 above].[1, 2, 3] In particular, heavy workload and lack of freedom in learning [defined by Ramsden[4] as control-centeredness] correlated with **surface** orientation (p<0.001).

The elements that promote **deep** learning orientation include matching the content to previous knowledge, the perceived relevance of subject matter [#5 above], good teaching (with appropriate level, pace, structure, explanation, enthusiasm and empathy) [#1 above], opportunities for individual choice [#3 above] and study skills training and support.[1, 5] In particular, good teaching plus freedom in learning [defined by Ramsden[5] as student-centeredness] correlated with **deep** learning orientation (p<0.01).

CPQ Scoring	**Sum of**
Good teaching	12, 16, 21
Openness to students	14, 18, 24
Freedom in learning	2, 11, 20
Clear Goals and standards	3, 8, 23
Vocational relevance	6, 10, 15
Social climate	4, 9, 13
(-) workload	(-) 5, 17, 22
(-) formal (lecture) teaching methods	(-) 1, 7, 19

CPQ	Total of these	ranges from –24 to 72; want a large number
Control-centered	10 plus workload minus freedom.	Range –2 to 22; want a small number.
Student-centered	Sum of good teaching plus freedom. Max 24;	want a large number.
Student/control	Ratio of student to control.	

Example data:

Table example data from the Course Perceptions Questionnaire

	Conventional lecture-style				Active learn	Problem-based		
	Science	Social Science	Engineering	average	n= 50	partial Engineering	partial enviro	full PBL
Overall	22.4	27.5	16.2	21.6	33.2 (7)	31.5	36.2	40.1
Student centered	9.6	13.5	9.7	9.8	13.9 (3.6)	14.2	18.2	20.1
Control centered	13.8	8.8	14.8	14.7	11.6 (3.5)	12.8	5.4	5.1
Components in Overall								
Good teaching	6	7.5	5.4	6	8.3 (1.9)	8.8	7.9	9.3
Openness to students	4.6	6.5	5.2	5.9	8.4 (1.6)	8.4	8.7	9.8
Freedom in learning	3.6	6.1	4.3	3.8	5.7 (2.5)	5.4	10.3	10.8
Clear goals, standards and assessment	6.3	8.3	5.4	8.7	8.6 (1.7)	7.6	5.1	4.8
Vocational relevance	7.5	4.1	6.5	6.8	8.2 (1.7)	8.4	4.7	6.8
Social climate	7.3	5.6	4.8	7.3	8.12 (2.2)	8	8.2	7.6
(Workload)	7.4	4.9	9.5	8.5	7.2 (2.5)	8.3	5.7	5.8
(Use of formal teaching methods)	5.5	5.6	6.7	8.3	6.7 (1.9)	6.8	3	2.7

Other options:

Questionnaires have been developed to measure the students' impressions of the learning environment.

- Course Perceptions Questionnaire,[6] CPQ, uses 40, 5-point Likert scale questions to score the eight elements of the environment listed above.

- mid 'CPQ'[7] uses 34 items for quality of "lecturing," clear standards, methods of assessment, relevance and workload.

- short CPQ[8, 9] uses 24 questions for the eight elements.

- Course Environment Questionnaire,[10] CEQ, uses 40, 5-point Likert scale questions to rate six elements: teaching, freedom and independence, clarity of goals, assessment and workload.

- Survey of the Learning Environment,[11] SLE, (Marshall) uses 54, 5-point Likert questions to rate seven elements: emotional climate toward the affective domain, supportiveness of staff for the students, flexibility in learning for the students, organization and coherence of the educational experience, vocational relevance, student-student interaction, extent to which students are encouraged to sustain outside and non-academic activities.

References

1. Noel Entwistle, "Influences on the quality of student learning- implications for medical education," *South African Medical Journal, 81 (20) June, 596–606* (1992)

2. C.M.L. Miller and M.R. Parlett "Up to the mark: a study of the examination game," Society for Research into Higher Education, Guildford (1974)

3. A.S. Becker et al., "Making the grade- the Academic Side of College Life," John Wiley, Chichester (1968)

4. P. Ramsden,. "How Academic Departments Influence Student Learning," *HERDSA News, 4, 3–5* (1982)

5. A. Frensson, "On qualitative differences in learning, IV: effects of intrinsic motivation and extrinsic test anxiety on process and outcome," *Br. J. Educ. Psychology, 47, 244–257* (1977)

6. P. Ramsden, "The Lancaster Approaches to Studying and Course Perceptions 6 Questionnaire: Lecturer's Handbook," Educational Methods Unit, Oxford Polytechnic (1983)

7. D.A. Watkins and J. Hattie, ""The Learning processes of Australian University Students: investigations of contextual and personological factors," *Bri. J. educ. Psychology, 51, 384–393* (1981)

8. C.K. Knapper, *Short version of the LASQ and CPQ*, University of Waterloo, Waterloo, Canada

9. D. Bertrand and Chris K. Knapper, "Contextual Influences on Student's Approaches to learning in Three Academic Departments," unpublished honours thesis, Psychology Department, University of Waterloo, Waterloo ON (1991)

10. P. Ramsden, "The Nature of Good Teaching in Higher Education," Chapter 6 in "Learning to Teach in Higher Education," Routledge (1992)

11. G. Feletti, J. Drinan and B. Maitland, "Students' approaches to learning and satisfaction with problem-based curricula for four different professions," *Assessment and Evaluation in Higher Education, 13, 163–176* (1983)

Course Perceptions Questionnaire (CPQ)
(reprinted with permission from Paul Ramsden and Christopher Knapper)

Please answer every line quickly by giving your immediate response. Indicate below your general approach to studying. You will be told whether you are to answer this questionnaire in terms of the departmental program or in terms of the individual course you are taking.

	4 Strongly agree	3 generally agree	2 doesn't apply or it is impossible to give a definite answer	1 generally disagree	0 strongly disagree
1. A great deal of time in this department (course) is taken up by timetabled classes (lectures, labs, tutorials, workshops, PBL cooperative learning group meetings).					
2. There is a real opportunity in this department (course) for students to choose the particular areas and topics they want to study.					
3. In this department (course) you usually have a clear idea where you're going and what is expected of you.					
4. A lot of students in this department (course) are friends of mine.					
5. The workload in this department (course) is too heavy.					
6. The content in this course (or the courses in this department) are related to student's future employment.					
7. In this department (course) you can learn nearly everything you need to know from the classes (and lectures); it isn't necessary to do much further reading/researching.					
8. In this department (course) it's always easy to know the standard of work expected of you.					
9. Students from this department (course) often get together socially.					
10. Instructor(s) in this department (course) are (is) keen to point out that you are receiving a professional training.					

... continue

	4 Strongly agree	3 generally agree	2 doesn't apply or it is impossible to give a definite answer	1 generally disagree	0 strongly disagree
11. In this department (course) we seem to be given a lot of choice about the work we have to do.					
12. Instructor(s) in this department (course) seem (s) to be good at pitching the teaching at the right level for us.					
13. This department (course) seems to foster a friendly climate that helps students get to know each other.					
14. Most of the instructors in this department (the instructor in this course) really try hard to get to know the students.					
15. The course(s) in this department seem(s) to be pretty well determined by job requirements.					
16. Faculty in this department (this instructor) make(s) a real effort to understand difficulties students may be having with their work.					
17. There seems to be too much work to get through in the course(s) in this department.					
18. Instructors in this department (this instructor) seem(s) to go out of their way to be friendly towards students.					
19. Lectures seem to be more important than tutorials, discussion groups, cooperative activities in this department (course).					
20. Students have a great deal of choice over how they learn in this department (course).					
21. The instructors in this department (This instructor) seem(s) ready to give help and advice on approaches to studying.					
22. There is a lot of pressure on students in this department (course).					
23. Instructors in this department (This instructor) generally make(s) it clear right from the start what will be required of students.					
24. Instructors in this department (This instructor) generally take(s) students' ideas and interests seriously.					

Appendix B
Approaches to Studying Questionnaire (ASQ)

Purpose: To provide feedback to students about their approaches to studying.

To be completed by: students

Description: 18, 5-point Likert scale questions to identify three subscales: strategic, surface and deep. The inventory was created in the UK by Paul Ramsden; this version was shortened and rewritten in terms of North American terminology by Christopher Knapper, Instructional Development, Queens University, Kingston, Ontario.

Results:

Strategic learners tend to be competitive, use well-organized study methods and hope for success. Oriented toward doing well, whatever this involves. They tend to do well (Correlation between this scale and success = +0.32).

Surface or rote learners attempt to memorize, are not interested in studying out of interest in the subject but only out of a concern to pass or gain qualifications. They keep narrowly to the syllabus as laid down in course descriptions and do not follow up interests of their own (if they have any). Despite their concern to pass they tend to do badly. (Correlation between the scale score and success rating = -0.25.)

Deep or search-for-meaning learners intend to make sense of the subject, show an interest in the subject itself and have a desire to learn. Students who score high on this scale follow up their own interests even if these are outside those parts of the course which are assessed, and want to understand about what they are studying. They find what they are learning to be interesting. They tend to do well (Correlation between scale score and success = +0.28).

Scoring:

Questions 1, 3, 6, 9, 12, 15 relate to Strategic learner

Questions 2, 5, 8, 11, 14, 18 relate to Surface or rote learner.

Questions 4, 7, 10, 13, 16, 17 relate to Deep or search-for-meaning learner.

The total is the sum of strategic plus deep minus rote.

Example Data:

Table 1. North American institutions using short forms for ASQ. The standard deviation is shown in square brackets [ ]

	Science, Chemistry		Psychology		Environmental resource		Engineering N = 1387	Chemical Engineering,		
								N = 84	N = 49	N = 59
Level	2nd	4th	2nd	4th	2nd	4th	all years	2nd	3rd	4th
Strategic	15.3	14.0	16.5	15.3	13.4	13.6	16.2 [3.1]	15.2 [2.8]	14.5 [3.2]	16.7 [3.1]
Surface	14.6	13.9	14.9	12.5	10.9	10.3	15.2 [3.2]	15.3 [3.3]	14.1 [3.5]	14.3 [3.4]
Deep	14.1	15.7	14.7	15.8	17.4	16.5	14.9 [3.7]	14.0 [3.6]	13.2 [3.4]	15.9 [3.5]
Total	14.8	15.8	16.3	18.6	19.9	19.8	15.9 [6.7]	13.9 [5.4]	13.6 [6.9]	18.3 [7]

Options:

Lancaster Approaches to Studying,[1] LASQ, uses 64, 5-point Likert scale questions to identify 16 subscales of which 12 are pertinent to the three subscales of strategic, surface and deep orientation.

- modified LASQ[2] (ASI) uses 49 questions to identify deep, strategic, surface learning plus non-academic orientation, study habits and methods and basic academic skills.

- short version LASQ (ASQ)[3,4] uses 18, 5-point Likert scale questions to identify three subscales: strategic, surface and deep.

- very short LASQ[5] uses 12, 5-point Likert scales questions to identify three subscales.

- Biggs' Study Process Questionnaire,[6] SPQ (1979), uses 42, 5-point Likert scale questions to identify six subscales: strategic (strategies and motivation), surface (strategies and motivation) and deep (strategies and motivation).

- Bigg's Study Behavior Questionnaire,[7] SBQ (1976), uses 80 questions to identify ten subscales: deep learning, surface learning, pragmatism, academic motivation, academic neuroticism, internality, study skill, test anxiety, openness, and class dependence.

- Schmeck *et al.*[8] (1977) Inventory of Learning Processes, ILP. (used by Watkins and Hattie20)

References:

1. P. Ramsden, "The Lancaster Approaches to Studying and Course Perceptions 6 Questionnaire: Lecturer's Handbook," Educational Methods Unit, Oxford Polytechnic (1983)

2. N. Entwistle and P. Ramsden, "Understanding Student Learning," Croon Helm, London (1983)

3. C.K. Knapper, "Short version of the LASQ and CPQ," University of Waterloo, Waterloo, Canada

4. D. Bertrand and Chris K. Knapper, "Contextual Influences on Student's Approaches to learning in Three Academic Departments," unpublished honours thesis, Psychology Department, University of Waterloo, Waterloo ON (1991)

5. K. Trigwell and M. Prosser, "Relating approaches to study and quality of learning outcomes at the course level," *Brit. J. Educ. Psychology, 61*, 265–275. (1991)

6. J.B. Biggs, "Study Process Questionnaire," University of Newcastle, Australia (1979)

7. J.B. Biggs, "Dimensions of study behavior: another look at ATI," *Br. J. educ. Psychology, 46, 68–80* (1976) SBQ (1976)

8. R.R. Schmeck et al., "Development of a self-report inventory for assessing individual differences in learning processes," *Appl. Psychol. Measures, 1, 413–431* (1977)

Approaches to Studying Questionnaire (ASQ)
(used with permission from Paul Ramsden and Christopher Knapper)

Please answer every line quickly by giving your immediate response.

	4 Strongly agree	3 generally agree	2 doesn't apply or it is impossible to give a definite answer	1 generally disagree	0 strongly disagree
1. I find it easy to organize my time effectively.					
2. I like to be told precisely what to do in essays or other set work.					
3. It's important to me to do really well in the course here.					
4. I usually set out to understand thoroughly the meaning of what I am asked to read.					
5. When I'm reading, I try to memorize important facts which may come in useful later.					
6. When I'm doing a piece of work, I try to bear in mind exactly what that particular professor seems to want.					
7. My main reason for being here is so that I can learn more about the subjects that really interest me.					
8. I'm more interested in the qualifications I'll get than in the courses I'm taking.					
9. I'm usually prompt in starting work in the evenings.					
10. I generally put a lot of effort into trying to understand things which initially seem difficult.					
11. Often I find I have to read things without having a chance to really understand them.					
12. If conditions aren't right for me to study, I generally manage to do something to change them.					

... continue

	4 Strongly agree	3 generally agree	2 doesn't apply or it is impossible to give a definite answer	1 generally disagree	0 strongly disagree
13. I often find myself questioning things I hear in class or read in books.					
14. I tend to read very little beyond what's required for completing assignments.					
15. It's important to me to do things better than my friends, if I possibly can.					
16. I spend a good deal of my spare time in finding out more about interesting topics which have been discussed in class.					
17. I find academic topics so interesting I should like to continue with them after I finish university.					
18. I find I have to concentrate on memorizing a good deal of what we have to learn.					

Appendix C
Perry Inventory (Moore Fitch, 1988)

Purpose: To provide feedback to students about their attitude and expectations toward learning.

To be completed by: students

Description: This version asks participants to select top 10 descriptors of ideal learning environment from among 34 descriptors.

Results: The 34 questions include 8 that characterize Perry level 2; 9 for level 3; 8 for level 4; 9 for level 5.

Scoring: Each question is coded. Total the second numeral in each code and divide by 10.

Example Data:

Year	Pavelich Moore[1]	Wise et al.[2]	Allen[3]	Fitch Culver[4]	Woods et al.[5]	n = 45 to 59[6]
1	3.27 (0.44)	3.27 (0.40)	2.3 to 3.1			
2	3.71 (0.53)					3.5 (0.4)
3		3.33 (0.35)			3.5	3.6 (0.5)
4	4.28 (0.50)	4.21 (0.50)		2.8 to 3.4	4.6	Post PBL 4.3 (0.4) 4.6 (0.5)

Other options:

Synonyms: general term: Levels of Intellectual Development[7]. Related inventories include King-Kitchener[8] "Model of Reflective Judgment"; Belensky et al.[9] "Women's Ways of Knowing"; Baxter Magolda's[10] "Model of Epistemological Development."

Learning Environment Preferences, by W. S. Moore[7] includes five sections with about a dozen responses per section. Participants rate each and rank to top three in each section.

Essay format. Participants write an essay on ideal learning environment. This is rated by trained experts.

Model of Reflective Judgment. King and Kitchener[8]. Presents seven stage model building on reasoning and reflective judgment. Questionnaire has been developed.

References:

1. Pavelich, M.J. and W.S. Moore (1996) "Measuring the effect of experiential education using the Perry model," *J. of Engineering Education, 85, 4,* 287–292

2. Wise, J. et al. (2004) "A Report on a Four-year longitudinal study of Intellectual Development in Engineering Undergraduates," *J of Adult Development, 11,* no. 2, 103–110

3. Allen, R.D. (1981) "Intellectual Development and the Understanding of Science: application of William Perry's Theory to Science Teaching", *J of College Science Teaching, 11,* 94–97

4. Fitch, M.A. and R.S. Culver (1984) "Educational Activities to Stimulate Intellectual Development in Perry's Scheme," Proceedings 1984 ASEE Annual Conference, 712–717

5. Woods et al. (1997) "Developing Problem Solving Skills: the McMaster Problem Solving program", *J Engineering Education, 86,* no. 2, 75–92

6. Woods, D.R. courses 2g, 3g and 4n. McMaster University, Hamilton

7. Moore, W.S. (1988) "The Measurement of Intellectual Development: an instrument manual," Center for the Study of Intellectual Development, Olympia, WA and W.S. Moore (1989) " The Learning Environment Preferences: exploring the construct validity of an objective measure of the Perry Scheme," J of College Student Development, 30, 504–514

8. King, P.M., and K. S. Kitchener (1994) "Developing Reflective Judgment: Understanding and Promoting Intellectual Growth and Critical Thinking in Adolescents and Adults" Jossey-Bass, San Francisco, CA

9. Belenky, M.F. et al. (1986) "Women's Ways of Knowing: the development of self, voice and mind," Basic Books, New York

10. Baxter Magolda, M.B. (2001) "A Constructivist Revision of the Measure of Epistemological Reflection," *J of College Student Development, 42, no. 6,* 520–534

Moore and Fitch Inventory for Learning Preference. LP-II
(Fitch, 1988, used with permission)

Each of us has an ideal learning environment. Think of how you learn best. Try not to focus on one particular course or one particular instructor. Focus on their significance in an ideal learning environment for you.

You have 10 check marks to make among the 34 questions. Put a checkmark in the * column next to the statement that best describes your ideal learning environment. The code column is for easy reference when we discuss the inventory.

Code *	My ideal learning environment
63	would provide assignments with practical everyday applications.
22	would have the professor give me all the theory and information I need to know.
74	would be where I have a lot of control over the course content and class discussion.
72	would be where I take effective notes on what is presented in class and reproduce that information on tests.
13	would emphasize class discussion but I would expect the professor to tell us the right answer.
24	would be where I have my own opinions and I can think for myself.
53	include grading that is by a prearranged point system (for homework, tests, final) since I think that is most fair.
42	would include straightforward, not "tricky" tests, covering only what has been taught and nothing else.
64	would let me learn on my own because I hate being spoon-fed by professors.
73	would be where the professor doesn't tell me the answers, rather he/she shows me how to find the answers for myself.
95	would provide a flexible class where I can explore independent learning options.
44	is where my opinion counts, but I have to support it with factual evidence.
52	would be where the professor is an expert who knows all the answers.
83	would provide experiences and material that are relevant to what I need to know later.
15	would be where learning is a mutual experience where I contribute to the teaching and learning in class.
12	would have the focus on having the right answers rather than on discussing methods on how to solve problems.
45	would value my classmates as sources of information, not only as companions.
14	would reward me with high grades for independent thought.
82	would be where the professor provides me with clear directions and guidance for all course activities and assignments.

... continue

Code *	My ideal learning environment
65	would take learning seriously and be where I feel personally motivated to learn the subject.
33	would reward me with good grades when I worked hard to learn the material.
55	would provide me with a professor who is a source of expertise only in a particular subject area.
54	would let me learn from classmates and peers.
35	would provide a classroom atmosphere of exploring and debating new ideas.
43	would encourage me to learn using lots of different learning methods.
84	would allow peers the right to have their own opinion.
25	would include exams and assessment as part of the learning process.
62	would be lectures since I can get the information I need to know most efficiently.
23	would have a professor who is not just an instructor, but more an explainer, entertainer and friend.
34	would be a "free flowing" class that does not follow a strict outline.
85	would provide a workshop or seminar atmosphere so that we can exchange ideas and evaluate our own perspectives on the subject matter.
93	would provide a relaxed atmosphere where discussion is encouraged.
32	would be where I could listen intently to the professor and not to classmates and peers for answers to the questions.
75	would be where I can make connections among various subject areas and am encouraged to construct an adequate argument.

Appendix D
Peer Evaluation of Educational Programs, PEEP

Purpose: To provide feedback to teachers about their proposed course.

To be completed by: three peers

Description: 30 criteria distributed among six categories to be rated from "highly satisfactory" = 1 to "highly unsatisfactory" = 7; Each criterion may be assigned a priority of relative importance for this particular course. Similarly, each overall category may be assigned a priority indicating relative importance.

Results: The Peer Evaluation of an Educational Program, PEEP. This inventory is a modified version of the PEEP developed by Howard Stone, University of Wisconsin, Madison. The inventory considers the six major factor influencing effective student learning. Instructors should provide a syllabus, a set of learning objectives, examples of proposed examinations or tests and any other pertinent information to peer evaluators. The PEEP evaluation is usually done before the course is given. The six categories are:

- Instructor's attitude toward learning with five criteria

- Course content and overall goals with five criteria

- Learning objectives with six criteria

- Assessment of student performance with five criteria

- Learning environment and activities with four criteria

- Evaluation of the Instructional Program with five criteria related to teacher's efforts to evaluate effectiveness.

Scoring: The overall rating for each category is the average of the ratings of the criteria. The overall rating (Section VII) is the arithmetic average of the overall ratings in each category.

In addition, each evaluator may elect to identify the relative priority of each criteria using the following scale: 1 low priority: for this particular course this criterion is not very important. 2 = average priority: for this particular course this criterion is important. 3 = for this particular course this criterion is extremely important.

If priorities are assigned, then in each category a weighted average is determined.

In Section VII, a similar priority rating can be assigned to each category

Example Data:

Course: Minimax   Instructor: D. A. Major

Overall weighted average = 1.95

All criteria given equal priority

1. Attitude: 2.4   Comment: syllabus missed addressing
                                   some of these well, in particular,
                                   expectation that students will succeed

2. Content: 1.2   Comment: well done

3. Objectives: 1.66

4. Assessment: 2.   Comment: self-assessment can be
                                   improved

5. Learning environment: 1.25

6. Evaluation: 3.2   Comment: no evidence that a scholarly
                                   approach is being taken; minimal peer
                                   periodic review.

References:

Howard Stone (1991) "Educational Resources: Data Gathering instruments for evaluating educational programs and teaching effectiveness in the Center for Health Sciences, University of Wisconsin, Madison," Center for Health Sciences, 1300 University Avenue, Madison, WI, USA

Peer Evaluation of Educational Programs, PEEP

Donald R. Woods, McMaster University, June 1997

(based on a form developed by Howard L. Stone, University of Wisconsin-Madison, 1991 and used with permission)

To be completed by a team of three peers before the course is presented. This is a measure about the potential for the course to be effective. Student evaluations measure the actual performance. This is about the potential of this course.

Course being reviewed: _____   Date: _____

Course credits: _____

Prerequisites for this course: _____

_____

This course is a prerequisite for the following courses: _____

Other courses to which the content of this course relates: _____

Rater's Name: _____

Scales		
Priority Scale		
1	2	3
Low priority	Average priority	High priority
Rating Scale		
1 2	3 4 5	6 7 NA
satisfactory	3. satisfactory with minor deficiencies 4. satisfactory with minimal exceptions 5. satisfactory but major deficiencies	unsatisfactory

Evaluation Criteria

I. Instructor's attitude toward learning

This may be difficult to assess based on the written information.

Priority Rating		Rating Scale Score
	Course description illustrates a focus on learning (instead of teaching).	
	Expectation that students will succeed is conveyed.	
	Student empowerment and options.	
	Elements present to promote deep rather than surface learning.	
	Strong teacher-student interaction indicated.	

Specific comments about attitude and approaches to learning:

_____

_____

II. Course Content and Overall Goals Identified

Priority Rating		Rating Scale Score
	A rationale for how the content of this course contributes to the achievement of the overall goals and objectives of the Program is stated.	
	The major content areas of the course are identified.	
	Content builds upon the prior learning experiences of the students.	
	Content will build an appropriate foundation for required subsequent learning experiences.	
	Content appears to have been included because it meets a high priority need for a graduate of this Program.	

Identify any specific or unnecessary overlaps in content with other courses:

_____

_____

... continue

III. Learning Objectives

Priority Rating		Rating Scale Score
	Specific objectives have been identified for each content area of the course.	
	Objectives representing knowledge, skills and attitudes can be identified.	
	The level of student achievement expected is stated in the learning objectives.	
	Objectives include criteria so that assessments to distinguish students who have achieved the objectives from those who have not can be made.	
	Objectives are achievable given the time and resources available.	
	Objectives are published and publicly available.	

Specific comments concerning the adequacy of the objectives:

_____

_____

IV. Assessment of Student Achievement

Priority Rating		Rating Scale Score
	Related to learning objectives.	
	Contains a mix of Bloom's levels including deep learning.	
	Opportunities for student self-assessment are provided.	
	A variety of assessment techniques have been developed for determining student progress in the course.	
	Opportunities to confront situations representing professional practice are included.	

Specific comments concerning the adequacy of the assessment techniques:

_____

_____

... continue

V. Learning Environment and learning Activities

Priority Rating		Rating Scale Score
	Learning activities for students apply the fundamental principles of how to improve learning.	
	Learning environment includes components to promote deep learning: flexibility, clarity in goals & assessment, minimum of formal lectures.	
	Efforts made to include professional practice situations.	
	Resources needed are available and planned for.	

Specific comments concerning the adequacy of the learning environment:

_____

_____

VI. Evaluation of instructional effectiveness

Priority Rating		Rating Scale Score
	Provisions for systematically securing student feedback are identified. Example: Ombudspersons.	
	Provisions for benchmarking and evaluating course effectiveness and learning environment. Example: Course Perceptions Questionnaire.	
	Evidence of a scholarly approach to teaching/ learning versus "diddlin' around."	
	Provisions for periodic peer review of the program are identified.	
	Consistency between "contract" with the Department in terms of course development and instructor's performance.	

Specific comments concerning the adequacy of Instructional Program Evaluation:

_____

_____

... continue

VII. Average of the Weighted Scores for each Section

Priority Rating		Rating Scale Score
	Instructor's attitude toward learning	
	Course content and overall goals	
	Learning objectives	
	Assessment of student performance	
	Learning environment and activities	
	Evaluation of the Instructional Program	
	Overall Rating of the Instructional Program	

Specific comments concerning the adequacy of the Instructional Program:

_____

_____

Appendix E
My Role Is Questionnaire, MRIQ

Purpose: To provide feedback to teachers about their perception of their role.

To be completed by: teacher

Description: 18 questions

Results: MRIQ: probes six elements related to attitudes of teachers

A: Teachers care about the students as people; scale 0 to 30; want a high number; typical response 22.1 with standard deviation of 3.6

B: Teachers expect students to succeed, instead of seeing their role as a hurdle the students must pass; scale 0 to 10; want a high number; typical response 6.2 with standard deviation of 1.6.

C: Teachers care about the student's long term; success scale 0 to 15; want a high number; typical response 10.7 with standard deviation of 2.4.

D: Teachers focus on students learning rather than on teacher "teaching"; scale 0 to 40; want a high number; typical response 26.7 with standard deviation of 3.9.

E: Teachers are willing to empower students with part of the learning process; scale 0 to 30; want a high number; typical response 10.6 with standard deviation of 2.7.

F: Teachers are willing to publish detailed goals; scale 0 to 5; want a high number; typical response 3.7 with standard deviation of 1.6.

Scoring:

A. [1,2,6,9]

1a _____	1b _____
5b _____	5a _____
6a _____	6b _____
10a _____	10b _____
11a _____	11b _____
15b+c _____	15a _____
TOTAL _____	_____

B.[1,9]

    2b _____   2a _____

    16b+c _____   16a _____

    TOTAL _____   _____

C.[2,3,6]

    9b _____   9a _____

    10a _____   10b _____

    17a _____   17b _____

    TOTAL _____   _____

D.[2,3,6]

    3a _____   3b _____

    8a _____   8b _____

    9b _____   9a _____

    10a _____   10b _____

    14a _____   14b _____

    16b+c _____   16a _____

    17a _____   17b _____

    18b _____   18a _____

    TOTAL _____   _____

E.[2,6,7,9]

    12a _____   12b _____

    13b _____   13a _____

    14a _____   14b _____

    16c _____   16a+b _____

    TOTAL _____   _____

F.[2,6,8,9]

    16b+c _____   16a _____

Example Data:

Data: total sample size for data reported above (n = 223).

	A 30	B 10	C 15	D 40	E 30	F 5
MPS teacher	23	9	10	30	12	5
Award teacher	25	8	12	29	10	4
PBL teacher	18	8	12	31	14	3
Community college, N = 80; Eastern Ontario	23.7	7.5	12	29.4	10	3.7
Temasek Polytech Singapore [15]	23.5 [2.6]	6.0 [1.7]	11.1 [1.6]	26.9 [3.1]	11.1 [1.4]	2.5 [1.2]
Temasek Poly Singapore, [90]	22.6 [3.6]	6.2 [1.6]	10.7 [2.4]	26.7 [4]	10.7 [2.7]	NA
Mac profs in Dept of ChE[8]	19.0 [1.9]	6.3 [1.4]	10.9 [1.2]	26.6 [2.2]	9 [2.3]	3.6 [1.2]
Korean Engng faculty [27]	21.4 [3.5]	7.0 [1.8]	10.4 [1.9]	26.7 [5.0]	9.6 [2.7]	3.4 [1.4]

References:

On the web:

see http://www.hebes.mdx.ac.uk/teaching/Research/PEPBL/mriq1.pdf

http://chemeng.mcmaster.ca/pbl/pblbook.pdf The inventory and scoring is on p 4–9
to 4–11/

In scoring MRIQ, each of the elements has superscripts that refer to the following
references that were used as the basis for including the item.

MRIQ references:

1. Chickering, A.W. and Z.F. Gamson, AAHE Bulletin March 3–7, 1987

2. Ramsden, Paul series of papers: HERDSA News 4, 3–5, 1985; Ramsden and
    Entwistle Brit JEducational Psychology, 51, 368–383, 1981; Marton and Saljo,
    1976 Brit J of Educational Psychology, 46, 4–11; Biggs, J.B. Higher Education
    Research and Development, 1, 33–55, 1982

3. Schmidt, H.G., "PBL: rationale and description" Med Ed, 17, 11–16, 1983, and
    Med Ed, 27, p 422–432, 1993

4. Bandura, A. American Psychologist 37, 122–147 1982

5. Dales Cone of Learning

6. Stone, H.L., "Data Gathering Instruments for Evaluating Educational Programs
    and Teaching Effectiveness in the Centre of Health Sciences," U of Wisconsin,
    Madison, 1991

7. Perry, W.G. jr., "Forms of Intellectual and Ethical development in the college
    years," Holt Rinehart and Winston, 1970

8. Woods, D.R. PBL: helping your students gain the most from PBL 1995 Chapter
    7. from the web http://www.chemeng.mcmaster.ca/innov1.htm and click on
    PBL

9. Woods, D.R., "Ideas to Improve learning," manuscript for book.

My Role Is Questionnaire (MRIQ) © Donald R. Woods 1992

The following 18 items are arranged with options (a and b or a,b and c). Each option represents a preference you may or may not hold. Rate your preferences for each item by giving a score from 0 to 5. 0 means you strongly disagree and strongly agree with the other option. 5 Means you strongly agree and strongly disagree with the other option. The scores for a and b, or a, b and c MUST ADD UP to 5 (0 and 5, 1 and 4, 2 and 3, etc.) Place your rating in the box **R** next to the statement. **Please do not use fractions.**

I think my role as a teacher is:

Statement	R	Statement	Statement R
1a. I have a basic conviction that I can make a difference.		1b. People come to me with basic attitudes and won't change.	
2a. My role is to maintain high standards and fail those who do not make the standards.		2b. My role is to help each succeed and make the most of his/her abilities.	
3a. My role is to uncover material so that students understand.		3b. My role is to cover the material in the curriculum.	
4a. My role is to make learning fun.		4b. Learning is serious business. My role is to be well prepared.	
5a. My responsibility is to teach subjects.		5b. My responsibility is to teach people.	
6a. Students must grow personally as well as intellectually.		6b. The sole purpose of university is intellectual growth.	
7a. Teaching. research, consulting are all opportunities to help others learn. The only difference is the client and the "class size". Teaching and research are a seamless continuum of learning.		7b. Teaching is the burden I must bear to allow me to do research.	
		7c. Research is the burden I must bear to allow me to teach in university.	
8a. Teaching and learning are a two-way responsibility. If students fail it is partly my fault.		8b. Learning is one-way; I do my thing, and it's up to the students to learn.	
9a. If students understand my presentation. they will automatically remember the material. Learning is rote memorisation and recall of facts.		9b. Understanding is not remembering. Students and I need opportunities to see new concepts in perspective to understand their limitations and to reach conclusions. Learning is active, independent and self-directed.	
10a. Students should learn knowledge and the processes for working with that knowledge. Knowledge cannot be separated from thinking.		10b. All students need to learn in college is knowledge.	
11a. The development of values is an integral part of my instructional plan. Values play a significant role in my student's future success.		11b. The development of values is the responsibility of the home and/or the religious component of the student's life. You can't measure "value" development; therefore, it is inappropriate to include this area in one's goals.	
12a. Students should self-assess. My role is to ensure that the assessment process used by the students is valid. I consider the goals, criteria and the evidence.		12b. Assessment of students is my responsibility. I create and mark all the exams that are used to measure the quality of student learning.	

I think my role as a teacher is:

Statement	R	Statement	Statement R
13a. My role is to design the whole learning process. Students just have to follow my design.		13b. My role is to empower students with all elements in the learning process: goals, choice of text, assessment, etc.	
I4a. I am a resource to help students learn; students have the principal responsibility for making and carrying out their own plans.		I4b. I am the source of knowledge. I have the advanced training to be shared with them.	
15a. My role is to help students with academic and intellectual issues. It's not my responsibility to get involved with their personal and social life.		15b. My role is to help students with academic and intellectual issues and to help them with personal problems.	
		15c. My role is to help students with academic and intellectual issues and to informally socialise and attend student events.	
16a. I prepare the detailed learning objectives, the assessment criteria but publish general guidelines for the students; to do otherwise provides too much detail; it's overwhelming for the students.		16b. I publish detailed learning objectives and assessment criteria.	
		16c. Students should prepare detailed learning objectives and assessment criteria. I monitor the process to ensure the standards are met.	
17a. My role is to help them solve problems similar to those they will encounter in professional practice.		17b. My role is to ensure that they know the fundamentals. I use problems that help develop and test that understanding.	
18a. I teach new knowledge. My role is to present well organized explanations expressed to match the student's learning style.		18b. All new knowledge bears some relationship to past. My role is to activate the past knowledge and help students see the relationship between the new and the old.	

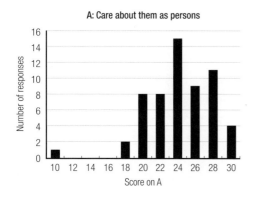

A: Care about them as persons

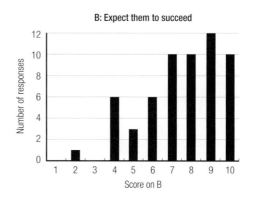

B: Expect them to succeed

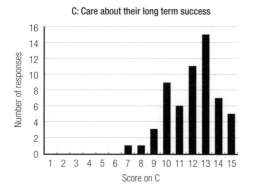

C: Care about their long term success

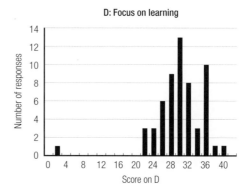

D: Focus on learning

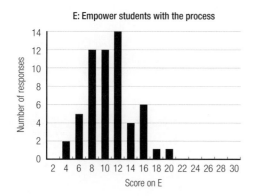

E: Empower students with the process

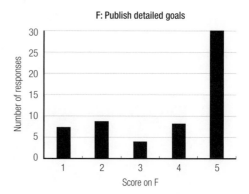

F: Publish detailed goals

Appendix F
Queen's University Exit Survey

Purpose: To provide feedback about the overall program

To be completed by: graduates upon graduation

Description: Selected questions from the survey include:

- 14 Likert-type questions related to the learning experience 1 to 5 and identify top three in importance.

- 22 Likert-type questions related to the development of higher-order thinking and process skills and attitudes and identify the top three in terms of importance.

Results: Provides feedback about the learning experience for the whole University experience and about the development of the "process skills" and attitudes.

Scoring: Numerical average and standard deviation can be computed or the results can be shown as bar charts. Examples of bar charts are published annually by Queen's University for each of nine faculties.

Example Data:
Interest in my learning: 4.5 (0.6)
Access: 4.45 (0.51)
Assess: 4.1 (0.56)   importance = 1
Feedback: 4.15 (0.75)   importance = 3
Positive: 4.28 (0.55)
Student evaluation: 3.98 (0.83)
TAs: 3.5 (1.0)
Participation: 4.38 (0.6)
Fair assess: 4.15 (0.5)
Theory-practice: 4.3 (0.8)
Choose: 4.1 (1.16)   importance = 2
Stimulate: 4.2 (0.6)
Enjoy: 4.2 (0.7)
Social: 4.1 (0.7)

References:

Office of the Registrar, "Undergraduate Learning Experiences at Queen's: Results from the exit poll," Queen's University, Kingston, ON (each year since 1994)

Motivating and rewarding university teachers to improve student learning

The Learning Experience

1 The following statements are concerned with your learning experience at Queen's. Think back to your experiences as a student at Queen's and indicate how much you agree or disagree with each statement by circling one of the numbers at the right.

	Strongly Disagree				Strongly Agree
a Instructors took an active interest in my learning	1	2	3	4	5
b Instructors were readily accessible outside class	1	2	3	4	5
c Instructors made an effort to check that students were understanding the material taught	1	2	3	4	5
d Instructors provided helpful feedback	1	2	3	4	5
e Instructors showed a positive attitude toward students	1	2	3	4	5
f Instructors encouraged feedback from the class regarding their teaching	1	2	3	4	5
g Teaching assistants were used appropriately	1	2	3	4	5
h Class participation was actively encouraged	1	2	3	4	5
i Assessment methods (exams and marking) were fair	1	2	3	4	5
j My program had a good balance between theory and practice	1	2	3	4	5
k I was generally able to enrol in the courses I wanted	1	2	3	4	5
l Overall, my learning experience was intellectually stimulating	1	2	3	4	5
m Overall, my learning experience has been enjoyable	1	2	3	4	5
n There was ample scope for organized social activities at Queen's	1	2	3	4	5

1b Which three of the statements listed above, in order of importance, were most important to you?

Please circle the letter corresponding to the statements listed above. (Circle one letter only for each rating).

Most important	a	b	c	d	e	f	g	h	i	j	k	l	m	n
Second most important	a	b	c	d	e	f	g	h	i	j	k	l	m	n
Third most important	a	b	c	d	e	f	g	h	i	j	k	l	m	n

2 Please indicate the degree to which your education (both inside and outside the classroom) at Queen's contributed to your learning and development in each of the following areas?

		Very Little				A Great Deal
a	Writing skills	1	2	3	4	5
b	Speaking skills	1	2	3	4	5
c	Critical judgment	1	2	3	4	5
d	Creative thinking	1	2	3	4	5
e	Problem-solving skills	1	2	3	4	5
f	Mathematical skills	1	2	3	4	5
g	Computing skills	1	2	3	4	5
h	Ability to use a foreign language	1	2	3	4	5
i	Leadership skills	1	2	3	4	5
j	Ability to compete	1	2	3	4	5
k	Ability to work independently	1	2	3	4	5
l	Ability to work well with others	1	2	3	4	5
m	Self-confidence	1	2	3	4	5
n	Appreciation of literature	1	2	3	4	5
o	Understanding of science	1	2	3	4	5
p	Appreciation of fine arts	1	2	3	4	5
q	Sensitivity to ethical issues	1	2	3	4	5
r	Awareness of political and social issues	1	2	3	4	5
s	Awareness of the rights and responsibilities of citizenship	1	2	3	4	5
t	Appreciation of other races, cultures and religions	1	2	3	4	5
u	Desire for further education	1	2	3	4	5
v	Lifelong learning skills	1	2	3	4	5

2b From the above list, please indicate in order of importance the three areas which were most valuable in contributing to your learning and development.

Please circle the letter corresponding to the factors listed above. (Circle one letter only for each rating.)

Most important   a b c d e f g h i j k l m n o p q r s t u v

Second most important a b c d e f g h i j k l m n o p q r s t u v

Third most important   a b c d e f g h i j k l m n o p q r s t u v

Appendix G
Student course evaluation

Purpose: To provide feedback about the student's perception of the learning environment.

To be completed by: students taking the course

Results: This example was developed for the Faculty of Engineering at McMaster University by Dr Alan Blizzard and Dale Roy of the Center for Leadership and Learning and Professor Bob Hudspith, Faculty of Engineering. (The form is reproduced with permission from the Faculty of Engineering)

Scoring: Arithmetic average for the overall ratings for the first five items. Distribution information about the feedback in Parts 2, 3 and 4. Unattributed written comments are listed.

Example: At McMaster University, the student evaluations are required for every course. The completed forms are collected by a student and delivered to the Dean's Office. The results are perused first by the Dean, then they are passed on to the department chair and then ultimately to the individual faculty member. Usually, the Dean will intercede and talk with individuals whose evaluations have been low. Usually, the chair writes a covering letter to each faculty member.

Appendix G Example student course evaluation

FACULTY OF ENGINEERING
STUDENT COURSE EVALUATION

Student ratings of course instructors are an important element in the evaluation of an instructor for promotion, tenure and merit salary decisions. Your considered responses to the following questions are important; they will help to reward effective instructors, and will indicate to the instructor what you thought was particularly effective and where you think improvements might be possible.

- On the answer sheet: Print the name and number of the course (eg. Engineer 1D04), the date and the instructor's name.

- Please record all your answers on the answer sheet provided.

- This questionnaire is confidential – your instructor and/or tutors will never have knowledge of your identity.

- You must record your student number and signature on the answer sheet in order for your comments to be considered.

PLEASE DO NOT WRITE ON THIS SHEET
WRITE ONLY ON THE ANSWER SHEET THAT HAS BEEN SEPARATELY PROVIDED FOR YOUR USE

PART ONE: OVERALL RATINGS

---

1. How much of the course material seemed valuable to you? (Choose one)

    1) 0-50%   2) 51-60%   3) 61-70%   4) 71-90%   5) 81-100%

2. How heavy was the work load in this course (compared to other courses at this level)?

    1) much lighter   2) lighter   3) about the same   4) heavier   5) much heavier

3. Were you encouraged to use independent critical judgment? (Choose one)

    1) not at all   2) not much   3) reasonably   4) fairly strongly   5) strongly

4. OVERALL, how do you rate the value of this course compared with others you have taken at McMaster? (Choose one)

    1) far below average   2) below average   3) about the same as others

    4) above average   5) far above average

5. OVERALL, what is your opinion of the effectiveness of the instructor as a teacher? (Choose one)

Very Poor	Poor		Acceptable			Good		Very Good	Excellent
1	2	3	4	5	6	7	8	9	10

PART TWO: DETAILED COMMENTS

This section lists comments you might want to make on various aspects of the course. The comments on various aspects are organized in two columns, those that indicate what was particularly effective, and those that indicate what particularly need improvement. Choose only the items you think are both relevant and particularly important. Select more than one comment per question if you wish.

ASPECTS NEEDING IMPROVEMENT	EFFECTIVE ASPECTS

EXPECTATIONS

6. 1) unclear explanation of course objectives 2) course did not correspond with outline	7. 1) clear explanation of course objectives 2) course fulfilled outline well 3) practical aspects presented: "real world applications" 4) clear explanation of how course relates to your discipline

RELATIONSHIP OF CLASS ACTIVITIES TO COURSE OBJECTIVES

8. 1) too much lecturing 2) not enough lecturing 3) ineffective use of group work and/or discussion 4) ineffective use of learning technologies-video, learnlink, etc. 5) too few in-class exercises	9. 1) appropriate amount of lecturing 2) effective use of group work and/or discussion 3) effective use of learning technologies-video, learnlink, etc. 4) appropriate use of in-class exercises

LECTURING

10. 1) usually too slow 2) usually too fast 3) boring 4) needs more examples 5) speech difficult to hear or understand 6) visual aids (use of chalkboard and/or overhead) not helpful 7) assumes too much prior knowledge	11. 1) very interesting 2) clear overheads/slides 3) clear explanations 4) well organized 5) clear voice 6) enthusiastic

INSTRUCTOR'S RESPONSE TO STUDENTS

12. 1) condescending 2) unclear answers to questions 3) discourage questions 4) seldom available 5) not approachable	13. 1) clear or well explained answers to questions 2) direct or "to the point" 3) willing to answer questions 4) usually available 5) good attitude towards students

GIVEN THE OBJECTIVES OF THE COURSE

14. Insufficient help in developing skills in: 1) writing and speaking 2) creative thinking 3) problem-solving 4) computing 5) working independently 6) working with others	15. Appropriate development of skills in: 1) writing and/or speaking 2) creative thinking 3) problem-solving 4) computing 5) working independently 6) working with others

ASSIGNMENTS

16. 1) too few/none 2) not fairly marked/grading unclear 3) too many 4) too long 5) too difficult 6) not returned on time	17. 1) expectations clearly defined 2) returned on time 3) clear explanation of grade 4) constructive/useful comments 5) fairly marked

ASPECTS NEEDING IMPROVEMENT	EFFECTIVE ASPECTS
TESTS	

18. 1) not enough 2) mark distribution unclear 3) too difficult 4) not fairly marked 5) too long	19. 1) sufficient number 2) appropriate level 3) good coverage 4) fairly marked 5) well supervised

LABORATORIES	

20. 1) not valuable 2) not interesting 3) too long 4) unorganized	21. 1) interesting 2) related well to course 3) well structured 4) gave hands-on experience with course content

TUTORIALS	

22. 1) not helpful 2) too few	23. 1) helpful 2) well conducted

TEACHING ASSISTANTS	

24. 1) speech difficult to hear or understand 2) not approachable 3) lack of knowledge of material 4) difficult to locate/not in for office hours	25. 1) helpful comments 2) available 3) good attitude to students 4) able to answer questions

TEXTS, LIBRARY RESERVES, HANDOUTs AND USE OF RESOURCE MATERIAL	

26. 1) text not useful 2) courseware not useful 3) too few reserve copies available 4) not enough detailed solutions available 5) not enough relevant practice problems or other resources	27. Effective use of: 1) texts 2) custom courseware 3) library reserves 4) handouts 5) electronic postings

---

PART THREE: CLASSROOM/LABORATORY FACILITIES AND EQUIPMENT

28. Were there problems with the classroom facilities? (Choose all that apply)

1) overcrowded	2) too hot / too cold	3) poor ventilation
4) inadequate lighting	5) uncomfortable seats	6) shortage of equipment
7) difficult to use	8) difficult to hear	9) too many students per station

29. Were there problems with the laboratory and/or laboratory equipment? (Choose all that apply)

1) overcrowded	2) inadequate lighting	3) shortage of equipment
4) outdated equipment	5) unreliable equipment	6) too many students per station

---

PART FOUR: WRITTEN COMMENTS

Written comments are valued by the Faculty of Engineering. Please add any comments to the designated area on your answer sheet. Remember to record your student number and signature on the answer sheet in order for your comments to be considered.

ALL INFORMATION IS CONFIDENTIAL

YOUR IDENTITY WILL NOT BE REVEALED TO INSTRUCTORS OR T.A.'S

Developed for the Faculty by Alan Blizzard and Dale Roy, Centre for Leadership and Learning and Bob Hudspith, Faculty of Engineering, McMaster University (reproduced courtesy of the Faculty of Engineering)

Appendix H
Example course loading form

Purpose: To provide feedback to chair about the teacher's perception of the load required to "teach a course." To provide a "contract" between the teacher and the Department.

To be completed by: teacher for each course (graduate and undergraduate) to be taught over two semesters.

Description: select relative factors for the relative time commitment to prepare, deliver and mark.

Results: identify a relative weighting for each of the following: how close the course is to your research area, the class size, anticipated preparation time and marking assistance. For "full teaching load over two semesters" the total should be about 550 hours.

Scoring: total factors, subtract 3 and multiply by the base course hours to obtain total time.

Example Data:

3 lectures/week and 10 week semester = base hour = 30 h.

Course is close to area of research select = 1.05

Undergraduate course, 30 students factor = 1.10

Preparation time. I am expected to revise one course each semester and I pick this one so the factor = 2

I have no TAs, factor = 2.

Total factor = 1.05 + 1.10 + 2 + 2 = 6.15 - 3 = 3.15

Therefore the loading for this course = 30 h x 3.15 = 94.5 h.

Over two semesters I am expected to have a load of 550 h. So I have about 350 h left to account for.

For preparation time for graduate courses, the bracketed numerals represent updated values suggested from those new faculty who say it takes about 12 hours to prepare for a 1 hour graduate lecture. In the 1980's when this form was used, we felt it took about 5 h / 1 hour of class time if you were creating a new graduate course. I now believe the number is probably somewhere between the two extremes. Indeed, for young faculty creating a new graduate course I strongly recommend that they teach only 1/2 of a graduate course and team up with someone else to team teach it. With such an arrangement this "averages" out to be the unbracketed numbers. I would discuss this with your colleagues and agree on the values.

References:

D. R. Woods, "Ideas on Encouraging Academic Excellence," *Engineering Education*, 74, p. 99 to 102 (1983).

Course loading: **Course name** _____

Nominal total syllabus hours for "lecture"   _____
Nominal total syllabus hours for "tutorials"   _____
Total base hours   _____

- Is this course in your area of research?
  Yes,   x 1.00
  Far removed   x 1.35   pick a factor between 1 and 1.35   _____

- Number of students/class

Undergraduate	Graduate	Factor
<20	< 3	x 1.00
30	5	x 1.10
40	8	x 1.15
50	15	x 1.20
60	20	x 1.23
80	25	x 1.26
>100	>30	x 1.30	_____

- Preparation time

	Undergraduate	Graduate
Given this course before very often	x 1.3	x 2
Will make minor revisions	x 1.7	x 3 (6)
Will make major revisions	x 2	x 4 (8)
First time	x 3	x 5 (12)	_____

- Marking assistance

TAs do all but exam	x 1.05
TAs do some	x 1.5
I do it all	x 2.0	_____

                                        Total of four factors _____

Total commitment: (Total base hours) x (Total of factors - 3.00) = _____

References

Abraham, M.R. and Cracolice, M.S. (1994). "Doing Research on College Science Teaching," *Journal of College Science Teaching, Dec/Jan*, pp. 150–153.

Accreditation Board for Engineering and Technology, ABET (2008). From http://www.abet.org.

Aleamoni, L.M. (1979). "Evaluation of Teaching: Developing a Comprehensive System to Improve and Reward Instructional Effectiveness," Paper presented at the AIChE Meeting, San Francisco, November.

Anderson, Lorin W., Krathwohl, David R., Airasian, Peter W., Cruikshank, Kathleen A., Mayer, Richard E., Pintrich, Paul R., Raths, James and Wittrock, Merlin C. (2001). *A Taxonomy for Learning, Teaching, and Assessing: A Revision of Bloom's Taxonomy of Educational Objectives*. Addison Wesley Longman, Inc.

Angelo, T.A. and Cross K.P. (1993). *Classroom Assessment Techniques: A Handbook for College Teachers*. 2nd ed. San Francisco, CA: Jossey-Bass.

Angus, J.C., et al. (1999). "Ranking Graduate Programs," *Chemical Engineering Education, 33(1)*, pp. 72–83.

Anon (1999). "3.2 Research Interests: Linking Staff Research and the Curriculum." http://www.brookes.ac.uk/services/ocsd/link1/cdesign1/trdobu.html.

Bell, A.H., and Smith, D.M. (2004). *Winning with Difficult People*. Hauppauge, NY: Barron's.

Benvenuto, M.A. "In the Age of Interactive Learning Some Students Want the Same Old Song and Dance," *The Chronicle of Higher Education*, June 4, 1999, B9.

Bert, Ray (1999). "What Do Assistant Professors Want?" *Prism, May/June*.

Bertrand, D. and Knapper, C.H. (1994). *Contextual Influences on Student's Approaches to Learning in Three Academic Departments*. Waterloo, ON: University of Waterloo.

Bligh, D., cited by Gibbs and Openshaw (1983). pp. 20.

Block, P. (1990). *The Empowered Manager*. San Francisco, CA: Jossey Bass.

Bloom, B.S., et al. (1956). *Taxonomy of Educational Objectives: Classification of Educational Goals: Handbook I: Cognitive Domain*. New York, NY: McKay Publishers.

Bok, D. (1990). *Universities and the Future of America*. Durham: Duke University Press.

Boyer, E. (1990). *Scholarship Revisited*. Princeton, NJ: Carnegie Foundation.

Boud, D. and Falchikov N. (1989). "Quantitative Studies of Student Self-assessment in Higher Education: A Critical Analysis of Findings," *Higher Education, 18*, pp. 529–549.

Brent, R., et al. (1999). "A Model Program for Promoting Effective Teaching in Colleges in Engineering." In *Proceedings ASEE Annual Conference*, and available on the web http://www.asee.org/conferences.

Brew, Angela and Boud, David (1996). "Preparing for New Academic Roles: A Holistic Approach to Development," *International Journal of Academic Development, Nov*, pp. 17–25.

Brinkman, R. and Kirschner R. (1994). *Dealing with People You Can't Stand*. New York, NY: McGraw Hill.

Brookfield, S.D. (1990). *The Skillful Teacher*. San Francisco, CA: Jossey-Bass.

Brown, B., Crooks, D., Fawcett, M., Ellis, P., Parsons, M., Rideout, L., Noesgaard, C., and Sergeant, D. (1996). *Teaching Portfolio*. Hamilton, ON: School of Nursing, McMaster University.

Buros, O.K. (Annually). *The Mental Measures Yearbook*. Highland Park, NJ: Gryphon Press.

Cabell Publishing (Annually). *Cabell's Directory of Publishing Opportunities in Education*.

Canadian Engineering Accreditation Board (1999). http://ccpe.ca/english/schools.

Candy, P. (1996). "Promoting Lifelong Learning: Academic Developers and University as a Learning Organization," *International Journal for Academic Development, 1*, pp. 7–18.

Cashin, W.E. (1995). "Student Ratings of Teaching: The Research Revisited." *IDEA Paper No. 32*. Manhattan, KS: Center for Faculty Evaluation and Development, Division of Continuing Education, Kansas State University.

Cava, Roberta (1990). *Difficult People*. Toronto, Key Porter Books.

Centra, J.A. (1980). "The How and Why of Evaluating Teaching," *Engineering Education, Dec*, pp. 205–210.

Centra, J.A. (1983). "Research Productivity and Teaching Effectiveness," *Research in Higher Education, 18(2)*, pp. 379–389.

Chickering, A.W., and Gamson, Z.F. (1987) "Seven Principles for Good Practice in Undergraduate Education," *AAHE Bulletin, 39(7)*, pp. 3–7.

Coles, C.R. (1985). "Differences between Conventional and Problem-based Curricula in the Student's Approaches to Studying," *Medical Education, 19,* pp. 308–309.

Cote, James E. and Allahar, A.L. (2007). *Ivory Tower Blues: A University System in Crisis*. Toronto, Ontario: University of Toronto Press.

Covey, S.R. (1989). *The Seven Habits of Highly Effective People*. New York, NY: Simon and Schuster Inc.

Davidson, C. I., and Ambrose, S.A. (1994). "Reviewing Research Proposals and Papers." In *The New Professor's Handbook*, Chapter 10. Bolton, MA: Anker Publishing Co.

Elbe, Kenneth E. (1988). *The Craft of Teaching: A Guide to Mastering the Professor's Art*. 2nd ed. San Francisco: Jossey-Bass.

Entwistle, Noel J. (1992). "Influences on the Quality of Student Learning — Implications for Medical Education," *South African Medical Journal, 81(20)*, pp. 596–606.

Office of Institutional Research, Evergreen State College (2008). *End-of-program Review and HECB Accountability Report*. From http://www.evergreen.edu/institutionalresearch.

Felder, R.M. (1994). "The Myth of the Superhuman Professor," *Journal of Engineering Education, April*, pp. 105–110.

Felder, R.M. (1998). "ABET Criteria 2000: An Exercise in Engineering Problem Solving," *Chemical Engineering Education, 32(2)*, pp. 126–127.

Felder, R.M., et al. (2000). "The Future of Engineering Education, II. Teaching Methods that Work," *Chemical Engineering Education, 34(1)*, pp. 26–39.

Felder, R.M. and Brent R. (1996). "If You've Got It, Flaunt It: Uses and Abuses of Teaching Portfolios," *Chemical Engineering Education, 30(3)*, pp. 188–189.

Felder, R.M and Brent R. (2005). "Understanding Student Differences," *Journal of Engineering Education, 94(1),* pp. 57–72.

Feldman, Kenneth A. (1976). "The Superior College Teacher from the Student's View," *Research in Higher Education, 5(3),* pp. 243–288.

Feldman, Kenneth A. (1987). "Research Productivity and Scholarly Accomplishment of College Teachers Related to Their Instructional Effectiveness," *Research in Higher Education, 26,* pp. 227–298.

Gibbs, Graham (undated). *A–Z of Student-focused Teaching Strategies*. Headington, UK: Educational Methods Unit, Oxford Polytechnic.

Gibbs, G., cited by Gibbs and Openshaw (1983) p. 20.

Gibbs, G. and Openshaw, Don (1983). "Rewarding Excellent Teachers," *Occasional Paper 14*.

Gibbs, G., et al. (1992). *Lecturing to More Students: 1 Problems and Course Design Strategies*. Oxford, UK: The Oxford Center for Staff Development, Oxford Polytechnic.

Gibbs, G., Knapper, C. and Piccinin, S. (2009). *Departmental Leadership of Teaching in Research Intensive Environments*. London, England: The Leadership Foundation for Higher Education.

Gmelch, W.H., et al. (1986). "Dimensions of Stress Among University Faculty: Factor-analytic Results from a National Study," *Research in Higher Education, 24(3)*, pp. 266–286.

Gourman, J. (1996). *The Gourman Report: A Rating of Undergraduate Programs in America and International Universities*. 8th ed. Los Angeles, CA: National Education Standards.

Gourman, J. (1998). *The Gourman Report: A Rating of Graduate and Professional Programs in America and International Universities*. 10th ed. Los Angeles, CA: National Education Standards.

Gray, P.J., Froh, R.C. and Diamond, R.M. (1992). *A National Study of Research Universities on the Balance between Research and Undergraduate Teaching*. Center for instructional Development, Syracuse University.

Gregory, R.D., et al. (1995). "Using a Student Experience Questionnaire for Improving Teaching and Learning." In *Improving Student learning — Through assessment and Evaluation*, edited by Gibbs, G., pp. 210–216. Oxford: Oxford Centre for Staff Development.

Guyatt, G.H., et al. (1993). "Users' Guide to the Medical Literature: I. How to Get Started," *Journal of American Medical Association, 270(17)*, pp. 2093–2095.

Guyatt, G.H., et al. (1993). "Users' Guide to the Medical Literature: II. How to Use an Article about Therapy or Prevention A. Are the Results of the Study Valid?" *Journal of American Medical Association, 270(21)*, pp. 2598–2601.

Guyatt, G.H., et al. (1994). "Users' Guide to the Medical Literature: II. How to Use an Article about Therapy or Prevention, B. What Were the Results and Will They Help Me in Caring for My Patients?" *Journal of American Medical Association, 271(1)*, pp. 59–63.

Guyatt, G.H., et al. (1994). "Users' Guide to the Medical Literature: III. How to Use an Article about a Diagnostic Test A. Are the Results of the Study Valid?" *Journal of American Medical Association, 271(5)*, pp. 389–291.

Guyatt, G.H., et al. (1994). "Users' Guide to the Medical Literature: IV. How to Use an Article about a Diagnostic Test B. What Are the Results and Will They Help Me in Caring for My Patients?" *Journal of American Medical Association, 271(9)*, pp. 703–707.

Hestenes, D., Wells, M. and Swackhamer, G. (1992). "Force Concept Inventory," *The Physics Teacher, 30(3)*, pp. 141–158.

Higher Learning Commission. (2003). "The Criteria for Accreditation," from http://www.ncahlc.org/download/Handbook03.pdf.

Howard, G.M. (1985). Engineering, University of Connecticut, Storrs. Personal communication.

Indiana University East: Beginning Teacher Mentor Program/Burnout. Web 2008.

Instructional Development Centre. (1983). "Teaching and Promotion: Three Paths," in *Teaching and Learning Notes, 6, 1, Jan.* McMaster University, Hamilton.

Jenkins, A., et al. (1998). "Teaching and Research: Student Perspectives and Policy Implications," *Studies in Higher Education, 23(2)*, pp. 127–141.

Jenkins, A., Healy, M. and Zetter, R. (2007). *Linking Teaching and Research in Disciplines and Departments*. Higher Education Academy. From http://www.heacademy.ac.uk/assets/York/documents/LinkingTeachingAndResearch_April07.pdf.

Johnstone, A. H. and El-Banna, H. (1986). "Capacities, Demands and Processes — A Predictive Model for Science Education," *Education in Chemistry, 23*, pp. 80–84.

Kelly, Diana K. (1990). "Reviving the 'Deadwood': How to Create an Institutional Climate to Encourage the Professional Growth and Revitalization of Mid-career Faculty in a Community College." Unpublished graduate paper, Claremont Graduate University.

Kepner, C.H and Tregoe B.B. (1981). *The New Rational Manager.* Princeton, NJ: Princeton Research Press.

King, P.M. and Kitchener, K.S. (1994). *Developing Reflective Judgment: Understanding and Promoting Intellectual Growth and Critical Thinking in Adolescents and Adults*. San Francisco, CA: Jossey-Bass.

Kimbell, R., Stables, K., Wheeler, T., Wosniak, A. and Kelly, V. (1991). *The Assessment of Performance in Design and Technology*. London: School Examinations and Assessment Council.

Kingman, J.F.C. (1982). *Research Student and Supervisor: A Discussion Document on Good Supervisory Practice*. Swindon, England: Science and Engineering Research Council.

Kouzes, J.M. and Posner, B.Z. (1989). *The Leadership Challenge*. San Francisco, CA: Jossey-Bass.

Knapper, C. (1994, 2011). Queen's University, Kingston. Personal communication.

Knapper, C. and Rogers, Pats. (1994). *Increasing the Emphasis on Teaching in Ontario Universities*. Toronto, ON: Ontario Council on University Affairs.

Kreber, Carolin (1997). "Faculty's Implicit Theories of Academic Work." Ph.D. Thesis, University of Toronto.

Kreber, C. (2000). "How Teaching Award Winners Conceptualize Academic Work: Further Thoughts on the Meaning of Scholarship," *Teaching in Higher Education, 5(1)*, pp. 61–78.

Kuh, G.D, et al. (2005) *Student Success in College: Creating Conditions that Matter*. San Francisco, CA: Jossey-Bass.

Lepkowski, W. (1996). "Research Universities Face Tough Challenge as Budgets Shrink." *Chemistry and Engineering News*, June 24, 1996, pp. 32–33.

Lindsay, R. (1999). "Teaching and Research — The Missing Link?" From http://www.brookes.ac.uk/services/ocsd/link1/research1/rlindsay.html.

Littlefield, V.M. (1999). "My Syllabus? It's Fine. Why Do You Ask? Or the Syllabus: A Tool for Improving Teaching and Learning." Presented at the Society for Teaching and Learning in Higher Education, Calgary, Canada.

Locke, E.N., et al. (1981). "Goal Setting and Task Performance, 1969–1980," *Psychological Bulletin, 90a*, pp. 125–152.

Maclean's Magazine. (2010). *2010 University Rankings*, November, 22.

Martin, Elaine. (1999). "Matrix Template for Scholarly Teaching."

Martin, Elaine. (1999). "What is Scholarly Teaching?"

McKay, M. and Fanning, P. (1987). *Self Esteem*. Oakland, CA: New Harbinger Publications.

McKeachie, W.J. (1999). *McKeachie's Teaching Tips: Strategies, Research and Theory for College and University Teachers*. 10th ed. Boston: Houghton Mifflin.

McMaster Education Services, Health Sciences (1994). "...So You Have to Prepare a Teaching Dossier: A Brief Guide." Hamilton, ON: Faculty of Health Sciences, McMaster University.

Mentkowski, M., et al. (2000). *Learning that Lasts: Integrating Learning, Development and Performance in College and Beyond*. San Francisco: Jossey-Bass Publishers.

Miller, Ron. (2008). "Thermal and Transport Science Concept Inventory: Fluids, heat, Thermo," Colorado School of Mines, Colorado. Personal communication.

Miller, W.R. and Rollnick, S. (2002). *Motivational Interviewing: Preparing People for Change*, 2nd ed. New York, NY: Guildford Press.

Moonwomon, B. (undated). "Sick and Tired: A Case Study on Faculty Workload and Health. From http://www.sonoma.edu/senate/apc/sickandtired.htm.

Murphy, Linda L., Conoley, Jane Close and Impara, James C. Eds. (1994). *Tests in Print IV: An Index to Tests, Test Reviews, and the Literature on Specific Tests*. NE: Buros Institute of Mental Measurements, University of Nebraska-Lincoln.

Murray, H.G. (1980). *Evaluating University Teaching: A Review of Research*. Toronto: Ontario Confederation of University Faculty Associations.

National Survey of Student Engagement (2008). http://www.nsse.iub.edu.

Natural Sciences and Engineering Research Council of Canada, Ottawa. http://www.nserc.ca.

Noll, R.G. (1996). Cited by Lepkowski (1996).

OCUA. (1994a). *The Structure of Academic Work*. Toronto, ON: Task Force on Resource Allocation, Ontario Council on University Affairs.

OCUA. (1994b). *Undergraduate Teaching, Research and Consulting/Community Service: What Are the Functional Interactions? — A Literature Survey*. Toronto, ON: Task Force on Resource Allocation, Ontario Council on University Affairs.

Paulsen, M.B. and Feldman, K.A. (1995). "Toward a Reconceptualization of Scholarship," *Journal of Higher Education, 66(6)*, pp. 615–640.

Perry, W.G., Jr. (1968). *Forms of Intellectual and Ethical Growth in the College Years*. New York, NY: Holt, Rinehart and Winston.

Peterson, G.D. (1995). *ABET Engineering Criteria 2000*. Baltimore, MD: Accreditation Board for Engineering and Technology, Inc.

Peterson, G.D. (1997). *Engineering Criteria 2000: Criteria for Accrediting Programs in Engineering in the United States*. 3rd ed. Baltimore, MD: Accreditation Board for Engineering and Technology, Inc.

Piper, David Warren. (1977). *The Changing University*. Windsor, England: Humanities Press.

Popham, W.J. and Baker, E.L. (1970). *Establishing Instructional Goals*. Englewood Cliffs, NJ: Prentice Hall.

Queen's University. (1992). "Queen's Index: 20 Indicators of Performance," *Special Issue, Queen's Alumni News, 66(6), Nov–Dec.*, pp. 14–21.

Queen's University. (2008). "Exit Poll." http://www.queensu.ca/registrar/aboutus/reports/exitpoll/exitpoll_2008.pdf.

Queen's University. (2008). "NSEE Data, Benchmarking and Plans." http://www.queensu.ca/irp/accountability/surveys.html.

Queen's University. (2008). "Institutional Research and Planning, Performance Indicators, 2000 Update: Measuring Excellence." http://www.queensu.ca/irp.

Queen's University, Office of the University Registrar. (1999). *Undergraduate Learning Experiences at Queen's: Results from the Exit Poll 1998, Spring*. Kingston: Queen's University.

Ramsden, P. (1983). *The Lancaster Approaches to Studying and Course Perceptions Questionnaires: Lecturer's Handbook*. Oxford: Educational Methods Unit, Oxford Polytechnic.

Ramsden, P. (1992). *Learning to Teach in Higher Education*. London: Routledge.

Ramsden, P. and Entwistle, N.J. (1981). "Effects of Academic Departments on Students' Approaches to Studying," *British Journal of Educational Psychology, 51*, pp. 368–382.

Ramsden, P. and Moses, I. (1992). "Associations between Research and Teaching in Australian Higher Education," *Higher Education, 23(3)*, pp. 273–295.

Regan-Smith, M.G., Obenshain, S.S., Seitz, H., Richards, B., Woodward, C., and Small, P.A. (1994). "Rote Learning in Medical School," *Journal of American Medical Association, 272(17)*, pp. 1380–81.

Reklaitis, R. (1992). "Being Effective Chairpersons," paper presented at the AIChE National Meeting, Miami Beach, FL, Fall.

Rice, R.E. (1992). "Toward a Broader Conception of Scholarship: The American Context," in *Research and Higher Education: The United States and the United Kingdom*, edited by Whiston, T.G. and Geiger, R.L., Chapter 9. Buckingham, UK: The Society for Research into Higher Education and Open University Press.

Rocha, J.A., et al. (1998). "Experiencias de acreditacion de programas de ingenieria Quimica en Mexico," *Revista del IMIQ, 5-6, Mayo-junio*, pp. 35–41.

Rosenthal, J.T., Cogan, M.L., Marshall, R., Meiland, J.W., Wion, P.K. and Molotsky, I.F. (1994). "The Work of Faculty: Expectations, Priorities and Rewards," *ACADEME*, Jan–Feb, pp. 35–48.

Roy, D. (1995). *The Evaluation of Teaching: Best Practice*. Hamilton, ON: Instructional Development Center, McMaster University.

Rugarcia, A. (1996). "Acreditacion de programas de ingenieria," *Educacion Quimica, Abril*, pp. 92–95.

Schon, D.A. (1987). *Educating the Reflective Practitioner: Toward a Design for Teaching and Learning in the Professions*. San Francisco, CA: Jossey-Bass.

Seldin, Peter. (1991). *The Teaching Portfolio: A Practical Guide to Improved Performance and Promotion/Tenure Decisions*. Bolton, MA: Anker Publishing Co.

Shore, B.M., Foster, S.F., Knapper, C.K., Nadeau, G.G., Neill, N. and Sims, V. (1986). *Guide to the Teaching Dossier, its Preparation and Use*. 2nd ed. Ottawa: Canadian Association of University Teachers.

Simpson, E. (1996). Dean, Faculty of Humanities, McMaster University, Hamilton, ON. Personal communication.

Sloan, E.D. (1989). "Extrinsic versus Intrinsic Motivation in Faculty Development," *Chem. Engr. Education, 23(3)*, pp.134–137 & 187.

Solomon, Muriel. (1990). *Working with Difficult People*. Englewood Cliffs, NJ: Prentice Hall.

Steif, P.S. and Dantzler, J.A. (2005). "A Statics Concept Inventory: Development and Psychometric Analysis," *Journal of Engineering Education, 94(4)*, pp. 363–371.

Stice, J.E. (1997). "Goals and Assessment." Workshop at the NSF workshop, University of Wisconsin, Madison, WI.

Stice, J.E., et al. (2000). "The Future of Engineering Education, IV. Learning How to teach," *Chemical Engineering Education, 34(2)*, pp. 118–127.

Stone, Howard (1991). *Data Gathering Instruments for Evaluating Educational Programs and Teaching Effectiveness in the Center for Health Sciences, University of Wisconsin — Madison.* Madison, WI: Educational Resources, Center for Health Sciences.

Terenzini, P.T. and Pascarella, E.T. (1994). "Living with Myths: Undergraduate Education in America," *Change, Jan/Feb*, pp. 28–32.

University of Michigan (1997). *Inventory of Institutional Support for Student Assessment.* Ann Arbor, MI: National Center for Postsecondary Improvement.

University of Texas at Austin, cited by Knapper and Rogers (1994).

University Committee on Teaching and Learning (1992). *Report on Recognition and Reward of Teaching at McMaster University.* Hamilton, ON: McMaster University.

University of Alberta. (1999). http://www.ualberta.ca/~uts/Dossier.html.

University of Victoria. (1999). http://learn.terc.uvic.ca/teaching.htm.

University of Victoria. (1999). "Student Ratings of Instruction for Summative Purposes." http://learn.terc.uvic.ca/Ratings.htm.

University of Technology, Sydney. (1999). "Why Evaluate Teaching and Courses?" http://www.clt.uts.edu.au/eval.html.

Wankat, P.C. and F.S. Oreovicz (1993) "Teaching Engineering," McGraw Hill, New York.

Wankat, P.C. (1997). Workshop given at the Technical University of Nova Scotia, Halifax, NS. Personal Communication.

Weinstein, C.E., Schulte, A. and Palmer, D.R. (1987). *Learning and Studies Strategy Inventory (LASSI).* Clearwater, FL: H&H Publishing.

White, J.A. (1990). "TQM: It's Time, Academia!" *IEEE Education News*, 3(2), pp. 1–6.

Whitehead, A.N. (1929). *The Aims of Education.* New York, NY: Macmillan.

Wood, Terri and McCarthy, Chris. (2002). "Understanding and Preventing Teacher Burnout," *ERIC, ERIC Digest.* http://www.ericdigests.org/2004-1/burnout.htm.

Wood, P.E. (1993). McMaster University, Hamilton ON. Personal communication.

Woods, D.R. (1983). "Ideas on Encouraging Academic Excellence," *Engineering Education, 74*, pp. 99–102.

Woods, D.R. (1991). "Total Quality Management: It's Overdue for Academia." Paper presented at the ABET meeting, Chicago, IL.

Woods, D.R. http://chemeng.mcmaster.ca/innov1.htm. Self-assessment targets. MPS 3.

Woods, D.R. (1994). *Problem-based Learning: How to Gain the Most from PBL.* Waterdown, ON: Woods, Publisher.

Woods, D.R. and Wood, P.E. (1996). "The Future of Engineering Education: A Canadian Perspective." In *Proceedings of New Approaches to Undergraduate Education VIII Conference, July 23–27*, pp. 128–149. Kingston, ON.

Woods, D.R. et al. (1997). "Developing Problem Solving Skills: the McMaster Problem Solving Program," *Journal of Engineering Education, 86(2)*, pp. 75–91.

Woods, D.R. (1998). *Problem-based Learning: Helping Your Students Gain the Most from PBL*, 2nd ed. Waterdown, ON: Woods, Publisher. http://www.chemeng. mcmaster.ca/innov1.htm and PBL.

Woods, D.R. (1998). "Unit 3: Self-assessment Targets." In *McMaster Problem Solving Program*. http://www.chemeng.mcmaster.ca/innov1.htm.

Woods, D.R. (1999). "Unit 49: Coping Creatively with Change." In *McMaster Problem Solving Program*. http://www.chemeng.mcmaster.ca/innov1.htm.

Woods, D.R., (1999a). *Ideas for Teachers to Improve Learning*, 3rd ed. Hamilton, ON: Chemical Engineering Department, McMaster University.

Woods, D.R. (1999b). *Problem-based Learning: Resources to Gain the Most from PBL*, 2nd ed. Waterdown, ON: Woods, Publisher. http://www.chemeng. mcmaster.ca/innov1.htm and PBL.

Woods, D.R. (1999c). *Analysis of Student Course Evaluations versus Faculty's Research Publications*. McMaster University. Internal publication.

Woods, D.R., Hrymak, A.N. and Wright, Heather. (2000). "Approaches to Learning and Learning Environments in Problem-based versus Lecture-based Learning." Conference paper published in the conference proceedings. American Society for Engineering Education, Conference, St Louis MO, June.

Woods D.R. (2006). "A For the sake of argument... If the Conventional Lecture is Dead, Why is it Alive and Thriving?" *Chemical Engineering Education, 40(2), Spring*. Inside front cover page.

Woods, D.R. (2007a). "Helping Students Gain the Most from their PBL Experience," in *Management of Change*, edited by Graaff, E. De and Kolmos, A., pp. 181–195. Sense Publishers.

Woods, D.R. (2007c). "Stress Management," MPS 5. http://www.chemeng.mcmaster.ca/MPS/default1.htm.

Woods, D.R. (2011). "Unit 5: Stress Management." In *McMaster Problem Solving Program.* http://www.chemeng.mcmaster.ca/innov1.

Woods, D.R. and Sheardown, H. (2009). "Ideas for Creating and Overcoming Student Silences," *Chemical Engineering Education, 44(2),* pp. 125–130.

Wright, A. (1992). "Student Ratings of Instruction: Principles for Practice," *Focus on University Teaching and Learning Newsletter, 4.*

Wright, A. (1996). "Teaching Improvement Practices in Canadian Universities," *Teaching and Learning in Higher Education, 18,* pp. 5–8.

York University Senate Committee on Teaching and Learning (1993). *Teaching Documentation Guide.* North York, ON: York University.

Index

P